MUCH ADO
ABOUT NOTHING

The RSC Shakespeare

Edited by Jonathan Bate and Eric Rasmussen
Chief Associate Editors: Héloïse Sénéchal and Jan Sewell
Associate Editors: Trey Jansen, Eleanor Lowe, Lucy Munro, Dee Anna Phares

Much Ado about Nothing

Textual editing: Eric Rasmussen
Introduction and Shakespeare's Career in the Theatre: Jonathan Bate
Commentary: Eleanor Lowe and Héloïse Sénéchal
Scene-by-Scene Analysis: Esme Miskimmin
In Performance: Penelope Freedman (RSC stagings), Jan Sewell (overview)
The Director's Cut (interviews by Jonathan Bate and Kevin Wright):
Marianne Elliott, Nicholas Hytner
Playing Beatrice: Harriet Walter

Editorial Advisory Board

The RSC Shakespeare

WILLIAM SHAKESPEARE

MUCH ADO ABOUT NOTHING

Edited by
Jonathan Bate and Eric Rasmussen

Introduced by Jonathan Bate

Macmillan

The right of Jonathan Bate and Eric Rasmussen to be identified as the authors of the editorial apparatus to this work by William Shakespeare has been asserted by them in accordance with the Copyright, Designs and Patents Act 1988.

Published 2009 by
MACMILLAN PUBLISHERS LTD
registered in England, company number 785998, of Houndmills,
Basingstoke, Hampshire RG21 6XS.
Companies and representatives throughout the world.

ISBN-13 978–0–230–23209–9 hardback
ISBN-13 978–0–230–23210–5 paperback

This book is printed on paper suitable for recycling and made from fully managed and sustained forest sources. Logging, pulping and manufacturing processes are expected to conform to the environmental regulations of the country of origin.

A catalogue record for this book is available from the British Library.

10   9   8   7   6   5   4   3   2   1
18   17   16   15   14   13   12   11   10   09

Printed in China

Essex County Council Libraries

CONTENTS

INTRODUCTION

COUPLES

On what basis do you choose a partner with whom to share your life? Sexual desire or social compatibility? Surface appearance or inner character? And how much freedom should young people have in making such an important choice? Is there anything to be said for the older way of doing things whereby parents play a central part in the process of arrangement and approval? These questions are no less pressing in today's multicultural societies than they were in the transitional age during which Shakespeare wrote his plays. And of all those plays, *Much Ado about Nothing* is the one that offers the most modern view of the game of boy meets girl that used to be called courtship.

Shakespeare knew that human motives and interactions are never simple. One of his favourite devices for exploring the complexity of our affairs is the double plot. In ancient Athens, Aristotle had said that a good play needs unity of action in order to keep the audience's focus. Shakespeare defied that rule and opted instead for stereoscopic vision. The double plot of *Much Ado* offers two versions of courtship. We might call them the romantic and the realistic, or the ancient and the modern.

There is an old story that goes back to ancient Greek romance and that reappeared in the early Renaissance. It received its most influential telling in an epic Italian romance by Ludovico Ariosto called *Orlando Furioso*. It tells of how a girl is wrongly accused of infidelity to the man she loves. He is tricked into believing that he has witnessed her letting another man into her bedroom window. The trick is that he is actually witnessing another woman disguised as his beloved. Accusations fly and an unhappy ending seems inevitable, but after various twists and turns the lovers are reunited.

1

This – adapted through various intermediary versions and reworked with many distinctively Shakespearean touches – is the origin of the Claudio and Hero story about which the play makes much ado. Coming as it does from the romance tradition, the relationship is focused on honour (a girl's chastity is non-negotiable) and on the combination of idealization and desire that we call 'romantic love'. One of the intermediate versions of the story, also known to Shakespeare, introduced the element of social class: its main characters are a knightly follower of Piero King of Aragon and the daughter of the poor but honourable Lionato de'Lionati of Messina. From here, Shakespeare took a series of questions about what constitutes a *suitable* marriage, how to reconcile the romantic desires of the young with the more down-to-earth matters of status, respect and money that are of concern to their parents.

Hero is the archetypal romance heroine. Her identity is defined by her sexual honesty: the accusation of infidelity almost literally kills her. Claudio is also bound by traditional notions of honour. Appearance is everything and all that matters is what *men* say. He doesn't believe Hero's denials of the false accusations and neither does his lord, Don Pedro, who makes clear that men must stand together: 'I stand dishonoured, that have gone about / To link my dear friend to a common stale' (a 'stale' means a whore).

Claudio's friend Benedick is given a choice at the climax of the accusation scene: to stick with the men or to stand up for Hero. The person who forces him to make that choice is Hero's cousin, Beatrice. She knows what is the right thing to do, but cannot do it herself because she is a woman: 'Is a not approved in the height a villain, that hath slandered, scorned, dishonoured my kinswoman? O that I were a man! What, bear her in hand until they come to take hands, and then, with public accusation, uncovered slander, unmitigated rancour — O God, that I were a man! I would eat his heart in the market-place.' If Benedick is to retain Beatrice's respect, he will have to take on the role that she cannot: he will have to challenge his friend Claudio to a duel.

The glorious relationship between Beatrice and Benedick has no equivalent in any of the older versions of the Claudio and Hero story.

It is Shakespeare's unique invention. And it takes over the audience's interest. This is a completely different, completely new, astonishingly modern relationship. The starting point is not sexual desire, not the romantic idea of falling in love at first sight. Nor is it honour or status. Beatrice is an orphan, not a daughter to be married off as a commodity. There is a general assumption that she will end up as an old maid. Her dazzling wit is her only defence against the loneliness of her likely fate.

We all know the problem with the romantic view of love: what is left when the gloss wears off, when the first mad passion is over? We have faith in Beatrice and Benedick because with them it is the other way round. Compatibility comes first, romance later. Their 'merry war' of words reveals that they are intellectual equals and mutual respect will flow from there. 'In each of them,' the actor Harriet Walter notes in her interview on playing the part of Beatrice, 'submitting to love was linked with an idea of loss of power and control. But having had such a long drawn-out and often antagonistic courtship, they can be said to really know one another and to have seen the worst of one another.' A partnership based on equality and respect, not on idealization or status: that is what makes Beatrice and Benedick so very real and so very modern.

TRAGEDY AVERTED

Comedy is tragedy averted. A young woman prepares herself for marriage. Then we witness the ceremony itself. Whenever we go to a wedding we cannot help relishing the dramatic pause when the priest asks the couple, 'If either of you know any inward impediment why you should not be conjoined, I charge you on your souls to utter it.' On this occasion the drama turns into a crisis: in front of the whole congregation Claudio the groom accuses Hero the bride of infidelity on the very eve of her wedding day. She faints, he storms out, her father says that he hopes she is dead since she has brought such shame on his household. The play has begun with the end of a war, a move from the language of martial bonding to that of courtship and coupling. Its atmosphere has been all holiday. No more.

The change of mood extends even to the other pair of lovers. The relationship between Benedick and Beatrice has hitherto been characterized by sharp but always light-hearted banter; now Beatrice raises the stakes dramatically, forcing Benedick to choose between love and friendship. Suddenly we have moved into the *Othello*-world of sexual accusation and death threat. Don John, the chief plotter of all the mischief, is no Iago – he is a cardboard cut-out villain, an archetypal melancholy man ('I cannot hide what I am: I must be sad when I have cause, and smile at no man's jests') – so in our rational minds we do not believe he will triumph, but we end the fourth act feeling that a substantial act of atonement will be required of Claudio.

Comedy makes room for little acts of grace; it allows the second chance which tragedy denies. In *Much Ado*, the grace comes from two agencies: the Friar who arranges the mock-death and resurrection of Hero, and the Watchmen who stumble upon the truth of Don John's plot. We expect God to work his benign way through friars. It may seem strange that providence also works by means of the bumbling, malaprop-prone Dogberry. It is, however, one of the laws of the comic universe that appearance ('semblance') is deceptive. Those who think they are clever, like Don John, end up looking foolish; those whom we at first think are foolish, like Dogberry, turn out to be peculiarly wise. Their wisdom is that of the heart, not the intellect. Jesus said that to understand the kingdom of heaven one has to make oneself as a child: Dogberry, like Bottom in *A Midsummer Night's Dream*, is one of Shakespeare's natural children. He is 'condemned into everlasting redemption' for his simplicity and goodness.

MUCH ADO ABOUT NOTING

The play's title is multiply suggestive. There is much ado about the nothing that Hero has done wrong. Shakespeare often makes 'nothing' a euphemism for female genitals, because women lack a male 'thing' between their legs, so there is an obscene second sense. 'Nothing' seems to have been pronounced 'noting', which provides a further rich sense: the play is full of 'noting' in the sense of watching and overhearing, whether in the famous scenes in which Benedick and Beatrice are deliberately allowed to overhear conversations of great interest to them, or the plan to let Claudio 'witness' the infidelity of his betrothed. Messina is full of hearsay.

Disguise is a closely related motif: Don Pedro woos Hero on behalf of, and in the guise of, Claudio. This plan is eavesdropped upon by scheming Borachio ('Being entertained for a perfumer, as I was smoking a musty room, comes me the prince and Claudio, hand in hand in sad conference. I whipped me behind the arras and there heard it agreed upon that the prince should woo Hero for himself, and having obtained her, give her to Count Claudio') and also misheard by a servant of Leonato's brother ('The prince and Count Claudio, walking in a thick-pleached alley in my orchard, were thus overheard by a man of mine: the prince discovered to Claudio that he loved my niece your daughter and meant to acknowledge it this night in a dance'). In each narrative of noting, an imagined detail – interlaced branches in a garden walk, a musty room hung with tapestry – creates a sense of location even as Shakespeare writes for a bare stage. As befits a work in which prose outweighs verse by a ratio of more than two to one, the texture of the play offers far more realism than romance: instead of the (sometimes parodically overblown) love-poetry we find in many of the other comedies, the focus here is on less hyperbolic but more heartfelt matters such as a bride's delight in the precise fashion and cut of her wedding dress.

It is unlikely to have taken a bright Elizabethan boy-actor more than about an hour to learn the little part of Hero. Traditionally the leading actress – Dora Jordan in the eighteenth century, Ellen Terry in the nineteenth, Peggy Ashcroft in the twentieth – has played Beatrice, and one suspects that the Chamberlain's Men's best boy would have done so in the original Shakespearean production. Claudio says of Hero 'Silence is the perfectest herald of joy'. She is the embodiment of the silent woman, talked about far more than she talks. Hero says far less than the other major characters, but we hear her name more often than that of any other character. And when we begin to look at her in this light we come to the centre of the play, for talking about people is the play's central activity.

SECOND CHANCE

The early nineteenth-century critic William Hazlitt was a great admirer of Hero's fortitude. Writing about *Much Ado* in his book *Characters of Shakespear's Plays* (1817), he noted that 'The justification of Hero in the end, and her restoration to the confidence and arms of her lover, is brought about by one of those temporary consignments to the grave of which Shakespeare seems to have been fond.' Hazlitt suggested that Shakespeare explained the theory behind this favourite plot twist in a crucial speech of the Friar's:

> She dying, as it must so be maintained,
> Upon the instant that she was accused,
> Shall be lamented, pitied and excused
> Of every hearer, for it so falls out
> That what we have we prize not to the worth
> Whiles we enjoy it; but, being lacked and lost,
> Why, then we rack the value, then we find
> The virtue that possession would not show us
> Whiles it was ours. So will it fare with Claudio:
> When he shall hear she died upon his words,
> Th'idea of her life shall sweetly creep
> Into his study of imagination,
> And every lovely organ of her life
> Shall come apparelled in more precious habit,
> More moving-delicate and full of life,
> Into the eye and prospect of his soul
> Than when she lived indeed.

Silence is associated with death and Hero's name is also associated with death: it is evocative of the title of the Roman poet Ovid's highly influential tales of deserted and despairing lovers, the *Heroides* (as well as the name of one of the characters in that collection, Hero mourning for her drowned lover, Leander). Death is the logic of the Hero-ine's exclusion from the first part of the play: in her habitual reticence, she is almost like a dead person from the start. But the Friar's suggestion is a kind of appropriation of death: he recognizes that the kind of death into which Hero has been forced can become the basis for a new life. The moment people believe she really is dead, they will start to value her. His recognition of this is based on what Hazlitt calls the theory behind Shakespeare's predilection for temporary consignments to the grave, namely the intuition of the human tendency not to value someone or something fully until we have lost it.

The idea remained very important to Shakespeare right through to the end of his career. Prospero in *The Tempest* only realizes how much he loves Ariel when he releases him. The point about the temporary consignment to the grave is that it gives a second chance. It allows one to experience the loss that makes one value what one has lost, and then it gives back the lost object. And this time, so the theory goes, one will really value it. 'Come, lady, die to live', says the Friar: it is only the apparent death, played out in elaborate fullness, that can provide a sufficiently firm basis for a subsequent fullness of life. When Hero is brought back to the stage, the language dwells sustainedly on this notion of dying to live. Hero dies while her slanders lived and lives once they die.

A temporary consignment to the grave is powerful in a play because a play serves a similar function. Claudio will come to value his Hero through having lived through her death. We will come to value our Heros through living through the stage-deaths of others like them. The great sixteenth-century French essayist Michel de Montaigne wrote an essay on Cicero's dictum 'That to philosophize is to learn how to die'; Shakespeare would suggest that to play-go is to learn how to live by seeing others pretend to die. As defenders of the stage were quick to point out when the theatre was attacked by puritans as immoral, the drama may serve an educative function for the audience. It may make us learn to value life through the surrogate experience of loss. Profound comedy must always be close to tragedy; the apparent death is necessary for the achievement of a comic fullness of life. One way of putting it would be to say that *The Winter's Tale*, with its hinged tragicomic structure, is the logical conclusion of Shakespeare's work. That play is certainly the fully matured reworking of *Much Ado*.

The temporary consignment to the grave is not only an analogue for the audience's experience in the theatre, and for the tragic element in comedy, it is also central to most myths and religions. Christ spends three days in the grave; Christianity is built on the idea of dying to one's self in order to achieve fuller life in Christ. Shakespeare made much of certain classical myths of temporary death and rebirth: the dying god, Adonis; Proserpina, goddess of spring, who dies to live and who is the archetype of Marina and Perdita; Orpheus bringing Eurydice back from the underworld. The ultimate original for the Hero plot is a Greek myth, that of Alcestis. Shakespeare could conceivably have known a Latin translation of Euripides' play on the subject, but he certainly received the story at secondhand through the prose romances that were the direct sources of *Much Ado*.

The plot of Alcestis may be summarized briefly: a man called Admetus is allowed an extra length of life, provided that at the appointed hour of his death someone else can be persuaded to die for him; Admetus' father and mother refuse; Alcestis, his loyal wife, consents and accordingly dies; just after her death, Herakles happens to be passing, on his way to perform one of his labours; despite his wife's recent death, Admetus entertains Herakles in accordance with the laws of hospitality; the latter discovers what has happened and goes to Death, the messenger who is taking Alcestis to the underworld, wrestles her from him and restores her to her husband who by this time feels guilty and repentant that he has let her die in his place. The story is played out on the level of myth, not in a civic community like Shakespeare's Messina, but the idea of a second chance is the key shared motif.

Much Ado shares with Euripides' Alcestis the idea of transformation being wrought by an image of the dead wife working on the mind. Alcestis expires on stage. Euripides gives a strong emphasis to her liminal position, both dead and not dead, no longer living but not yet received into the underworld. A gap is thus left open for recovery and return. When Herakles does return, it is with a veiled woman. Initially he says that it is a woman whom he has won; he asks Admetus to look after her while he goes off to perform his labour.

Admetus says that he doesn't want a woman in the house, especially one whose form is so like that of Alcestis. Herakles talks of a potential remarriage and the widower reacts angrily; there is a sense of him being tested and this time not failing. Eventually Admetus gives way to the strong will of Herakles and says he will take the woman into the house. The revelation and reunion then occur. It is a beautiful sequence, close in spirit and style to the reanimation of Hermione in *The Winter's Tale*. Strikingly, though, Alcestis does not speak. This motif is taken into the mythic structure when Herakles explains that she will not be allowed to speak for three days, by which time her obligations to the gods of the underworld will have been washed away. Alcestis functions as the archetypal silenced woman, and in this she is a precedent for the Hero who is allowed to say so little throughout the play and is given only two brief factual speeches on her unveiling at the climax. There are plenty of differences, not least in that there is no accusation of infidelity on Admetus' part. Alcestis is not a direct source for the Hero plot; rather, it is a powerful mythic prototype for the silencing of the woman and its extension, her temporary consignment to the grave. As in *All's Well that Ends Well* and *The Winter's Tale*, the actual death of the myth is replaced by a self-conscious stage trick. Superhuman interventions like that of Herakles are replaced by domesticated divine agents: the Friar's scheme in this play, Helen's self-contrived devices in *All's Well*, Paulina's priestess-like art in *The Winter's Tale*. Silence is not given a mythic-religious cause but becomes a psychological and social reality. But the strong sense of a second chance, of dying to live, draws the texts together.

DOUBLE ENDING

If we read Hero as an analogue for the female victims of Ovid's *Heroides*, then Claudio is like one of the men in those poems: thoroughly untrustworthy and self-interested. This would accord with the bad press he's always had: Charles Gildon at the beginning of the eighteenth century accused him of 'barbarous' conduct towards Hero, A. C. Swinburne at the end of the nineteenth century called him 'a pitiful fellow', and most theatre-goers today have little sympathy for him. But if, on the other hand, Hero is an Alcestis, Claudio is an Admetus who repents of and learns from his earlier unfair conduct. To accept the play as romance we have to go with this reading. The Friar's plan has got to work: the mock-death must make Claudio see Hero's virtues, must make him into a nobler lover. We must therefore take seriously such lines in the final act as 'I have drunk poison whiles he uttered it' and 'Sweet Hero! Now thy image doth appear / In the rare semblance that I loved it first'. And we must accept the sincerity of Claudio's vow of an annual sackcloth visit to Hero's monument. We must accept the magic of the reunion and, as in *The Winter's Tale*, we must, in the Friar's words, 'let wonder seem familiar'.

In an Elizabethan collection of romances called *A Petite Pallace of Pettie his Pleasure*, which Shakespeare almost certainly read, the moral of the Admetus and Alcestis story is addressed to women readers: 'you should die to yourselves and live to your husbands'. An old-fashioned plea for wifely submissiveness. But Shakespeare orders the matter differently: he retains the motif of the woman dying and then living again, but he does so in order that the husbands should die to themselves and live to their wives, for in *Much Ado*, as in *The Winter's Tale*, it is the husband who must be transformed by loss in order that he may become worthy of his wife.

As spectators we have been much more attracted to the witty lovers than the (supposedly) romantic ones. Since we cannot wait for the union of Benedick and Beatrice, we join Claudio in the rush towards it. Only on a second reading or viewing do we stop to worry about the kind of husband he will make for Hero. The question that matters to us is how on earth Beatrice and Benedick will stop insulting each other long enough to agree a marriage contract. The answer comes from Leonato when he says 'Peace! I will stop your mouth' – and forces the lovers into a kiss. We know that the wit-combat will resume, but for a moment at the end of the play we imagine the suspension of all quarrels in a kiss and then a dance. Technically, the Beatrice and Benedick story is a sub-plot that Shakespeare introduced into a romance story he inherited from

Renaissance Italy; theatrically, they steal the show, and the benign plot whereby they are tricked into acknowledging their love for each other is the most memorable thing in the play. The simultaneously ardent and reluctant conjunction of 'Signior Mountanto' and 'Lady Disdain' helps us to forget about Claudio's deficiencies. Small wonder that King Charles I wrote 'Bennedike and Betrice' beneath the title of the play in his copy of Shakespeare's Second Folio and that in the nineteenth century Hector Berlioz dispensed with the other pair altogether in composing his opera *Béatrice et Bénédict*.

Though Don Pedro facilitates Claudio's desire for Hero, it is Beatrice who intrigues him. When he offers to repeat his match-making and get her a husband, for a moment he is half-serious in offering her himself. The exchange is one of the loveliest moments anywhere in Shakespearean comedy:

> BEATRICE   Good lord, for alliance! Thus goes everyone to the world but I, and I am sunburnt. I may sit in a corner and cry 'Hey-ho for a husband!'
>
> DON PEDRO   Lady Beatrice, I will get you one.
>
> BEATRICE   I would rather have one of your father's getting. Hath your grace ne'er a brother like you? Your father got excellent husbands, if a maid could come by them.
>
> DON PEDRO   Will you have me, lady?
>
> BEATRICE   No, my lord, unless I might have another for working days: your grace is too costly to wear every day. But I beseech your grace pardon me. I was born to speak all mirth and no matter.
>
> DON PEDRO   Your silence most offends me, and to be merry best becomes you, for out of question, you were born in a merry hour.
>
> BEATRICE   No, sure, my lord, my mother cried, but then there was a star danced, and under that was I born. Cousins, God give you joy!

Beatrice bookends this encounter with references to the pair who have found love; her merriment in the interim masks a profound loneliness that Don Pedro himself retains at the end of the play. 'Prince, thou art sad;' says Benedick, 'get thee a wife, get thee a wife.' Everyone needs to join the dance of matrimony, he suggests – otherwise one will end up a despised exile like Don John. But the note of realism that comes from the grounded prose voice of the sparring partners is sounded one last time, in a light-hearted reference to cuckoldry that simultaneously reactivates and defuses the matter of infidelity that has created all the ado in the first place: 'There is no staff more reverend than one tipped with horn.' A truce has been called, but the merry and not so merry war between the sexes is always liable to resume. Its only armistice is that of death.

ABOUT THE TEXT

Shakespeare endures through history. He illuminates later times as well as his own. He helps us to understand the human condition. But he cannot do this without a good text of the plays. Without editions there would be no Shakespeare. That is why every twenty years or so throughout the last three centuries there has been a major new edition of his complete works. One aspect of editing is the process of keeping the texts up to date – modernizing the spelling, punctuation and typography (though not, of course, the actual words), providing explanatory notes in the light of changing educational practices (a generation ago, most of Shakespeare's classical and biblical allusions could be assumed to be generally understood, but now they can't).

But because Shakespeare did not personally oversee the publication of his plays, editors also have to make decisions about the relative authority of the early printed editions. Half of the sum of his plays only appeared posthumously, in the elaborately produced First Folio text of 1623, the original 'Complete Works' prepared for the press by Shakespeare's fellow-actors, the people who knew the plays better than anyone else. The other half had appeared in print in his lifetime, in the more compact and cheaper form of 'Quarto' editions, some of which reproduced good quality texts, others of which were to a greater or lesser degree garbled and error-strewn. In the case of a few plays there are hundreds of differences between the Quarto and Folio editions, some of them far from trivial.

If you look at printers' handbooks from the age of Shakespeare, you quickly discover that one of the first rules was that, whenever possible, compositors were recommended to set their type from existing printed books rather than manuscripts. This was the age before mechanical typesetting, where each individual letter had to be picked out by hand from the compositor's case and placed on a stick (upside down and back to front) before being laid on the press. It was an age of murky rush-light and of manuscripts written in a secretary hand that had dozens of different, hard-to-decipher forms. Printers' lives were a lot easier when they were reprinting existing books rather than struggling with handwritten copy. Easily the quickest way to have created the First Folio would have been simply to reprint those eighteen plays that had already appeared in Quarto and only work from manuscript on the other eighteen.

But that is not what happened. Whenever Quartos were used, playhouse 'promptbooks' were also consulted and stage directions copied in from them. And in the case of several major plays where a reasonably well-printed Quarto was available, the Folio printers were instructed to work from an alternative, playhouse-derived manuscript. This meant that the whole process of producing the first complete Shakespeare took months, even years, longer than it might have done. But for the men overseeing the project, John Hemings and Henry Condell, friends and fellow-actors who had been remembered in Shakespeare's will, the additional labour and cost were worth the effort for the sake of producing an edition that was close to the practice of the theatre. They wanted all the plays in print so that people could, as they wrote in their prefatory address to the reader, 'read him and again and again', but they also wanted 'the great variety of readers' to work from texts that were close to the theatre-life for which Shakespeare originally intended them. For this reason, the *RSC Shakespeare*, in both *Complete Works* and individual volumes, uses the Folio as base text wherever possible. Significant Quarto variants are, however, noted in the Textual Notes.

Much Ado about Nothing is one of the plays where the Folio text was printed from the Quarto, though with some reference to a playhouse manuscript, which provided some additional stage directions. Most modern editors use the Quarto as their copy-text but import stage directions, act divisions and some corrections from Folio. Our Folio-led editorial practice follows the reverse procedure, using Folio as copy-text, but deploying Quarto as a 'control text' that offers assistance in the correction and identification of compositors' errors. Differences are for the most part minor.

The following notes highlight various aspects of the editorial process and indicate conventions used in the text of this edition:

Lists of Parts are supplied in the First Folio for only six plays, not including *Much Ado about Nothing*, so the list here is editorially supplied. Capitals indicate that part of the name which is used for speech headings in the script (thus 'BENEDICK a lord from Padua').

Locations are provided by the Folio for only two plays. Eighteenth-century editors, working in an age of elaborately realistic stage sets, were the first to provide detailed locations. Given that Shakespeare wrote for a bare stage and often an imprecise sense of place, we have relegated locations to the explanatory notes at the foot of the page, where they are given at the beginning of each scene where the imaginary location is different from the one before. The whole of *Much Ado* is located in Messina, a city in north-east Sicily.

Act and Scene Divisions were provided in the Folio in a much more thoroughgoing way than in the Quartos. Sometimes, however, they were erroneous or omitted; corrections and additions supplied by editorial tradition are indicated by square brackets. Five-act division is based on a classical model, and act breaks provided the opportunity to replace the candles in the indoor Blackfriars playhouse which the King's Men used after 1608, but Shakespeare did not necessarily think in terms of a five-part structure of dramatic composition. The Folio convention is that a scene ends when the stage is empty. Nowadays, partly under the influence of film, we tend to consider a scene to be a dramatic unit that ends with either a change of imaginary location or a significant passage of time within the narrative. Shakespeare's fluidity of composition accords well with this convention, so in addition to act and scene numbers we provide a *running scene* count in the right margin at the beginning of each new scene, in the typeface used for editorial directions. Where there is a scene break caused by a momentary bare stage, but the location does not change and extra time does not pass, we use the convention *running scene continues*. There is inevitably a degree of editorial judgement in making such calls, but the system is very valuable in suggesting the pace of the plays.

Speakers' Names are often inconsistent in Folio. We have regularized speech headings, but retained an element of deliberate inconsistency in entry directions, in order to give the flavour of Folio.

Verse is indicated by lines that do not run to the right margin and by capitalization of each line. The Folio printers sometimes set verse as prose, and vice versa (either out of misunderstanding or for reasons of space). We have silently corrected in such cases, although in some instances there is ambiguity, in which case we have leaned towards the preservation of Folio layout. Folio sometimes uses contraction ('turnd' rather than 'turned') to indicate whether or not the final '-ed' of a past participle is sounded, an area where there is variation for the sake of the five-beat iambic pentameter rhythm. We use the convention of a grave accent to indicate sounding (thus 'turnèd' would be two syllables), but would urge actors not to overstress. In cases where one speaker ends with a verse half-line and the next begins with the other half of the pentameter, editors since the late eighteenth century have indented the second line. We have abandoned this convention, since the Folio does not use it, and nor did actors' cues in the Shakespearean theatre. An exception is made when the second speaker actively interrupts or completes the first speaker's sentence.

Spelling is modernized, but older forms are occasionally maintained where necessary for rhythm or aural effect.

Punctuation in Shakespeare's time was as much rhetorical as grammatical. 'Colon' was originally a term for a unit of thought in an argument. The semi-colon was a new unit of punctuation (some of the Quartos lack them altogether). We have modernized punctuation throughout, but have given more weight to Folio punctuation than many editors, since, though not Shakespearean, it reflects the usage of his period. In particular, we have used the colon far more than many editors: it is exceptionally useful as a way of indicating how many Shakespearean speeches unfold clause by clause in a developing argument that gives the illusion of enacting the process of thinking in the moment. We have also kept in mind the origin of punctuation in classical times as a way of assisting the actor and orator: the comma suggests the briefest of pauses for breath, the colon a middling one and a full stop or period a longer pause. Semi-colons, by contrast, belong to an era of punctuation that was only just coming in during Shakespeare's time and that is coming to an end now: we have accordingly only used them where they occur in our copy-texts (and not always then). Dashes are sometimes used for parenthetical interjections where the Folio has brackets. They are also used for interruptions and changes in train of thought. Where a change of addressee occurs within a speech, we have used a dash preceded by a full stop (or occasionally another form of punctuation). Often the identity of the respective addressees is obvious from the context. When it is not, this has been indicated in a marginal stage direction.

Entrances and Exits are fairly thorough in Folio, which has accordingly been followed as faithfully as possible. Where characters are omitted or corrections are necessary, this is indicated by square brackets (e.g. '[*and Attendants*]'). *Exit* is sometimes silently normalized to *Exeunt* and *Manet* anglicized to 'remains'. We trust Folio positioning of entrances and exits to a greater degree than most editors.

Editorial Stage Directions such as stage business, asides, indications of addressee and of characters' position on the gallery stage are only used sparingly in Folio. Other editions mingle directions of this kind with original Folio and Quarto directions, sometimes marking them by means of square brackets. We have sought to distinguish what could be described as *directorial* interventions of this kind from Folio-style directions (either original or supplied) by placing them in the right margin in a different typeface. There is a degree of subjectivity about which directions are of which kind, but the procedure is intended as a reminder to the reader and the actor that Shakespearean stage directions are often dependent upon editorial inference alone and are not set in stone. We also depart from editorial tradition in sometimes admitting uncertainty and thus printing permissive stage directions, such as an *Aside?* (often a line may be equally effective as an aside or a direct address – it is for each production or reading to make its own decision) or a *may exit* or a piece of business placed between arrows to indicate that it may occur at various different moments within a scene.

Line Numbers in the left margin are editorial, for reference and to key the explanatory and textual notes.

Explanatory Notes at the foot of each page explain allusions and gloss obsolete and difficult words, confusing phraseology, occasional major textual cruces, and so on. Particular attention is given to non-standard usage, bawdy innuendo and technical terms (e.g. legal and military language). Where more than one sense is given, commas indicate shades of related meaning, slashes alternative or double meanings.

Textual Notes at the end of the play indicate major departures from the Folio. They take the following form: the reading of our text is given in bold and its source given after an equals sign, with 'Q' indicating that it derives from the Quarto of 1600, 'F' from the First Folio of 1623, 'F2' a reading from the Second Folio of 1632 and 'Ed' from the subsequent editorial tradition. The rejected Folio ('F') reading is then given. A selection of Quarto variants and plausible unadopted editorial readings are also included. Thus, for example: '3.1.106, ta'en = F. Q = limed'. This indicates that at Act 3 scene 1 line 106 we have retained the Folio reading 'ta'en' but that 'limed' is an interestingly different reading in the Quarto.

KEY FACTS

MAJOR PARTS: (*with percentage of lines/number of speeches/scenes on stage*) Benedick (17%/134/8), Leonato (13%/120/9), Don Pedro (12%/135/8), Claudio (11%/125/8), Beatrice (10%/106/8), Dogberry (7%/52/4), Hero (5%/44/6), Borachio (5%/23/6), Don John (4%/40/6), Friar Francis (3%/16/2), Margaret (2%/26/3), Antonio (2%/23/4), Ursula (2%/19/3), Conrad (1%/23/1), Verges (1%/18/3), Balthasar (1%/11/2).

LINGUISTIC MEDIUM: 30% verse, 70% prose.

DATE: Late 1598. Not mentioned by Francis Meres in list of Shakespeare's plays in *Palladis Tamis* (registered for publication September 1598), but included part for Will Kemp, who left Shakespeare's acting company in early 1599.

SOURCES: The Hero/Claudio plot of a deception leading to a false supposition of infidelity has many precedents in the sixteenth-century Italian romance tradition; Shakespeare's primary sources seem to have been (1) the tale of Sir Timbreo and Fenicia in Matteo Bandello's *Novelle*, which included characters of Piero King of Aragon and Lionato of Messina (in Italian, 1554, no English translation, but Shakespeare might have known the French translation of Pierre de Belleforest, *Histoires Tragiques*, 1569), and (2) the tale of Renaldo and Ginevra in Ariosto's *Orlando Furioso*, book 5 (English translation by Sir John Harington, 1591). The Beatrice and Benedick plot is Shakespeare's innovation, though witty couples and characters who scorn love only to fall in love themselves have comic precedents, notably in the plays of John Lyly.

TEXT: Quarto published 1600, probably printed from Shakespeare's manuscript or a transcript of it. Generally good quality of printing.

On some occasions, actors' names instead of characters' appear in the speech headings (Kemp for Dogberry and Cowley for Verges). Folio printed from Quarto, though with some reference to a playhouse manuscript; extra stage directions inserted, also act divisions; some corrections and some errors introduced. Our text restores Quarto readings in cases judged to be compositor error, but retains Folio where changes appear to be intentional.

MUCH ADO ABOUT NOTHING

DON PEDRO, Prince of Aragon

BENEDICK a lord from Padua ⎱
CLAUDIO a lord from Florence ⎰ companions to Don Pedro

BALTHASAR, a singer, attendant upon Don Pedro

A BOY, servant to Benedict

DON JOHN, illegitimate brother of Don Pedro

BORACHIO ⎱ followers of
CONRAD ⎰ Don John

LEONATO, governor of Messina

Innogen, his silent wife

HERO, his daughter

BEATRICE, his niece, an orphan

ANTONIO, an old man, brother of Leonato

MARGARET ⎱ gentlewomen
URSULA ⎰ attendant upon Hero

FRIAR FRANCIS

DOGBERRY, Constable in charge of the Watch

VERGES, Headborough accompanying Dogberry

A SEXTON

WATCHMEN

Attendants and Messengers

NOTHING puns on 'noting' (i.e. musical notation/observation) and on 'no thing' (i.e. vagina)   **List of parts**
Headborough   parish officer

Act 1 Scene 1   *running scene 1*

*Enter Leonato Governor of Messina, Innogen his wife, Hero
his daughter and Beatrice his niece, with a Messenger*

LEONATO   I learn in this letter that Don Peter of Aragon   *Shows a letter*
comes this night to Messina.

MESSENGER He is very near by this: he was not three
leagues off when I left him.

5   **LEONATO** How many gentlemen have you lost in this
action?

MESSENGER But few of any sort, and none of name.

LEONATO A victory is twice itself when the achiever
brings home full numbers. I find here that Don Peter

10   hath bestowed much honour on a young Florentine
called Claudio.

MESSENGER Much deserved on his part and equally
remembered by Don Pedro. He hath borne himself
beyond the promise of his age, doing in the figure of a

15   lamb the feats of a lion. He hath indeed better
bettered expectation than you must expect of me to
tell you how.

LEONATO He hath an uncle here in Messina will be very
much glad of it.

20   **MESSENGER** I have already delivered him letters, and
there appears much joy in him, even so much that
joy could not show itself modest enough without a
badge of bitterness.

LEONATO Did he break out into tears?

25   **MESSENGER** In great measure.

LEONATO A kind overflow of kindness. There are no faces
truer than those that are so washed. How much
better is it to weep at joy than to joy at weeping!

BEATRICE I pray you, is Signior Mountanto returned

30   from the wars or no?

1.1   *Location: Messina, city in north-east Sicily*   ***Innogen*** a character who never speaks: she may have
been created in the writing and omitted in the performance   ***Hero*** named after the loyal lover of Leander
who killed herself after he drowned swimming the Hellespont to see her   ***Beatrice*** from the Latin beatrix
meaning 'she who blesses'   **1 Don Peter** i.e. Don Pedro   **Aragon** kingdom in northern Spain   **4 leagues** a
league is about three miles   **6 action** battle   **7 sort** high rank   **name** reputation/distinction/noble
status   **10 Florentine** person from the city of Florence, in north-west Italy   **13 remembered** rewarded
14 figure form/image   **23 badge of bitterness** i.e. the uncle's **tears** that demonstrate that his **joy** is
modest   **badge** badge worn by a nobleman's servant (a sign of inferiority and humility)   **26 kind** natural
27 truer more genuine/virtuous/honest   **29 Mountanto** from the fencing term 'montanto', an upward
thrust, suggestive of the verbal duelling Benedick engages in with Beatrice (there may also be a sexual play
on 'mount on to')

MESSENGER I know none of that name, lady: there was none such in the army of any sort.

LEONATO What is he that you ask for, niece?

HERO My cousin means Signior Benedick of Padua.

35 **MESSENGER** O, he's returned, and as pleasant as ever he was.

BEATRICE He set up his bills here in Messina and challenged Cupid at the flight: and my uncle's fool, reading the challenge, subscribed for Cupid and
40 challenged him at the bird-bolt. I pray you, how many hath he killed and eaten in these wars? But how many hath he killed? For indeed I promised to eat all of his killing.

LEONATO Faith, niece, you tax Signior Benedick too
45 much, but he'll be meet with you, I doubt it not.

MESSENGER He hath done good service, lady, in these wars.

BEATRICE You had musty victual and he hath holp to eat it: he's a very valiant trencherman, he hath an
50 excellent stomach.

MESSENGER And a good soldier too, lady.

BEATRICE And a good soldier to a lady. But what is he to a lord?

MESSENGER A lord to a lord, a man to a man, stuffed
55 with all honourable virtues.

BEATRICE It is so indeed, he is no less than a stuffed man. But for the stuffing — well, we are all mortal.

LEONATO You must not, sir, mistake my niece. There is a kind of merry war betwixt Signior Benedick and her:
60 they never meet but there's a skirmish of wit between them.

BEATRICE Alas, he gets nothing by that. In our last conflict four of his five wits went halting off, and now is the whole man governed with one: so that if he

---

34 Benedick from the Latin *benedictus* meaning 'blessed'   **Padua** northern Italian city known for its university   **35 pleasant** amusing/merry   **37 bills** notices advertising a public entertainment   **38 Cupid** god of love who shot love-inducing arrows into people's hearts   **flight** archery with flight-arrows (light, well-feathered arrows)   **fool** probably a professional fool employed by Leonato for entertainment
39 subscribed for took up the challenge on behalf of   **40 bird-bolt** blunt arrow safe enough to be used by children or fools   **44 Faith** in faith (i.e. truly)   **tax** censure/disparage   **45 meet** even   **48 musty victual** mouldy, stale food   **holp** helped   **49 valiant trencherman** hearty eater (**valiant** plays on the sense of 'courageous' as Beatrice implies that the only thing Benedick tackles with boldness is food)   **trencher** wooden plate   **50 stomach** appetite (puns on the sense of 'courage')   **52 he to** he compared to/faced with   **54 stuffed** full/replete   **56 stuffed man** figure stuffed to resemble a man/man sated with food   **59 betwixt** between   **63 five wits** five mental faculties (imagination, memory, fantasy, estimation, common sense)   **halting** limping

65   have wit enough to keep himself warm, let him bear
it for a difference between himself and his horse, for it
is all the wealth that he hath left to be known a
reasonable creature. Who is his companion now? He
hath every month a new sworn brother.

70   **MESSENGER** Is't possible?

BEATRICE Very easily possible: he wears his faith but as
the fashion of his hat — it ever changes with the next
block.

MESSENGER I see, lady, the gentleman is not in your
75   books.

BEATRICE No. An he were, I would burn my study. But I
pray you, who is his companion? Is there no young
squarer now that will make a voyage with him to the
devil?

80   **MESSENGER** He is most in the company of the right
noble Claudio.

BEATRICE O lord, he will hang upon him like a disease:
he is sooner caught than the pestilence, and the taker
runs presently mad. God help the noble Claudio. If he
85   have caught the Benedick, it will cost him a
thousand pound ere he be cured.

MESSENGER I will hold friends with you, lady.

BEATRICE Do, good friend.

LEONATO You'll ne'er run mad, niece.

90   **BEATRICE** No, not till a hot January.

MESSENGER Don Pedro is approached.

*Enter Don Pedro, Claudio, Benedick, Balthasar and John the
bastard*

DON PEDRO Good Signior Leonato, are you come to meet
your trouble? The fashion of the world is to avoid
cost, and you encounter it.

95   **LEONATO** Never came trouble to my house in the
likeness of your grace, for trouble being gone,
comfort should remain. But when you depart from
me, sorrow abides and happiness takes his leave.

---

66 difference in heraldry the sign that distinguished the junior branch of a family (in this case Benedick)
67 known . . . creature identified as one in possession of the faculty of reason (i.e. human)   **69 sworn
brother** brother-in-arms (one who swore brotherly loyalty and support in combat to a friend)   **71 faith**
fidelity/oath of brotherhood   **73 block** mould for shaping new fashions of hats   **75 books** good books,
favour   **76 An** if   **78 squarer** brawler/quarrelsome rogue   **83 pestilence** plague/disease   **84 presently**
immediately   **86 ere** before   **87 hold** remain   **89 run mad** i.e. by catching (falling in love with) **the
Benedick**   **93 trouble** i.e. Don Pedro and his companions who will put Leonato, as host, to the **cost** and
effort of entertaining them   **fashion** usual practice   **96 likeness** appearance

DON PEDRO You embrace your charge too willingly. I
100   think this is your daughter.

LEONATO Her mother hath many times told me so.

BENEDICK Were you in doubt, sir, that you asked her?

LEONATO Signior Benedick, no, for then were you a
child.

105   **DON PEDRO** You have it full, Benedick. We may guess by
this what you are, being a man. Truly the lady
fathers herself. Be happy lady, for you are like an
honourable father.

BENEDICK If Signior Leonato be her father, she would
110   not have his head on her shoulders for all Messina, as
like him as she is.   *Don Pedro and Leonato talk aside*

BEATRICE I wonder that you will still be talking, Signior
Benedick: nobody marks you.

BENEDICK What, my dear Lady Disdain! Are you yet
115   living?

BEATRICE Is it possible disdain should die while she hath
such meet food to feed it as Signior Benedick?
Courtesy itself must convert to disdain, if you come
in her presence.

120   **BENEDICK** Then is courtesy a turncoat. But it is certain I
am loved of all ladies, only you excepted: and I would
I could find in my heart that I had not a hard heart,
for truly I love none.

BEATRICE A dear happiness to women: they would else
125   have been troubled with a pernicious suitor. I thank
God and my cold blood, I am of your humour for
that. I had rather hear my dog bark at a crow than a
man swear he loves me.

BENEDICK God keep your ladyship still in that mind, so
130   some gentleman or other shall scape a predestinate
scratched face.

BEATRICE Scratching could not make it worse an 'twere
such a face as yours were.

BENEDICK Well, you are a rare parrot-teacher.

---

99 charge responsibility/expense   **103 for … child** i.e. so I had nothing to fear from a seducer such as
you   **105 have it full** have been amply answered   **107 fathers herself** i.e. shows who her father is through
her resemblance to him   **110 head** i.e. with its white hair   **113 marks** pays attention to   **117 meet**
suitable (puns on 'meat' which meant food generally)   **120 turncoat** one who changes their appearance or
loyalties   **121 would** wish   **124 dear happiness** great good fortune   **125 pernicious** ruinous/
wicked   **126 humour for that** disposition on that issue   **130 scape** escape   **predestinate** inevitable
132 an 'twere if it were   **134 rare parrot-teacher** marvellous chatterer (literally, one who repeats herself
as if teaching a parrot)

135 BEATRICE A bird of my tongue is better than a beast of
           yours.

     BENEDICK I would my horse had the speed of your
           tongue, and so good a continuer. But keep your way,
           a God's name, I have done.

140 BEATRICE You always end with a jade's trick. I know
           you of old.

     DON PEDRO That is the sum of all, Leonato.— Signior   *To the others*
           Claudio and Signior Benedick, my dear friend
           Leonato hath invited you all. I tell him we shall
145   stay here at the least a month, and he heartily prays
           some occasion may detain us longer. I dare swear he
           is no hypocrite, but prays from his heart.

     LEONATO If you swear, my lord, you shall not be   *To Don John*
           forsworn.— Let me bid you welcome, my lord.
150   Being reconciled to the prince your brother, I owe
           you all duty.

     DON JOHN I thank you. I am not of many words, but I
           thank you.

     LEONATO Please it your grace lead on?

155 DON PEDRO Your hand, Leonato. We will go together.
                      Exeunt all but Benedick and Claudio

     CLAUDIO Benedick, didst thou note the daughter of
           Signior Leonato?

     BENEDICK I noted her not, but I looked on her.

     CLAUDIO Is she not a modest young lady?

160 BENEDICK Do you question me as an honest man should
           do, for my simple true judgement? Or would you
           have me speak after my custom, as being a professed
           tyrant to their sex?

     CLAUDIO No, I pray thee speak in sober judgement.

165 BENEDICK Why, i'faith, methinks she's too low for a high
           praise, too brown for a fair praise, and too little for a
           great praise. Only this commendation I can afford
           her, that were she other than she is, she were
           unhandsome, and being no other but as she is, I do
170   not like her.

---

135 beast of yours i.e. because beasts do not have the power of speech   **138 so … continuer** was able to
go on for so long   **140 jade** over-used or worthless horse/whore   **trick** knack (of stopping abruptly)/sexual
act   **149 forsworn** proved wrong   **150 Being** as you are   **158 noted her not** did not pay her any special
attention   **162 after my custom** in my usual way/as is my habit   **165 low** short   **high** elevated/elaborate
(puns on the sense of 'tall')   **166 brown** brown-haired   **fair** fine/flattering (puns on the sense of 'light-
complexioned/pale-haired')   **167 afford** offer/allow

CLAUDIO Thou think'st I am in sport. I pray thee tell me truly how thou lik'st her.

BENEDICK Would you buy her, that you inquire after her?

175 **CLAUDIO** Can the world buy such a jewel?

BENEDICK Yea, and a case to put it into. But speak you this with a sad brow? Or do you play the flouting jack, to tell us Cupid is a good hare-finder and Vulcan a rare carpenter? Come, in what key shall a man take
180 you to go in the song?

CLAUDIO In mine eye, she is the sweetest lady that ever I looked on.

BENEDICK I can see yet without spectacles and I see no such matter. There's her cousin, an she were not
185 possessed with a fury, exceeds her as much in beauty as the first of May doth the last of December. But I hope you have no intent to turn husband, have you?

CLAUDIO I would scarce trust myself, though I had sworn the contrary, if Hero would be my wife.

190 **BENEDICK** Is't come to this? In faith, hath not the world one man but he will wear his cap with suspicion? Shall I never see a bachelor of threescore again? Go to, i'faith, an thou wilt needs thrust thy neck into a yoke, wear the print of it and sigh away Sundays.
195 Look, Don Pedro is returned to seek you.

Enter Don Pedro [and] John the bastard

DON PEDRO What secret hath held you here, that you followed not to Leonato's?

BENEDICK I would your grace would constrain me to tell.

DON PEDRO I charge thee on thy allegiance.

200 **BENEDICK** You hear, Count Claudio. I can be secret as a dumb man, I would have you think so. But on my allegiance, mark you this, on my allegiance — he is in love. With who? Now that is your grace's part.

---

171 **in sport** joking, being playful   176 **case** plays on the sense of 'vagina' (**jewel** could also mean 'virginity')   177 **sad** serious   **flouting jack** mocking rascal   178 **hare-finder** one with eyesight sharp enough to spot a quick hare (the mockery of a **flouting Jack** as **Cupid** was blind)   **Vulcan** Roman god of fire, traditionally depicted as a blacksmith   180 **go** be in tune/harmonize   185 **fury** fierce passion/rage/ avenging spirit   191 **wear . . . suspicion** get married and invite suspicion when wearing his cap that it covers horns (signs of being a cuckold – i.e. having an unfaithful wife)   192 **threescore** sixty   **Go to** away with you (an expression of impatience)   194 **yoke** wooden apparatus worn on the neck of a captive and used to subdue and prevent escape; a similar device is used to couple oxen together for ploughing   **print** imprint   **sigh away Sundays** which must now be spent dutifully with one's wife   198 **constrain** compel   199 **charge** order   203 **part** i.e. to ask **with who?**

Mark how short his answer is: with Hero, Leonato's
205   short daughter.
CLAUDIO If this were so, so were it uttered.
BENEDICK Like the old tale, my lord: 'It is not so, nor
    'twas not so, but indeed, God forbid it should be so!'
CLAUDIO If my passion change not shortly, God forbid it
210   should be otherwise.
DON PEDRO Amen, if you love her, for the lady is very
    well worthy.
CLAUDIO You speak this to fetch me in, my lord.
DON PEDRO By my troth, I speak my thought.
215   **CLAUDIO** And in faith, my lord, I spoke mine.
BENEDICK And by my two faiths and troths, my lord, I
    spoke mine.
CLAUDIO That I love her, I feel.
DON PEDRO That she is worthy, I know.
220   **BENEDICK** That I neither feel how she should be loved,
    nor know how she should be worthy, is the opinion
    that fire cannot melt out of me: I will die in it at the
    stake.
DON PEDRO Thou wast ever an obstinate heretic in the
225   despite of beauty.
CLAUDIO And never could maintain his part but in the
    force of his will.
BENEDICK That a woman conceived me, I thank her.
    That she brought me up, I likewise give her most
230   humble thanks. But that I will have a recheat winded
    in my forehead, or hang my bugle in an invisible
    baldrick, all women shall pardon me. Because I will
    not do them the wrong to mistrust any, I will do
    myself the right to trust none. And the fine is — for
235   the which I may go the finer — I will live a bachelor.
DON PEDRO I shall see thee, ere I die, look pale with love.

---

206 If … uttered if this were indeed the case it would be uttered in this way   **207 'It … so!'** the quotation is supposedly from an old story in which it is uttered by a woman who has discovered that her lover is a robber   **213 fetch me in** trick me (into confessing)   **214 troth** good faith   **216 my … troths** Benedick owes loyalty to both Claudio, his **sworn brother**, and to Don Pedro, prince and military leader   **223 stake** a wooden post to which **heretics** were tied for burning   **224 heretic** one who holds blasphemous opinions or whose ideas are in opposition to accepted views   **225 despite** contempt   **226 maintain** justify   **in … will** by wilful obstinacy   **230 recheat** notes sounded on a horn for calling hounds together at a hunt (here symbolic of the cuckolded husband's horns)   **winded** blown   **231 bugle** horn (here suggestive of both the cuckold's horn and the penis)   **232 baldrick** shoulder belt used to hold a **bugle** (also suggestive of the vagina, particularly as it is **invisible** – i.e. hidden)   **234 fine** conclusion   **235 finer** more finely dressed (without a wife to support)

BENEDICK With anger, with sickness, or with hunger, my lord, not with love: prove that ever I lose more blood with love than I will get again with drinking, pick out mine eyes with a ballad-maker's pen, and hang me up at the door of a brothel-house for the sign of blind Cupid.

DON PEDRO Well, if ever thou dost fall from this faith, thou wilt prove a notable argument.

BENEDICK If I do, hang me in a bottle like a cat and shoot at me, and he that hits me, let him be clapped on the shoulder and called Adam.

DON PEDRO Well, as try. 'In time the savage bull doth bear the yoke.'

BENEDICK The savage bull may, but if ever the sensible Benedick bear it, pluck off the bull's horns and set them in my forehead, and let me be vilely painted, and in such great letters as they write 'Here is good horse to hire', let them signify under my sign 'Here you may see Benedick the married man.'

CLAUDIO If this should ever happen, thou wouldst be horn-mad.

DON PEDRO Nay, if Cupid have not spent all his quiver in Venice, thou wilt quake for this shortly.

BENEDICK I look for an earthquake too, then.

DON PEDRO Well, you will temporize with the hours. In the meantime, good Signior Benedick, repair to Leonato's, commend me to him, and tell him I will not fail him at supper, for indeed he hath made great preparation.

BENEDICK I have almost matter enough in me for such an embassage, and so I commit you—

---

238 prove i.e. should you prove   **more ... drinking** the heavy sighs brought on by love were thought to drain the heart of blood, while drinking wine was believed to fortify the blood flow   **240 ballad-maker** writer of ballads (songs of love)   **241 hang ... Cupid** brothels had signs painted on their walls   **for** in the place of   **244 argument** topic for discussion   **245 hang ... me** cats were sometimes suspended in baskets (bottles) and used for archery practice   **247 Adam** a reference to Adam Bell, a famous archer   **248 try** tell   **'In ... yoke'** a proverb that may have been popularized by its use in Thomas Kyd's play *The Spanish Tragedy*   **251 pluck ... forehead** another reference to cuckoldry   **253 in ... write** in lettering that is as big as that usually used to write   **254 sign** sign used to advertise a sideshow or public spectacle which consisted of a picture of the attraction with a description written under it   **257 horn-mad** completely mad/ enraged (like a charging bull or a furious cuckold)   **258 spent ... Venice** shot all of his arrows in Venice, famous for its sexual freedom and prostitution (**spent** puns on its sense of 'to ejaculate' and arrows are phallic)   **quiver** case for arrows (puns on **quake**)   **260 look for** await/expect   **261 temporize ... hours** become more temperate (milder) with time/waste time or procrastinate (**hours** may pun on 'whores')   **264 fail him** i.e. fail to attend   **266 matter** wit/sense   **267 embassage** message/mission

CLAUDIO To the tuition of God. From my house, if I had
        it—
270   DON PEDRO The sixth of July. Your loving friend,
        Benedick.
    BENEDICK Nay, mock not, mock not; the body of your
        discourse is sometime guarded with fragments, and
        the guards are but slightly basted on neither. Ere you
275   flout old ends any further, examine your conscience.
        And so I leave you.   *Exit*
    CLAUDIO My liege, your Highness now may do me good.
    DON PEDRO My love is thine to teach: teach it but how,
        And thou shalt see how apt it is to learn
280   Any hard lesson that may do thee good.
    CLAUDIO Hath Leonato any son, my lord?
    DON PEDRO No child but Hero, she's his only heir.
        Dost thou affect her, Claudio?
    CLAUDIO O, my lord,
285   When you went onward on this ended action,
        I looked upon her with a soldier's eye
        That liked, but had a rougher task in hand
        Than to drive liking to the name of love.
        But now I am returned, and that war-thoughts
290   Have left their places vacant, in their rooms
        Come thronging soft and delicate desires,
        All prompting me how fair young Hero is,
        Saying I liked her ere I went to wars.
    DON PEDRO Thou wilt be like a lover presently
295   And tire the hearer with a book of words.
        If thou dost love fair Hero, cherish it,
        And I will break with her and with her father,
        And thou shalt have her. Wast not to this end
        That thou began'st to twist so fine a story?
300   CLAUDIO How sweetly you do minister to love,
        That know love's grief by his complexion!
        But lest my liking might too sudden seem,
        I would have salved it with a longer treatise.

---

268 To ... Benedick Claudio and Don Pedro imitate the conventional ending of a letter   tuition care/
guidance   272 body basic material   273 guarded with fragments adorned with scraps
274 guards ... neither ornamental scraps are only loosely stitched on anyway   275 flout old ends mock
(me) with old tags of letters/fragments of cloth   277 do me good help me   279 apt quick/ready
283 affect love/favour   285 ended action recently ended military action   289 that now that
292 prompting reminding/urging   295 book of words lovers traditionally wrote lots of poetry
297 break broach the matter   299 twist weave   300 minister to tend to/administer a cure to
303 salved accounted for/applied soothing ointment to   treatise narrative

DON PEDRO What need the bridge much broader than
      the flood?
305   The fairest grant is the necessity.
    Look, what will serve is fit: 'tis once, thou lovest,
    And I will fit thee with the remedy.
    I know we shall have revelling tonight.
    I will assume thy part in some disguise
310   And tell fair Hero I am Claudio,
    And in her bosom I'll unclasp my heart,
    And take her hearing prisoner with the force
    And strong encounter of my amorous tale.
    Then after, to her father will I break,
315   And the conclusion is, she shall be thine.
    In practice let us put it presently.   *Exeunt*

[Act 1 Scene 2]   *running scene 2*

Enter Leonato and an old man [Antonio] brother to Leonato
[meeting]

LEONATO How now, brother, where is my cousin, your
    son? Hath he provided this music?
ANTONIO He is very busy about it. But brother, I can tell
    you strange news that you yet dreamt not of.
5   LEONATO Are they good?
ANTONIO As the event stamps them, but they have a
    good cover: they show well outward. The prince and
    Count Claudio, walking in a thick-pleached alley in
    my orchard, were thus overheard by a man of mine:
10   the prince discovered to Claudio that he loved my
    niece your daughter and meant to acknowledge it
    this night in a dance, and if he found her accordant,
    he meant to take the present time by the top and
    instantly break with you of it.
15   LEONATO Hath the fellow any wit that told you this?
ANTONIO A good sharp fellow. I will send for him, and
    question him yourself.

---

304 flood river   **305 The ... necessity** the best gift is the gift that is needed   **306 what ... fit** whatever is useful and will suffice is suitable   **'tis once** once and for all   **307 fit** supply   **311 in her bosom** privately   **unclasp** open (as if undoing the clasps of a book)   **313 encounter** conversational address/ military assault   **1.2**   **1 cousin** a general term for any relative or close friend   **5 they** i.e. the **news** **6 As ... them** as the outcome (**event**) determines/proves   **stamps** prints (the book metaphor continues with **cover**)   **7 show well outward** look promising   **8 thick-pleached alley** walk overarched by densely intertwining branches   **10 discovered** revealed   **12 accordant** of the same opinion/agreeable **13 take ... top** seize the opportunity   **15 wit** good sense/acumen

LEONATO No, no; we will hold it as a dream till it appear
itself. But I will acquaint my daughter withal, that
20   she may be the better prepared for an answer, if
peradventure this be true. Go you and tell her of it.
[Enter Attendants]
Cousins, you know what you have to do.— O, I cry
you mercy, friend, go you with me and I will use your
skill.— Good cousin, have a care this busy time.

Exeunt

[Act 1 Scene 3]   *running scene 3*

Enter Sir [Don] John the Bastard and Conrad his companion

CONRAD   What the goodyear, my lord, why are you
thus out of measure sad?

DON JOHN There is no measure in the occasion that
breeds, therefore the sadness is without limit.

5   **CONRAD** You should hear reason.

DON JOHN And when I have heard it, what blessing
bringeth it?

CONRAD If not a present remedy, yet a patient
sufferance.

10   **DON JOHN** I wonder that thou — being as thou sayest
thou art, born under Saturn — goest about to apply a
moral medicine to a mortifying mischief. I cannot
hide what I am: I must be sad when I have cause,
and smile at no man's jests, eat when I have
15   stomach, and wait for no man's leisure, sleep when
I am drowsy, and tend on no man's business, laugh
when I am merry, and claw no man in his humour.

CONRAD Yea, but you must not make the full show of
this till you may do it without controlment. You have
20   of late stood out against your brother, and he hath
ta'en you newly into his grace, where it is impossible
you should take true root but by the fair weather that
you make yourself. It is needful that you frame the
season for your own harvest.

18 **hold** regard   **appear** manifests   19 **withal** with it   21 **peradventure** perhaps   22 **cry you mercy** beg your pardon   23 **friend** i.e. one of the attendants, a musician   **1.3   1 What the goodyear** what the devil   **2 out of measure** immoderately   **3 measure** proportion/moderation/limit   **occasion that breeds** circumstances that provoke (my **sadness**)   **8 present** immediate   **9 sufferance** endurance   **11 Saturn** those born under the influence of Saturn were thought to be naturally morose and melancholy   **12 mortifying mischief** fatal disease   **16 tend on** attend/see to   **17 claw** soothe/flatter   **19 controlment** restraint   **20 stood ... brother** i.e. opposed Don Pedro in the recent war   **21 grace** favour   **23 frame** create

25   **DON JOHN** I had rather be a canker in a hedge than a
     rose in his grace, and it better fits my blood to be
     disdained of all than to fashion a carriage to rob love
     from any. In this — though I cannot be said to be a
     flattering honest man — it must not be denied but I
30   am a plain-dealing villain. I am trusted with a muzzle
     and enfranchised with a clog: therefore I have
     decreed not to sing in my cage. If I had my mouth,
     I would bite. If I had my liberty, I would do my liking.
     In the meantime, let me be that I am, and seek not to
35   alter me.

     CONRAD Can you make no use of your discontent?

     DON JOHN I will make all use of it, for I use it only. Who
     comes here?

     Enter Borachio

     What news, Borachio?

40   **BORACHIO** I came yonder from a great supper. The
     prince your brother is royally entertained by Leonato,
     and I can give you intelligence of an intended
     marriage.

     DON JOHN Will it serve for any model to build mischief
45   on? What is he for a fool that betroths himself to
     unquietness?

     BORACHIO Marry it is your brother's right hand.

     DON JOHN Who, the most exquisite Claudio?

     BORACHIO Even he.

50   **DON JOHN** A proper squire! And who, and who? Which
     way looks he?

     BORACHIO Marry, on Hero, the daughter and heir of
     Leonato.

     DON JOHN A very forward March-chick. How came you
55   to this?

     BORACHIO Being entertained for a perfumer, as I was
     smoking a musty room, comes me the prince and
     Claudio, hand in hand in sad conference. I whipped

---

25 canker wild rose (puns on the sense of 'cancer')   **26 blood** disposition/illegitimate status   **27 of
by   fashion a carriage** invent a demeanour/behaviour   **30 trusted … muzzle** like a fierce dog, only
trusted when wearing a muzzle   **31 enfranchised … clog** only given liberty with a heavy block of wood
tied to my leg   **37 use it only** am always discontented/discontent is my only resource   **38 *Borachio*** from
the Spanish **borracho** meaning 'drunkard'   **44 model** architectural plan   **46 unquietness** i.e. a troubled
life   **48 exquisite** accomplished/perfect   **50 proper squire** fine lover (the tone is contemptuous)
54 forward precocious/eager/ardent/presumptuous   **March-chick** very young thing (could apply to Hero
or Claudio, though Claudio seems likely)   **56 entertained …   perfumer** employed as burner of sweet-
smelling herbs in the rooms of a house   **57 smoking** perfuming   **58 sad** serious

me behind the arras and there heard it agreed upon
60   that the prince should woo Hero for himself, and
having obtained her, give her to Count Claudio.

DON JOHN Come, come, let us thither: this may prove
food to my displeasure. That young start-up hath all
the glory of my overthrow. If I can cross him any
65   way, I bless myself every way. You are both sure, and
will assist me?

CONRAD To the death, my lord.

DON JOHN Let us to the great supper. Their cheer is the
greater that I am subdued. Would the cook were of
70   my mind. Shall we go prove what's to be done?

BORACHIO We'll wait upon your lordship.   *Exeunt*

Act 2 Scene 1   *running scene 4*

Enter Leonato, [Antonio] his brother, [Innogen] his wife,
Hero his daughter [attended by Margaret and Ursula], and
Beatrice his niece and a Kinsman

LEONATO Was not Count John here at supper?

ANTONIO I saw him not.

BEATRICE How tartly that gentleman looks. I never can
see him but I am heart-burned an hour after.

5   **HERO** He is of a very melancholy disposition.

BEATRICE He were an excellent man that were made just
in the midway between him and Benedick: the one is
too like an image and says nothing, and the other too
like my lady's eldest son, evermore tattling.

10   **LEONATO** Then half Signior Benedick's tongue in Count
John's mouth, and half Count John's melancholy in
Signior Benedick's face —

BEATRICE With a good leg and a good foot, uncle, and
money enough in his purse, such a man would win
15   any woman in the world, if he could get her good
will.

LEONATO By my troth, niece, thou wilt never get thee a
husband if thou be so shrewd of thy tongue.

---

59 arras large tapestry hung on a wall for insulation (with sufficient space behind it for a man to conceal
himself)   **63 start-up** upstart   **64 overthrow** i.e. defeat in the war   **cross** thwart   **65 sure** reliable,
loyal   **68 cheer** merriment, joy   **69 subdued** low in spirits/conquered   **70 prove** put to the test/find out
by experience   **2.1 *Kinsman*** like Innogen, a 'ghost' character who does not speak   **3 tartly** sourly,
bitterly   **4 am heart-burned** suffer heartburn (indigestion)   **8 image** statue   **9 my ... son** a widow's
eldest son (traditionally a favoured and indulged child)   **13 good leg** i.e. shapely   **18 shrewd** mischievous/
sharp

ANTONIO In faith, she's too curst.

20 **BEATRICE** Too curst is more than curst. I shall lessen
God's sending that way, for it is said: 'God sends a
curst cow short horns', but to a cow too curst he
sends none.

LEONATO So, by being too curst, God will send you no
25 horns.

BEATRICE Just, if he send me no husband, for the which
blessing I am at him upon my knees every morning
and evening. Lord, I could not endure a husband
with a beard on his face! I had rather lie in the
30 woollen.

LEONATO You may light upon a husband that hath no
beard.

BEATRICE What should I do with him? Dress him in my
apparel and make him my waiting-gentlewoman? He
35 that hath a beard is more than a youth, and he that
hath no beard is less than a man: and he that is more
than a youth is not for me, and he that is less than a
man, I am not for him. Therefore I will even take
sixpence in earnest of the bearward and lead his apes
40 into hell.

LEONATO Well then, go you into hell.

BEATRICE No, but to the gate, and there will the devil
meet me like an old cuckold with horns on his head,
and say 'Get you to heaven, Beatrice, get you to
45 heaven, here's no place for you maids.' So deliver I up
my apes, and away to Saint Peter, for the heavens.
He shows me where the bachelors sit, and there live
we as merry as the day is long.

ANTONIO Well, niece, I trust you will be ruled by your   *To Hero*
50 father.

BEATRICE Yes, faith, it is my cousin's duty to make
curtsy and say 'Father, as it please you': but yet for
all that, cousin, let him be a handsome fellow, or else
make another curtsy and say 'Father, as it please
55 me.'

---

19 curst perverse/shrewish   **25 horns** in her response Beatrice plays on the senses of 'cuckold's horns' and 'penis'   **26 Just** exactly right   **29 the woollen** rough wool blankets (rather than a husband with a scratchy beard)   **34 apparel** clothing   **39 in earnest** as an advance payment   **the … hell** proverbially, the fate of an old maid was to lead apes in hell   **bearward** keeper of bears (and possibly apes)   **45 maids** virgins   **46 Saint Peter** heaven's gatekeeper   **for the heavens** a mild exclamation, but also with the sense of 'in order to get to heaven' or '**away to St Peter** as one who is in charge of entry to heaven'   **47 bachelors** unmarried people of both sexes

LEONATO Well, niece, I hope to see you one day fitted
    with a husband.

BEATRICE Not till God make men of some other metal
    than earth. Would it not grieve a woman to be
60   overmastered with a piece of valiant dust? To make
    account of her life to a clod of wayward marl? No,
    uncle, I'll none: Adam's sons are my brethren, and
    truly I hold it a sin to match in my kindred.

LEONATO Daughter, remember what I told you: if the   *To Hero*
65   prince do solicit you in that kind, you know your
    answer.

BEATRICE The fault will be in the music, cousin, if you be
    not wooed in good time. If the prince be too
    important, tell him there is measure in everything,
70   and so dance out the answer. For hear me, Hero:
    wooing, wedding and repenting is as a Scotch jig, a
    measure and a cinque-pace: the first suit is hot and
    hasty like a Scotch jig, and full as fantastical, the
    wedding mannerly-modest as a measure, full of state
75   and ancientry, and then comes repentance and, with
    his bad legs, falls into the cinque-pace faster and
    faster, till he sinks into his grave.

LEONATO Cousin, you apprehend passing shrewdly.

BEATRICE I have a good eye, uncle, I can see a church by
80   daylight.

LEONATO The revellers are entering, brother. Make good
    room.   *All put on their masks*

Enter Prince [Don] Pedro, Claudio, and Benedick, and
Balthasar, [Don] John, [Borachio, Margaret, Ursula and
other] Masquers with a drum   *Couples pair-up and begin dancing*

DON PEDRO Lady, will you walk a bout with your friend?

HERO So you walk softly, and look sweetly, and say
85   nothing, I am yours for the walk, and especially
    when I walk away.

---

56 fitted supplied (with suggestion of a vagina filled with a penis)   **58 metal** material (puns on 'mettle' meaning 'temperament')   **59 earth** a reference to the Christian notion that God made man from dust (whereas women were formed from one of Adam's ribs)   **61 wayward marl** unreasonable/changeable clay   **62 brethren** brothers   **63 match … kindred** marry a relative   **65 solicit** entreat/woo   **kind** manner (i.e. with talk of marriage)   **68 in good time** soon/in time to the music   **69 important** pressing, urgent   **measure** moderation (puns on the dance known as a measure)   **71 Scotch jig** a lively dance   **72 measure** a slow, stately dance   **cinque-pace** a lively dance involving five (**cinque**) steps (**pas**) and pronounced 'sink-a-pace' (thus leading to Beatrice's pun on **sink**)   **suit** wooing   **hot** passionate/vigorous   **73 fantastical** imaginative/full of wild movements   **74 mannerly-modest** decorously moderate   **state and ancientry** ceremonious dignity and old-fashioned formality   **76 bad legs** tottering or perhaps gout-ridden legs resulting from old age   **78 apprehend passing shrewdly** interpret things very severely/discern things very sharply   **83 friend** friend/lover   **84 So** so long as

DON PEDRO With me in your company?

HERO I may say so when I please.

DON PEDRO And when please you to say so?

90 **HERO** When I like your favour, for God defend the lute
should be like the case.

DON PEDRO My visor is Philemon's roof, within the
house is Jove.

HERO Why then your visor should be thatched.

95 **DON PEDRO** Speak low, if you speak love.   *They dance aside*

BALTHASAR Well, I would you did like me.

MARGARET So would not I for your own sake, for I have
many ill qualities.

BALTHASAR Which is one?

100 **MARGARET** I say my prayers aloud.

BALTHASAR I love you the better. The hearers may cry
'Amen'.

MARGARET God match me with a good dancer.

BALTHASAR Amen.

105 **MARGARET** And God keep him out of my sight when the
dance is done. Answer, clerk.

BALTHASAR No more words: the clerk is answered.   *They dance aside*

URSULA I know you well enough, you are Signior
Antonio.

110 **ANTONIO** At a word, I am not.

URSULA I know you by the waggling of your head.

ANTONIO To tell you true, I counterfeit him.

URSULA You could never do him so ill-well, unless you
were the very man. Here's his dry hand up and

115 down: you are he, you are he.

ANTONIO At a word, I am not.

URSULA Come, come, do you think I do not know you by
your excellent wit? Can virtue hide itself? Go to,
mum, you are he. Graces will appear, and there's an

120 end.   *They dance aside*

BEATRICE Will you not tell me who told you so?

BENEDICK No, you shall pardon me.

BEATRICE Nor will you not tell me who you are?

---

90 favour face   **91 case** a metaphorical reference to Don Pedro's (apparently unattractive) mask   **92 visor** mask   **Philemon's … Jove** the peasant Philemon entertained a disguised Jove (king of the gods) in his humble cottage   **94 thatched** i.e. like Philemon's cottage – perhaps a suggestion that Don Pedro is bald or balding, or that his mask lacks hair   **106 clerk** i.e. a parish clerk who led the responses during a church service   **110 At a word** in brief   **111 waggling** shaking, either the tremblings of old age or a gesture that accompanied his denial in the previous line   **112 counterfeit** imitate   **113 do … ill-well** imitate his inadequacies so well   **114 dry hand** a result of age   **up and down** all over/in every respect   **119 mum** silence   **Graces** attractive personal qualities/virtues

BENEDICK Not now.

125   **BEATRICE** That I was disdainful, and that I had my good
        wit out of the 'Hundred Merry Tales' — well, this was
        Signior Benedick that said so.

      BENEDICK What's he?

      BEATRICE I am sure you know him well enough.

130   **BENEDICK** Not I, believe me.

      BEATRICE Did he never make you laugh?

      BENEDICK I pray you, what is he?

      BEATRICE Why, he is the prince's jester, a very dull fool,
        only his gift is in devising impossible slanders. None

135   but libertines delight in him, and the commendation
        is not in his wit, but in his villainy, for he both
        pleaseth men and angers them, and then they laugh
        at him and beat him. I am sure he is in the fleet. I   *Aside?*
        would he had boarded me.

140   **BENEDICK** When I know the gentleman, I'll tell him
        what you say.

      BEATRICE Do, do: he'll but break a comparison or two on
        me, which peradventure — not marked or not
        laughed at — strikes him into melancholy, and then

145   there's a partridge wing saved, for the fool will eat no
        supper that night. We must follow the leaders.   *Music*

      BENEDICK In every good thing.

      BEATRICE Nay, if they lead to any ill, I will leave them at
        the next turning.

      Music for the Dance. [*Then*] *exeunt* [*dancing, all except Don*
      John, Borachio and Claudio]

150   **DON JOHN** Sure my brother is amorous on Hero and hath   *Aside to*
        withdrawn her father to break with him about it. The   *Borachio*
        ladies follow her and but one visor remains.

      BORACHIO And that is Claudio: I know him by his
        bearing.

155   **DON JOHN** Are not you Signior Benedick?   *To Claudio*

      CLAUDIO You know me well, I am he.

      DON JOHN Signior, you are very near my brother in his
        love. He is enamoured on Hero. I pray you dissuade

126 **'Hundred Merry Tales'** a popular collection of crude comic anecdotes   134 **only his** his only
impossible unbelievable   135 **libertines** those who disregard moral laws and follow their own inclinations
136 **villainy** wicked humour/discourtesy/low-minded jesting   137 **pleaseth … them** i.e. amuses some
with his rudeness but angers those he slanders   138 **in the fleet** amongst the dancers   139 **boarded**
tackled/accosted (puns on the sense of 'had sex with')   142 **break** as a lance might in jousting
comparison a sneering or unflattering analogy   145 **partridge wing** the part of the bird with virtually no
meat on it (Beatrice's comment is sarcastic)   146 **leaders** i.e. of the dance   150 **amorous on** courting
157 **near … love** i.e. close to/highly regarded by my brother

him from her, she is no equal for his birth. You may
160 do the part of an honest man in it.

CLAUDIO How know you he loves her?

DON JOHN I heard him swear his affection.

BORACHIO So did I too, and he swore he would marry
her tonight.

165 **DON JOHN** Come, let us to the banquet.

Exeunt [Don John and Borachio]

CLAUDIO Thus answer I in the name of Benedick,
But hear these ill news with the ears of Claudio.
'Tis certain so, the prince woos for himself.
Friendship is constant in all other things
170 Save in the office and affairs of love.
Therefore all hearts in love use their own tongues,
Let every eye negotiate for itself
And trust no agent, for beauty is a witch
Against whose charms faith melteth into blood.
175 This is an accident of hourly proof,
Which I mistrusted not. Farewell, therefore, Hero!

Enter Benedick

BENEDICK Count Claudio?

CLAUDIO Yea, the same.

BENEDICK Come, will you go with me?

180 **CLAUDIO** Whither?

BENEDICK Even to the next willow, about your own
business, count. What fashion will you wear the
garland of? About your neck, like an usurer's chain?
Or under your arm, like a lieutenant's scarf? You
185 must wear it one way, for the prince hath got your
Hero.

CLAUDIO I wish him joy of her.

BENEDICK Why, that's spoken like an honest drover, so
they sell bullocks. But did you think the prince would
190 have served you thus?

CLAUDIO I pray you leave me.

BENEDICK Ho, now you strike like the blind man: 'twas
the boy that stole your meat, and you'll beat the post.

---

165 banquet wine, fruit and sweetmeats served after the dance   **169 constant** unwavering/faithful
170 office service/business   **171 all** let all   **174 faith** loyalty/integrity   **blood** desire   **175 accident** ...
proof event that is shown to be the case very regularly   **176 mistrusted** suspected   **181 willow** a willow
garland was an emblem of unrequited love   **183 usurer's chain** heavy gold chain worn by wealthy
moneylenders   **184 lieutenant's scarf** sash worn diagonally across the chest as a symbol of rank
188 drover cattle-dealer   **so** in this way   **192 now** ... **post** i.e. strike out in anger (an allusion to a tale in
which a boy is punished for stealing meat from his blind master, and gets his revenge by causing the old man
to injure himself on a pillar)   **193 post** pillar/messenger (i.e. Benedick)

CLAUDIO If it will not be, I'll leave you.   *Exit*

195 **BENEDICK** Alas, poor hurt fowl, now will he creep into
            sedges. But that my Lady Beatrice should know me
            and not know me! The prince's fool! Ha? It may be I
            go under that title because I am merry. Yea, but so I
            am apt to do myself wrong. I am not so reputed: it is

200   the base, though bitter, disposition of Beatrice that
            puts the world into her person and so gives me out.
            Well, I'll be revenged as I may.
        Enter the Prince [Don Pedro]

     DON PEDRO Now, signior, where's the count? Did you
            see him?

205 **BENEDICK** Troth, my lord, I have played the part of Lady
            Fame. I found him here as melancholy as a lodge in a
            warren. I told him, and I think I told him true, that
            your grace had got the good will of this young lady,
            and I offered him my company to a willow-tree,

210   either to make him a garland, as being forsaken, or to
            bind him a rod, as being worthy to be whipped.

     DON PEDRO To be whipped? What's his fault?

     BENEDICK The flat transgression of a schoolboy, who,
            being overjoyed with finding a bird's nest, shows it

215   his companion, and he steals it.

     DON PEDRO Wilt thou make a trust a transgression? The
            transgression is in the stealer.

     BENEDICK Yet it had not been amiss the rod had been
            made, and the garland too: for the garland he might

220   have worn himself and the rod he might have
            bestowed on you, who, as I take it, have stolen his
            bird's nest.

     DON PEDRO I will but teach them to sing, and restore
            them to the owner.

225 **BENEDICK** If their singing answer your saying, by my
            faith you say honestly.

     DON PEDRO The Lady Beatrice hath a quarrel to you: the
            gentleman that danced with her told her she is much
            wronged by you.

---

194 **If … be** i.e. if you will not leave me   195 **hurt fowl** injured bird   196 **sedges** coarse rush-like plants
(where a wounded **fowl** might hide)   197 **not know me** not know my true nature   198 **so** in this way (i.e.
by being merry)   201 **puts … out** assumes that the world shares her opinions and represents me in that
way   205 **Lady Fame** i.e. a gossip   206 **Fame** rumour   **lodge … warren** dwelling (probably of a
gamekeeper) in an enclosed area used for breeding game (i.e. an isolated place)   210 **forsaken** rejected (by a
lover)   211 **bind … rod** bind together a bundle of twigs as rod for punishment   213 **flat transgression**
plain sin   216 **a trust** an act of trust   224 **them** i.e. the birds   225 **If … honestly** if what they sing agrees
with what you say you have taught them (i.e. to marry Claudio) then you speak honourably   227 **to** with

230   **BENEDICK** O, she misused me past the endurance of a
block! An oak but with one green leaf on it would
have answered her. My very visor began to assume
life and scold with her. She told me — not thinking I
had been myself — that I was the prince's jester, and
235   that I was duller than a great thaw, huddling jest
upon jest with such impossible conveyance upon me
that I stood like a man at a mark, with a whole army
shooting at me. She speaks poniards, and every word
stabs. If her breath were as terrible as her
240   terminations, there were no living near her, she
would infect to the North Star. I would not marry
her, though she were endowed with all that Adam
had left him before he transgressed. She would have
made Hercules have turned spit, yea, and have cleft
245   his club to make the fire too. Come, talk not of her,
you shall find her the infernal Ate in good apparel. I
would to God some scholar would conjure her, for
certainly, while she is here, a man may live as quiet
in hell as in a sanctuary, and people sin upon
250   purpose, because they would go thither: so indeed all
disquiet, horror and perturbation follows her.

    Enter Claudio and Beatrice, Leonato [and] Hero

  DON PEDRO Look, here she comes.

  BENEDICK Will your grace command me any service to
the world's end? I will go on the slightest errand now
255   to the Antipodes that you can devise to send me on:
I will fetch you a tooth-picker now from the furthest
inch of Asia, bring you the length of Prester John's
foot, fetch you a hair off the great Cham's beard, do
you any embassage to the Pygmies, rather than hold
260   three words' conference with this harpy. You have
no employment for me?

---

230 **misused** abused   231 **block** block of wood   235 **great thaw** the dull period during which roads
became muddy and impassable and people were unable to go out   **huddling** heaping up   236 **impossible
conveyance** incredible skill   237 **mark** archer's target (at which a man would have stood to note where
the arrows landed)   238 **poniards** daggers   240 **terminations** terms of expression   242 **all . . .
transgressed** i.e. the delights and dominion of the Garden of Eden before the Fall   244 **Hercules . . . too** in
Greek legend the Queen of Lydia, Omphale, made Hercules dress as a woman and spin wool while she took
over his **club** and lion's skin; turning a roasting **spit** was one of the lowliest domestic tasks   **cleft** split
246 **Ate** goddess of discord and vengeance   247 **conjure** exorcize (the sending of evil spirits back to hell had
to be carried out in Latin so a **scholar** would be required)   248 **here** i.e. on earth   249 **sanctuary** holy
place of safety   255 **Antipodes** the other side of the world   256 **tooth-picker** toothpick   257 **Prester
John** Christian ruler of a wealthy Eastern kingdom   258 **Cham** Kubla Khan, emperor of the Mongols
259 **Pygmies** race of very small people thought to live in Asia   260 **harpy** fierce mythical creature with the
face of a woman and body of a bird

DON PEDRO None, but to desire your good company.

BENEDICK O God, sir, here's a dish I love not: I cannot endure this Lady Tongue.   *Exit*

265 **DON PEDRO** Come, lady, come, you have lost the heart of Signior Benedick.

BEATRICE Indeed, my lord, he lent it me awhile, and I gave him use for it, a double heart for his single one: marry, once before he won it of me with false dice,
270 therefore your Grace may well say I have lost it.

DON PEDRO You have put him down, lady, you have put him down.

BEATRICE So I would not he should do me, my lord, lest I should prove the mother of fools. I have brought
275 Count Claudio, whom you sent me to seek.

DON PEDRO Why, how now, count? Wherefore are you sad?

CLAUDIO Not sad, my lord.

DON PEDRO How then? Sick?

280 **CLAUDIO** Neither, my lord.

BEATRICE The count is neither sad, nor sick, nor merry, nor well: but civil count, civil as an orange, and something of a jealous complexion.

DON PEDRO I'faith, lady, I think your blazon to be true,
285 though I'll be sworn, if he be so, his conceit is false. Here, Claudio, I have wooed in thy name, and fair Hero is won: I have broke with her father, and his good will obtained. Name the day of marriage, and God give thee joy!

290 **LEONATO** Count, take of me my daughter, and with her my fortunes. His grace hath made the match, and all grace say 'Amen' to it.

BEATRICE Speak, count, 'tis your cue.

CLAUDIO Silence is the perfectest herald of joy. I were but
295 little happy, if I could say how much. Lady, as you are mine, I am yours. I give away myself for you and dote upon the exchange.

BEATRICE Speak, cousin, or, if you cannot, stop his mouth with a kiss, and let not him speak neither.   *Claudio and Hero kiss?*

---

268 use financial interest on a loan (plays on the sense of 'usage')   **double** twice as loving/duplicitous
269 false dice i.e. false promises, deception   **271 put him down** defeated him with wit (Beatrice's response plays on the sense of 'sexually subdued')   **273 do** puns on the sense of 'have sex with'   **276 Wherefore** why   **282 civil count** grave/sober count (puns on 'Seville', the Spanish city well-known as a producer of bitter-tasting oranges)   **283 jealous complexion** i.e. yellow, a colour associated with melancholy and jealousy   **284 blazon** description   **285 conceit** understanding of things, notion   **292 grace** i.e. God
294 herald messenger/proclaimer   **297 dote upon** love dearly

300 **DON PEDRO** In faith, lady, you have a merry heart.

BEATRICE Yea, my lord, I thank it, poor fool, it keeps on the windy side of care. My cousin tells him in his ear that he is in her heart.

CLAUDIO And so she doth, cousin.

305 **BEATRICE** Good lord, for alliance! Thus goes everyone to the world but I, and I am sunburnt. I may sit in a corner and cry 'Hey-ho for a husband!'

DON PEDRO Lady Beatrice, I will get you one.

BEATRICE I would rather have one of your father's
310 getting. Hath your grace ne'er a brother like you? Your father got excellent husbands, if a maid could come by them.

DON PEDRO Will you have me, lady?

BEATRICE No, my lord, unless I might have another for
315 working days: your grace is too costly to wear every day. But I beseech your grace pardon me. I was born to speak all mirth and no matter.

DON PEDRO Your silence most offends me, and to be merry best becomes you, for out of question, you
320 were born in a merry hour.

BEATRICE No, sure, my lord, my mother cried, but then there was a star danced, and under that was I born. Cousins, God give you joy!

LEONATO Niece, will you look to those things I told you
325 of?

BEATRICE I cry you mercy, uncle.— By your grace's   *To Don Pedro*
pardon.   *Exit*

DON PEDRO By my troth, a pleasant-spirited lady.

LEONATO There's little of the melancholy element in her,
330 my lord: she is never sad but when she sleeps, and not ever sad then, for I have heard my daughter say, she hath often dreamt of unhappiness and waked herself with laughing.

DON PEDRO She cannot endure to hear tell of a husband.

---

302 windy ... care windward (i.e. advantageous/safe) side of trouble   **305 Good ... alliance!** Thank God for family unions/marriage!   **goes ... world** everyone gets married   **306 sunburnt** Elizabethans considered a tanned complexion unattractive   **307 'Hey-ho ... husband!'** a playful expression of regret that was also the title of a ballad   **310 getting** conception (a punning response to Don Pedro's sense of 'obtain')   **317 matter** substance/serious content   **318 Your ... me** i.e. I would much rather you talked on than were silent   **319 becomes** suits   **321 cried** i.e. at the pain of labour   **326 cry you mercy** beg your pardon   **By ... pardon** with your grace's (Don Pedro's) pardon (for my departure)   **329 melancholy element** the body was thought to consist of four elements, or humours, one of which was black bile, an excess of which caused melancholy   **331 ever** always

335 **LEONATO** O, by no means: she mocks all her wooers out
of suit.

DON PEDRO She were an excellent wife for Benedick.

LEONATO O lord, my lord, if they were but a week
married, they would talk themselves mad.

340 **DON PEDRO** Count Claudio, when mean you to go to
church?

CLAUDIO Tomorrow, my lord. Time goes on crutches till
love have all his rites.

LEONATO Not till Monday, my dear son, which is hence a
345 just seven-night, and a time too brief, too, to have all
things answer my mind.

DON PEDRO Come, you shake the head at so long a
breathing. But I warrant thee, Claudio, the time shall
not go dully by us. I will in the interim undertake one
350 of Hercules' labours, which is to bring Signior
Benedick and the Lady Beatrice into a mountain of
affection, th'one with th'other. I would fain have it a
match, and I doubt not but to fashion it, if you three
will but minister such assistance as I shall give you
355 direction.

LEONATO My lord, I am for you, though it cost me ten
nights' watchings.

CLAUDIO And I, my lord.

DON PEDRO And you too, gentle Hero?

360 **HERO** I will do any modest office, my lord, to help my
cousin to a good husband.

DON PEDRO And Benedick is not the unhopefullest
husband that I know. Thus far can I praise him: he
is of a noble strain, of approved valour and confirmed
365 honesty. I will teach you how to humour your cousin
that she shall fall in love with Benedick, and I, with   *To Leonato*
your two helps, will so practise on Benedick that, in   *and Claudio*
despite of his quick wit and his queasy stomach, he
shall fall in love with Beatrice. If we can do this,
370 Cupid is no longer an archer: his glory shall be ours,
for we are the only love-gods. Go in with me, and I
will tell you my drift.   *Exeunt*

---

335 suit courtship   **344 a just seven-night** precisely a week   **348 breathing** interval   **warrant** assure
350 Hercules' labours in Greek legend, Hercules carried out twelve seemingly impossible tasks (**labours**)
imposed on him by King Eurystheus   **352 fain** gladly   **354 minister** provide   **357 watchings** staying
awake   **360 modest** proper, seemly   **362 unhopefullest** least promising   **364 strain** descent, lineage
approved tested/proven   **365 honesty** honour   **367 practise on** work upon craftily   **368 queasy
stomach** feelings of sickness/delicate stomach/poor appetite (for love and marriage)   **372 drift** plan,
intention

[Act 2 Scene 2]

Enter [Don] John and Borachio

DON JOHN It is so: the Count Claudio shall marry the
daughter of Leonato.

BORACHIO Yea, my lord, but I can cross it.

DON JOHN Any bar, any cross, any impediment will be
5   medicinable to me: I am sick in displeasure to him,
and whatsoever comes athwart his affection ranges
evenly with mine. How canst thou cross this
marriage?

BORACHIO Not honestly, my lord, but so covertly that no
10   dishonesty shall appear in me.

DON JOHN Show me briefly how.

BORACHIO I think I told your lordship a year since, how
much I am in the favour of Margaret, the waiting
gentlewoman to Hero.

15 **DON JOHN** I remember.

BORACHIO I can at any unseasonable instant of the night
appoint her to look out at her lady's chamber
window.

DON JOHN What life is in that, to be the death of this
20   marriage?

BORACHIO The poison of that lies in you to temper. Go
you to the prince your brother, spare not to tell him
that he hath wronged his honour in marrying
the renowned Claudio — whose estimation do you
25   mightily hold up — to a contaminated stale, such a
one as Hero.

DON JOHN What proof shall I make of that?

BORACHIO Proof enough to misuse the prince, to vex
Claudio, to undo Hero, and kill Leonato. Look you for
30   any other issue?

DON JOHN Only to despite them, I will endeavour
anything.

BORACHIO Go, then, find me a meet hour to draw Don
Pedro and the Count Claudio alone. Tell them that
35   you know that Hero loves me, intend a kind of zeal
both to the prince and Claudio — as in a love of your

2.2 5 medicinable healing **6 comes athwart** impedes, is an obstacle to **ranges evenly** goes smoothly,
directly **16 unseasonable** inappropriate/odd **17 appoint** instruct **21 temper** mix **24 renowned**
well-reputed/honourable **estimation** worth **25 stale** prostitute **28 vex** torment, afflict **29 undo**
ruin **30 issue** outcome **31 despite** spite, wreak malice on **33 meet** suitable **draw** bring together
35 intend pretend **zeal** ardent loyalty **36 as in** as follows/such as

brother's honour, who hath made this match, and
his friend's reputation, who is thus like to be cozened
with the semblance of a maid — that you have
40   discovered thus. They will scarcely believe this
without trial: offer them instances, which shall bear
no less likelihood than to see me at her chamber
window, hear me call Margaret Hero, hear Margaret
term me Claudio, and bring them to see this the very
45   night before the intended wedding — for in the
meantime I will so fashion the matter that Hero shall
be absent — and there shall appear such seeming
truths of Hero's disloyalty that jealousy shall be
called assurance and all the preparation overthrown.
50   DON JOHN Grow this to what adverse issue it can, I will
put it in practice. Be cunning in the working this,
and thy fee is a thousand ducats.
BORACHIO Be thou constant in the accusation, and my
cunning shall not shame me.
55   DON JOHN I will presently go learn their day of marriage.

Exeunt

[Act 2 Scene 3]   *running scene 5*

Enter Benedick, alone

BENEDICK Boy!
[*Enter Boy*]
BOY Signior?
BENEDICK In my chamber-window lies a book: bring it
hither to me in the orchard.
5   BOY I am here already, sir.
BENEDICK I know that, but I would have thee hence and
here again.   *Exit* [*Boy*]
I do much wonder that one man, seeing how much
another man is a fool when he dedicates his
10   behaviours to love, will, after he hath laughed at
such shallow follies in others, become the argument
of his own scorn by falling in love: and such a man is

38 like likely   cozened cheated   39 semblance outward appearance   41 trial evidence   instances
proofs   46 fashion the matter arrange matters/contrive affairs   48 jealousy suspicion   49 preparation
i.e. for the wedding   50 Grow ... can no matter how harmful the outcome   51 working carrying out
of   52 ducats gold (sometimes silver) coins used in Europe   53 constant unchanging/resolved
2.3   5 I ... sir i.e. I will return so quickly that it will seem as if I had never left (in his reply Benedick
jestingly takes the Boy literally)   11 argument subject

Claudio. I have known when there was no music
with him but the drum and the fife, and now had he
15   rather hear the tabor and the pipe. I have known
when he would have walked ten mile afoot to see a
good armour, and now will he lie ten nights awake
carving the fashion of a new doublet. He was wont to
speak plain and to the purpose — like an honest man
20   and a soldier — and now is he turned orthography,
his words are a very fantastical banquet, just so
many strange dishes. May I be so converted and see
with these eyes? I cannot tell: I think not. I will not
be sworn, but love may transform me to an oyster,
25   but I'll take my oath on it, till he have made an oyster
of me, he shall never make me such a fool. One
woman is fair, yet I am well: another is wise, yet I am
well: another virtuous, yet I am well: but till all
graces be in one woman, one woman shall not come
30   in my grace. Rich she shall be, that's certain: wise, or
I'll none: virtuous, or I'll never cheapen her: fair, or
I'll never look on her: mild, or come not near me:
noble, or not I for an angel: of good discourse, an
excellent musician, and her hair shall be of what
35   colour it please God. Ha! The prince and Monsieur
Love! I will hide me in the arbour.   *He hides in the arbour*
Enter [Don Pedro], Leonato, Claudio and [Balthasar]
DON PEDRO Come, shall we hear this music?
CLAUDIO Yea, my good lord. How still the evening is,
As hushed on purpose to grace harmony.
40   **DON PEDRO** See you where Benedick hath hid himself?
CLAUDIO O, very well, my lord: the music ended,
We'll fit the kid-fox with a pennyworth.
DON PEDRO Come, Balthasar, we'll hear that song again.
BALTHASAR O, good my lord, tax not so bad a voice
45   To slander music any more than once.

---

14 drum ... fife i.e. war-like instruments   **fife** a flute-like instrument   **15 tabor ... pipe** i.e. instruments
associated with festivity   **tabor** a small drum   **16 afoot** on foot   **18 carving** designing   **doublet** close-
fitting jacket with flared base   **wont** accustomed   **20 orthography** stylistically polished and elaborate
21 fantastical fanciful, imaginative   **24 transform ... oyster** turn me into a lowly creature/silence me as
an oyster snaps shut   **29 graces** virtues   **30 grace** favour   **31 none** have none of her   **cheapen** bid
for   **32 or come** or she shall come   **33 noble** puns on the name of a gold coin   **angel** puns on the name of
a gold coin   **39 As** as if   **41 the music ended** i.e. once the music has ended   **42 fit ... pennyworth** i.e.
give him more than he bargained for   **kid-fox** cunning young fox   **44 tax** order

DON PEDRO It is the witness still of excellency
    To put a strange face on his own perfection.
    I pray thee sing, and let me woo no more.
BALTHASAR Because you talk of wooing, I will sing,
50   Since many a wooer doth commence his suit
    To her he thinks not worthy, yet he woos,
    Yet will he swear he loves.
DON PEDRO Nay, pray thee come,
    Or if thou wilt hold longer argument,
55   Do it in notes.
BALTHASAR Note this before my notes:
    There's not a note of mine that's worth the noting.
DON PEDRO Why, these are very crotchets that he
      speaks:
    Note notes, forsooth, and nothing. *Music*
60 **BENEDICK** Now, divine air! Now is his soul ravished.
    Is it not strange that sheep's guts should hale *Aside*
    souls out of men's bodies?
    Well, a horn for my money, when all's done.
BALTHASAR [*Sings*] *the song*
65   Sigh no more, ladies, sigh no more,
    Men were deceivers ever:
    One foot in sea and one on shore,
    To one thing constant never.
    Then sigh not so, but let them go,
70   And be you blithe and bonny,
    Converting all your sounds of woe
    Into hey nonny, nonny.

    Sing no more ditties, sing no moe,
    Of dumps so dull and heavy:
75   The fraud of men was ever so,
    Since summer first was leafy.
    Then sigh not so, etc.
DON PEDRO By my troth, a good song.
BALTHASAR And an ill singer, my lord.

---

46 It ... **perfection** it is always proof of excellence that it claims not to recognize its own skill   **48 woo** entreat, coax   **51 her ... worthy** Balthasar also refers to himself as one who is an unworthy singer, but whose skills have yet been courted by Don Pedro   **58 crotchets** whimsical fancies/musical notes
59 Note ... nothing pay attention to your musical notes, in truth, and nothing else (**nothing** puns on 'noting' which was pronounced in a similar manner)   **60 air** melody   **61 sheep's guts** from which an instrument's strings were made   **hale** haul   **63 horn** hunting horn, a more masculine instrument (possibly with an unconscious play on cuckold's horns)   **70 blithe and bonny** joyful and healthily beautiful
73 ditties songs   **moe** more   **74 dumps** low spirits (puns on the sense of 'sad songs')

80   DON PEDRO Ha, no, no, faith: thou sing'st well enough
        for a shift.
      BENEDICK An he had been a dog that should have   *Aside*
        howled thus, they would have hanged him, and I
        pray God his bad voice bode no mischief. I had as lief
85   have heard the night-raven, come what plague could
        have come after it.
      DON PEDRO Yea, marry, dost thou hear, Balthasar? I
        pray thee get us some excellent music, for tomorrow
        night we would have it at the Lady Hero's chamber
90   window.
      BALTHASAR The best I can, my lord.
      DON PEDRO Do so: farewell.   *Exit Balthasar*
        Come hither, Leonato. What was it you told me of
        today, that your niece Beatrice was in love with
95   Signior Benedick?
      CLAUDIO O, ay! Stalk on, the fowl sits.—   *Aside to Don Pedro*
        I did never think that lady would have loved any man.   *Aloud*
      LEONATO No, nor I neither, but most wonderful that she
        should so dote on Signior Benedick, whom she hath
100   in all outward behaviours seemed ever to abhor.
      BENEDICK Is't possible? Sits the wind in that corner?   *Aside*
      LEONATO By my troth my lord, I cannot tell what to
        think of it, but that she loves him with an enraged
        affection: it is past the infinite of thought.
105   DON PEDRO Maybe she doth but counterfeit.
      CLAUDIO Faith, like enough.
      LEONATO O God! Counterfeit? There was never
        counterfeit of passion came so near the life of
        passion as she discovers it.
110   DON PEDRO Why, what effects of passion shows she?
      CLAUDIO Bait the hook well, this fish will bite.   *Aside to them*
      LEONATO What effects, my lord? She will sit you — you
        heard my daughter tell you how.
      CLAUDIO She did indeed.
115   DON PEDRO How, how, I pray you? You amaze me: I
        would have thought her spirit had been invincible
        against all assaults of affection.

---

81 for a shift for the purpose/for lack of a better alternative   **82 An** if   **84 as lief** as soon/rather   **85 night-raven** the call of which was supposed to foretell disaster   **96 Stalk on** i.e. as a hunter would advance upon his prey (a sitting **fowl**)   **98 wonderful** extraordinary/astonishing   **101 Sits ... corner?** Is that the way the wind is blowing? (i.e. is that the way things are)   **103 enraged affection** furiously passionate love   **105 counterfeit** pretend   **109 discovers** reveals   **112 sit you** sit

LEONATO I would have sworn it had, my lord, especially
  against Benedick.

120 **BENEDICK** I should think this a gull, but that the white-   *Aside*
  bearded fellow speaks it: knavery cannot sure hide
  himself in such reverence.

CLAUDIO He hath ta'en th'infection — hold it up.   *Aside to them*

DON PEDRO Hath she made her affection known to
125 Benedick?

LEONATO No, and swears she never will. That's her
  torment.

CLAUDIO 'Tis true indeed, so your daughter says: 'Shall
  I,' says she, 'that have so oft encountered him with
130 scorn, write to him that I love him?'

LEONATO This says she now when she is beginning to
  write to him, for she'll be up twenty times a night,
  and there will she sit in her smock till she have writ a
  sheet of paper: my daughter tells us all.

135 **CLAUDIO** Now you talk of a sheet of paper, I remember a
  pretty jest your daughter told us of.

LEONATO O, when she had writ it, and was reading it
  over, she found 'Benedick' and 'Beatrice' between the
  sheet?

140 **CLAUDIO** That.

LEONATO O, she tore the letter into a thousand
  halfpence, railed at herself, that she should be so
  immodest to write to one that she knew would flout
  her. 'I measure him', says she, 'by my own spirit, for I
145 should flout him if he writ to me, yea, though I love
  him, I should.'

CLAUDIO Then down upon her knees she falls, weeps,
  sobs, beats her heart, tears her hair, prays, curses: 'O
  sweet Benedick! God give me patience!'

150 **LEONATO** She doth indeed, my daughter says so, and the
  ecstasy hath so much overborne her that my
  daughter is sometime afeard she will do a desperate
  outrage to herself: it is very true.

DON PEDRO It were good that Benedick knew of it by
155 some other, if she will not discover it.

CLAUDIO To what end? He would but make a sport of it
  and torment the poor lady worse.

---

120 gull trick/deception   **123 hold it up** keep up the trick/keep going   **133 smock** slip   **140 That** (yes)
that one   **142 halfpence** fragments (a halfpenny was a small coin)   **railed** ranted/chastised abusively
151 ecstasy frenzy   **overborne** overwhelmed   **153 outrage** violence

DON PEDRO An he should, it were an alms to hang him.
She's an excellent sweet lady and, out of all
160   suspicion, she is virtuous.

CLAUDIO And she is exceeding wise.

DON PEDRO In everything, but in loving Benedick.

LEONATO O, my lord, wisdom and blood combating in so
tender a body, we have ten proofs to one that blood
165   hath the victory. I am sorry for her, as I have just
cause, being her uncle and her guardian.

DON PEDRO I would she had bestowed this dotage on me:
I would have daffed all other respects and made her
half myself. I pray you tell Benedick of it and hear
170   what he will say.

LEONATO Were it good, think you?

CLAUDIO Hero thinks surely she will die, for she says she
will die if he love her not, and she will die ere she
make her love known, and she will die if he woo her,
175   rather than she will bate one breath of her
accustomed crossness.

DON PEDRO She doth well: if she should make tender of
her love, 'tis very possible he'll scorn it, for the man,
as you know all, hath a contemptible spirit.

180   **CLAUDIO** He is a very proper man.

DON PEDRO He hath indeed a good outward happiness.

CLAUDIO 'Fore God, and in my mind, very wise.

DON PEDRO He doth indeed show some sparks that are
like wit.

185   **LEONATO** And I take him to be valiant.

DON PEDRO As Hector, I assure you: and in the
managing of quarrels you may see he is wise, for
either he avoids them with great discretion, or
undertakes them with a Christian-like fear.

190   **LEONATO** If he do fear God, a must necessarily keep
peace. If he break the peace, he ought to enter into a
quarrel with fear and trembling.

DON PEDRO And so will he do, for the man doth fear God,
howsoever it seems not in him by some large jests he

---

158 alms charitable deed   **160 suspicion** doubt   **163 blood** passion/desire   **164 tender** young/delicate
167 dotage great love/infatuation   **168 daffed** doffed (i.e. cast off)   **respects** considerations   **made
... myself** i.e. married her   **175 bate** abate, modify   **177 make tender of** offer   **179 contemptible**
contemptuous/scornful   **180 proper** handsome   **181 good outward happiness** pleasingly attractive
appearance   **182 'Fore God** an exclamation roughly equivalent to 'indeed so, with God as my witness'
186 Hector the leader of the Trojans in the Trojan war, known for his bravery   **188 discretion** prudence,
good judgement   **194 by** to judge by   **large** coarse/unrestrained

195   will make. Well, I am sorry for your niece. Shall we
       go seek Benedick, and tell him of her love?

CLAUDIO Never tell him, my lord: let her wear it out with
       good counsel.

LEONATO Nay, that's impossible: she may wear her heart
200   out first.

DON PEDRO Well, we will hear further of it by your
       daughter. Let it cool the while. I love Benedick well,
       and I could wish he would modestly examine himself,
       to see how much he is unworthy to have so good a
205   lady.

LEONATO My lord, will you walk? Dinner is ready.

CLAUDIO If he do not dote on her upon this, I will never   *Aside to them*
       trust my expectation.

DON PEDRO Let there be the same net spread for her, and   *Aside to them*
210   that must your daughter and her gentlewoman
       carry. The sport will be when they hold one an
       opinion of another's dotage, and no such matter:
       that's the scene that I would see, which will be
       merely a dumb-show. Let us send her to call him in
215   to dinner.

                        Exeunt [Don Pedro, Claudio and Leonato]

BENEDICK This can be no trick: the conference was sadly   *He comes*
       borne, they have the truth of this from Hero. They   *forward*
       seem to pity the lady: it seems her affections have the
       full bent. Love me? Why, it must be requited. I hear
220   how I am censured: they say I will bear myself
       proudly, if I perceive the love come from her. They
       say too that she will rather die than give any sign of
       affection. I did never think to marry. I must not seem
       proud. Happy are they that hear their detractions
225   and can put them to mending. They say the lady is
       fair — 'tis a truth, I can bear them witness, and
       virtuous — 'tis so, I cannot reprove it, and wise, but
       for loving me — by my troth, it is no addition to her
       wit, nor no great argument of her folly, for I will be
230   horribly in love with her. I may chance have some

---

197 wear it out outlive it/use it up/grow tired of it   **198 counsel** reflection   **202 the while** in the
meantime   **203 modestly** in a reasonable, moderate way   **207 upon** after   **211 carry** carry out
they … dotage each believes that the other is in love   **212 no such matter** in fact there is no truth in
it   **214 dumb-show** play acted without words (as Benedick and Beatrice will be speechless)   **216 sadly
borne** seriously carried out   **218 have … bent** are engaged to their fullest extent (like a bow pulled as far
as possible)   **220 censured** judged/criticized   **224 their detractions** criticisms of themselves
227 reprove disprove/refute/reject   **229 argument** demonstration/evidence

odd quirks and remnants of wit broken on me
because I have railed so long against marriage. But
doth not the appetite alter? A man loves the meat in
his youth that he cannot endure in his age. Shall
235   quips and sentences and these paper bullets of the
brain awe a man from the career of his humour? No,
the world must be peopled. When I said I would die a
bachelor, I did not think I should live till I were
married. Here comes Beatrice. By this day, she's a fair
240   lady! I do spy some marks of love in her.

Enter Beatrice

BEATRICE Against my will I am sent to bid you come in
to dinner.

BENEDICK Fair Beatrice, I thank you for your pains.

BEATRICE I took no more pains for those thanks than
245   you take pains to thank me: if it had been painful, I
would not have come.

BENEDICK You take pleasure then in the message?

BEATRICE Yea, just so much as you may take upon a
knife's point and choke a daw withal. You have no
250   stomach, signior, fare you well.   *Exit*

BENEDICK Ha! 'Against my will I am sent to bid you
come in to dinner' — there's a double meaning in
that. 'I took no more pains for those thanks than you
took pains to thank me' — that's as much as to say,
255   'Any pains that I take for you is as easy as thanks.' If
I do not take pity of her, I am a villain: if I do not love
her, I am a Jew. I will go get her picture.   *Exit*

Act 3 Scene 1   *running scene 6*

Enter Hero, and two gentlewomen, Margaret and Ursula

HERO Good Margaret, run thee to the parlour,
There shalt thou find my cousin Beatrice
Proposing with the prince and Claudio.
Whisper her ear, and tell her I and Ursula
5   Walk in the orchard, and our whole discourse

231 **quirks** quips/witty conceits   **broken** cracked at my expense/snapped like a lance in jousting
235 **sentences** maxims, sayings   **paper ... brain** i.e. words, which cannot hurt   236 **awe** terrify/
restrain   **career ... humour** pursuit of his inclination **career** gallop of a horse, as in a tournament
243 **pains** efforts (Beatrice plays on the sense of literal pain in **painful**)   249 **choke** kill/silence   **daw**
jackdaw (proverbially a stupid bird, so also a rude reference to the talkative Benedick)   **withal** with
250 **stomach** appetite   257 **Jew** thought by many Elizabethans to be pitiless   **picture** a miniature, which
a lover might wear or carry with him   **3.1**   **3 Proposing** conversing

Is all of her. Say that thou overheard'st us,
And bid her steal into the pleachèd bower
Where honeysuckles, ripened by the sun,
Forbid the sun to enter, like favourites,
10 Made proud by princes, that advance their pride
Against that power that bred it: there will she hide her
To listen our purpose. This is thy office:
Bear thee well in it, and leave us alone.
MARGARET I'll make her come, I warrant you, presently.
                                                    [*Exit*]
15 HERO Now, Ursula, when Beatrice doth come,
As we do trace this alley up and down,
Our talk must only be of Benedick.
When I do name him, let it be thy part
To praise him more than ever man did merit:
20 My talk to thee must be how Benedick
Is sick in love with Beatrice. Of this matter
Is little Cupid's crafty arrow made,
That only wounds by hearsay.
Enter Beatrice [into the bower]
                                      Now begin:
For look where Beatrice like a lapwing runs
25 Close by the ground to hear our conference.
URSULA The pleasant'st angling is to see the fish   *To Hero*
Cut with her golden oars the silver stream,
And greedily devour the treacherous bait:
So angle we for Beatrice, who even now
30 Is couchèd in the woodbine coverture.
Fear you not my part of the dialogue.
HERO Then go we near her, that her ear lose nothing   *To Ursula*
Of the false sweet bait that we lay for it.   *They approach the bower*
No, truly, Ursula, she is too disdainful: *Aloud*
35 I know her spirits are as coy and wild
As haggards of the rock.
URSULA   But are you sure
That Benedick loves Beatrice so entirely?
HERO So says the prince and my new-trothèd lord.

---

10 advance ... it defy the very prince whose favour made them great   **12 purpose** matter of our conversation   **office** duty/task   **16 trace** range through, pass along   **23 hearsay** report/rumour/ something overheard   **24 lapwing** bird of the plover family known for running through the grass in a crouching fashion   **27 oars** i.e. fins   **30 couchèd ... coverture** lying hidden in the thick covering of honeysuckle   **35 coy** disdainful   **wild** unrestrained/wayward/rude/fierce   **36 haggards** untamed female hawks   **38 entirely** completely/sincerely   **39 new-trothèd** i.e. Claudio, newly betrothed

40 **URSULA** And did they bid you tell her of it, madam?

HERO They did entreat me to acquaint her of it,
But I persuaded them, if they loved Benedick,
To wish him wrestle with affection,
And never to let Beatrice know of it.

45 **URSULA** Why did you so? Doth not the gentleman
Deserve as full as fortunate a bed
As ever Beatrice shall couch upon?

HERO O god of love! I know he doth deserve
As much as may be yielded to a man.

50 But nature never framed a woman's heart
Of prouder stuff than that of Beatrice.
Disdain and scorn ride sparkling in her eyes,
Misprising what they look on, and her wit
Values itself so highly that to her

55 All matter else seems weak: she cannot love,
Nor take no shape nor project of affection,
She is so self-endeared.

URSULA Sure, I think so:
And therefore certainly it were not good

60 She knew his love, lest she make sport at it.

HERO Why, you speak truth. I never yet saw man,
How wise, how noble, young, how rarely featured,
But she would spell him backward: if fair-faced,
She would swear the gentleman should be her sister:

65 If black, why, nature, drawing of an antic,
Made a foul blot: if tall, a lance ill-headed:
If low, an agate very vilely cut:
If speaking, why, a vane blown with all winds:
If silent, why, a block movèd with none.

70 So turns she every man the wrong side out,
And never gives to truth and virtue that
Which simpleness and merit purchaseth.

URSULA Sure, sure, such carping is not commendable.

HERO No, not to be so odd and from all fashions

75 As Beatrice is cannot be commendable.
But who dare tell her so? If I should speak,

45 **Doth ... upon?** i.e. doesn't Benedick deserve a wife as good as Beatrice 46 **bed** marriage bed
47 **couch** lie 49 **yielded** given 53 **Misprising** undervaluing/scorning 55 **weak** of little worth/
contemptible 56 **project** conception, notion 57 **self-endeared** in love with herself 62 **How** however
rarely excellently 63 **spell him backward** declare he is the opposite **fair-faced** attractive/light-
complexioned 65 **black** dark-complexioned **antic** grotesque figure/grinning buffoon 66 **ill-headed**
with a poorly made or misshapen head 67 **agate** an agate stone would often have a tiny figure carved into
it before being set in a ring 72 **simpleness** plainness/integrity **purchaseth** earns/deserves 73 **carping**
fault-finding 74 **odd** at odds with **from** contrary to

       She would mock me into air: O, she would laugh me
       Out of myself, press me to death with wit.
       Therefore let Benedick, like covered fire,
80   Consume away in sighs, waste inwardly.
       It were a better death than die with mocks,
       Which is as bad as die with tickling.
URSULA Yet tell her of it: hear what she will say.
HERO No, rather I will go to Benedick
85   And counsel him to fight against his passion.
       And truly I'll devise some honest slanders
       To stain my cousin with. One doth not know
       How much an ill word may empoison liking.
URSULA O, do not do your cousin such a wrong.
90   She cannot be so much without true judgement —
       Having so swift and excellent a wit
       As she is prized to have — as to refuse
       So rare a gentleman as Signior Benedick.
HERO He is the only man of Italy,
95   Always excepted my dear Claudio.
URSULA I pray you be not angry with me, madam,
       Speaking my fancy: Signior Benedick,
       For shape, for bearing, argument and valour,
       Goes foremost in report through Italy.
100 **HERO** Indeed he hath an excellent good name.
URSULA His excellence did earn it ere he had it.
       When are you married, madam?
HERO Why, every day, tomorrow. Come, go in:
       I'll show thee some attires, and have thy counsel   *They step back*
105   Which is the best to furnish me tomorrow.   *from the bower*
URSULA She's ta'en, I warrant you: we have caught her,
       madam.
HERO If it prove so, then loving goes by haps:
       Some Cupid kills with arrows, some with traps.
                             Exeunt [Hero and Ursula]
BEATRICE What fire is in mine ears? Can this be true?   *She comes*
110   Stand I condemned for pride and scorn so much?   *forward*
       Contempt farewell, and maiden pride adieu!
       No glory lives behind the back of such.

---

78 press … death pressing a person to death with heavy weights was the penalty for one who refused to plead guilty or innocent to a crime   **79 covered** covered with a tightly packed heap of fuel to ensure a long burning time   **85 counsel** advise   **86 honest slanders** i.e. slanders that will do no serious harm to her reputation   **92 prized** esteemed, valued   **94 only** i.e. best, unrivalled   **97 fancy** thought/preference/liking   **98 argument** skill in debate/powers of reasoning   **103 tomorrow** from tomorrow onwards **104 attires** ornamented headdresses with false hair attached to them   **105 furnish me** fit me out with, clothe me with   **107 haps** chance/accidents

And, Benedick, love on, I will requite thee,
Taming my wild heart to thy loving hand.
115 If thou dost love, my kindness shall incite thee
To bind our loves up in a holy band.
For others say thou dost deserve, and I
Believe it better than reportingly.   *Exit*

Act 3 Scene 2   *running scene 7*

Enter Prince [Don Pedro], Claudio, Benedick and Leonato

DON PEDRO I do but stay till your marriage be
consummate, and then go I toward Aragon.

CLAUDIO I'll bring you thither, my lord, if you'll
vouchsafe me.

5 **DON PEDRO** Nay, that would be as great a soil in the
new gloss of your marriage as to show a child his
new coat and forbid him to wear it. I will only be bold
with Benedick for his company, for from the crown of
his head to the sole of his foot he is all mirth. He hath

10 twice or thrice cut Cupid's bow-string and the little
hangman dare not shoot at him. He hath a heart as
sound as a bell and his tongue is the clapper, for what
his heart thinks his tongue speaks.

BENEDICK Gallants, I am not as I have been.

15 **LEONATO** So say I, methinks you are sadder.

CLAUDIO I hope he be in love.

DON PEDRO Hang him, truant! There's no true drop of
blood in him to be truly touched with love. If he be
sad, he wants money.

20 **BENEDICK** I have the toothache.

DON PEDRO Draw it.

BENEDICK Hang it.

CLAUDIO You must hang it first, and draw it afterwards.

DON PEDRO What? Sigh for the toothache?

25 **LEONATO** Where is but a humour or a worm.

114 Taming … hand i.e. as a hawk would learn to obey the falconer **116 band** bond (plays on sense of
'wedding ring') **118 reportingly** as it is reported/through hearsay **3.2 2 consummate** consummated/
accomplished **4 vouchsafe** permit **7 only … with** be bold only with (i.e. prevail upon) **11 hangman**
i.e. executioner **17 truant** knave **19 wants** lacks **21 Draw** extract (Claudio puns on the sense of
'disembowel', sometimes the fate of a hanged man) **22 Hang it** an expression of angry impatience
23 hang it teeth were hung up outside barbers' shops as advertisements for the dental work that barbers also
carried out (though Claudio also refers to the hanging, and drawing, of a criminal) **25 Where** where
there **humour … worm** toothache was thought to be caused either by the descent from the head into the
tooth of one of the four humours (fluids), or by a worm in the tooth

BENEDICK Well, everyone cannot master a grief but he
that has it.

CLAUDIO Yet say I, he is in love.

DON PEDRO There is no appearance of fancy in him,
30   unless it be a fancy that he hath to strange disguises
— as to be a Dutchman today, a Frenchman
tomorrow. Unless he have a fancy to this foolery,
as it appears he hath, he is no fool for fancy, as you
would have it to appear he is.

35 **CLAUDIO** If he be not in love with some woman, there is
no believing old signs: a brushes his hat o'mornings,
what should that bode?

DON PEDRO Hath any man seen him at the barber's?

CLAUDIO No, but the barber's man hath been seen with
40   him, and the old ornament of his cheek hath already
stuffed tennis-balls.

LEONATO Indeed, he looks younger than he did, by the
loss of a beard.

DON PEDRO Nay, a rubs himself with civet. Can you
45   smell him out by that?

CLAUDIO That's as much as to say the sweet youth's in
love.

DON PEDRO The greatest note of it is his melancholy.

CLAUDIO And when was he wont to wash his face?

50 **DON PEDRO** Yea, or to paint himself? For the which, I
hear what they say of him.

CLAUDIO Nay, but his jesting spirit, which is now crept
into a lute-string and now governed by stops.

DON PEDRO Indeed, that tells a heavy tale for him.
55   Conclude: he is in love.

CLAUDIO Nay, but I know who loves him.

DON PEDRO That would I know too. I warrant, one that
knows him not.

CLAUDIO Yes, and his ill conditions, and in despite of all,
60   dies for him.

DON PEDRO She shall be buried with her face upwards.

---

26 but except   **29 fancy** love (Don Pedro goes on to pun on the sense of 'whim')   **31 Frenchman
tomorrow** German and Spanish references follow hereafter in the Quarto (see Textual Notes); Folio's
omission of them may have been to avoid offence at court   **40 ornament ... tennis-balls** filling tennis balls
with beard-hair seems to have been an actual practice   **44 civet** a musky perfume obtained from the glands
of the civet cat   **45 smell him out** detect the truth/discern his presence by his smell   **48 note** sign
49 wont accustomed   **wash** clean/perfume   **50 paint** apply cosmetics   **53 lute-string** the lute was
considered the instrument of a lover   **governed** controlled/has the musical key determined   **stops** frets/
restraints/impediments   **54 heavy** sad   **59 ill conditions** bad characteristics   **60 dies** expires/orgasms
61 face upwards as a faithful Christian/in a sexual position, under Benedick

BENEDICK Yet is this no charm for the toothache. Old
signior, walk aside with me: I have studied eight or
nine wise words to speak to you, which these hobby-
65   horses must not hear. [*Exeunt Benedick and Leonato*]
DON PEDRO For my life, to break with him about
Beatrice.
CLAUDIO 'Tis even so. Hero and Margaret have by this
played their parts with Beatrice, and then the two
70   bears will not bite one another when they meet.
Enter [Don] John the Bastard
DON JOHN My lord and brother, God save you.
DON PEDRO Good den, brother.
DON JOHN If your leisure served, I would speak with you.
DON PEDRO In private?
75   **DON JOHN** If it please you. Yet Count Claudio may hear,
for what I would speak of concerns him.
DON PEDRO What's the matter?
DON JOHN Means your lordship to be married tomorrow?   *To Claudio*
DON PEDRO You know he does.
80   **DON JOHN** I know not that, when he knows what I
know.
CLAUDIO If there be any impediment, I pray you discover
it.
DON JOHN You may think I love you not: let that appear
85   hereafter, and aim better at me by that I now will
manifest. For my brother, I think he holds you well,
and in dearness of heart, hath holp to effect your
ensuing marriage — surely suit ill spent and labour
ill bestowed.
90   **DON PEDRO** Why, what's the matter?
DON JOHN I came hither to tell you, and, circumstances
shortened — for she has been too long a talking of —
the lady is disloyal.
CLAUDIO Who, Hero?
95   **DON PEDRO** Even she: Leonato's Hero, your Hero, every
man's Hero.
CLAUDIO Disloyal?

---

62 **Old signior** i.e. Leonato   64 **hobby-horses** jokers   66 **For** upon   68 **by this** by this time   71 **God
save you** a common greeting   72 **Good den** good evening   73 **If … served** if you have time
84 **let … hereafter** whether or not I love you will be apparent after I have imparted what I have to say
85 **aim … manifest** judge me more effectively according to what I will now reveal to you   86 **holds**
regards   91 **circumstances shortened** in brief/regardless of details   92 **a talking of** the subject of
conversation (either Claudio and Don Pedro's conversation or public gossip)

DON JOHN The word is too good to paint out her wickedness. I could say she were worse: think you
100 of a worse title, and I will fit her to it. Wonder not till further warrant. Go but with me tonight, you shall see her chamber window entered, even the night before her wedding-day. If you love her then, tomorrow wed her. But it would better fit your
105 honour to change your mind.

CLAUDIO May this be so?

DON PEDRO I will not think it.

DON JOHN If you dare not trust that you see, confess not that you know. If you will follow me, I will show you
110 enough, and when you have seen more and heard more, proceed accordingly.

CLAUDIO If I see anything tonight why I should not marry her tomorrow in the congregation where I should wed, there will I shame her.

115 **DON PEDRO** And, as I wooed for thee to obtain her, I will join with thee to disgrace her.

DON JOHN I will disparage her no farther till you are my witnesses. Bear it coldly but till night, and let the issue show itself.

120 **DON PEDRO** O day untowardly turned!

CLAUDIO O mischief strangely thwarting!

DON JOHN O plague right well prevented! So will you say when you have seen the sequel.   *Exeunt*

[Act 3 Scene 3]   *running scene 8*

Enter Dogberry and his compartner [Verges] with the Watch

DOGBERRY Are you good men and true?

VERGES Yea, or else it were pity but they should suffer salvation, body and soul.

DOGBERRY Nay, that were a punishment too good for
5 them, if they should have any allegiance in them, being chosen for the prince's watch.

---

98 **paint out** convey in full   100 **fit** suit/adapt   **Wonder** marvel/be incredulous   101 **warrant** proof   104 **fit** befit   108 **If … know** if you do not dare to admit that what you see with your own eyes is the case, then you had better say nothing about it/then you know nothing at all   118 **Bear it coldly** behave calmly   120 **untowardly turned** unfavourably changed   121 **mischief** misfortune/wickedness
3.3 *Dogberry* named after the berry of the wild cornel or dogwood, a type of shrub   *Verges* named after verjuice, the bitter juice that comes from unripe fruit   *Watch* a group of citizens who assisted with local policing   1 **true** reliable, honest   3 **salvation** a malapropism – Verges means 'damnation'   5 **allegiance** Dogberry means 'treachery'

VERGES Well, give them their charge, neighbour
    Dogberry.

DOGBERRY First, who think you the most desertless man
10   to be constable?

FIRST WATCHMAN Hugh Otecake, sir, or George Seacole,
    for they can write and read.

DOGBERRY Come hither, neighbour Seacole. God hath   *Second*
    blessed you with a good name: to be a well-favoured   *Watchman*
15   man is the gift of fortune, but to write and read   *steps forward*
    comes by nature.

SECOND WATCHMAN Both which, master constable—

DOGBERRY You have: I knew it would be your answer.
    Well, for your favour, sir, why, give God thanks, and
20   make no boast of it. And for your writing and
    reading, let that appear when there is no need of
    such vanity. You are thought here to be the most
    senseless and fit man for the constable of the watch:
    therefore bear you the lantern. This is your charge:
25   you shall comprehend all vagrom men, you are to bid
    any man stand, in the prince's name.

SECOND WATCHMAN How if a will not stand?

DOGBERRY Why, then, take no note of him, but let him
    go, and presently call the rest of the watch together,
30   and thank God you are rid of a knave.

VERGES If he will not stand when he is bidden, he is
    none of the prince's subjects.

DOGBERRY True, and they are to meddle with none but
    the prince's subjects. You shall also make no noise in
35   the streets, for for the watch to babble and talk is
    most tolerable and not to be endured.

WATCHMAN We will rather sleep than talk: we know
    what belongs to a watch.

DOGBERRY Why, you speak like an ancient and most
40   quiet watchman, for I cannot see how sleeping
    should offend: only have a care that your bills be not
    stolen. Well, you are to call at all the ale-houses, and
    bid them that are drunk get them to bed.

WATCHMAN How if they will not?

---

7 **charge** duties/responsibilities   9 **desertless** Dogberry's error for 'deserving'   11 **Otecake** from
'oatcake', a cake made of oatmeal   **Seacole** from 'sea coal', a more expensive type of fuel   14 **well-
favoured** good-looking   19 **favour** face/appearance   23 **senseless** Dogberry means 'sensible'   **fit**
suitable   25 **comprehend** malapropism for 'apprehend'   **vagrom** vagrant   26 **stand** stop   28 **take …
him** pay no attention to him   33 **meddle** be concerned/involved with   36 **tolerable** Dogberry means
'intolerable'   38 **belongs to** is the responsibility of   39 **ancient** experienced   41 **bills** long-handled
weapons with axe-like heads

45 **DOGBERRY** Why then, let them alone till they are sober:
        if they make you not then the better answer, you
        may say they are not the men you took them for.
    WATCHMAN Well, sir.

    DOGBERRY If you meet a thief, you may suspect him, by
50   virtue of your office, to be no true man: and for such
        kind of men, the less you meddle or make with them,
        why the more is for your honesty.
    WATCHMAN If we know him to be a thief, shall we not lay
        hands on him?

55 **DOGBERRY** Truly, by your office, you may, but I think
        they that touch pitch will be defiled. The most
        peaceable way for you, if you do take a thief, is to let
        him show himself what he is, and steal out of your
        company.

60 **VERGES** You have been always called a merciful man,
        partner.

    DOGBERRY Truly, I would not hang a dog by my will,
        much more a man who hath any honesty in him.
    VERGES If you hear a child cry in the night, you must
65   call to the nurse and bid her still it.

    WATCHMAN How if the nurse be asleep and will not hear
        us?

    DOGBERRY Why then, depart in peace, and let the child
        wake her with crying, for the ewe that will not hear
70   her lamb when it baas will never answer a calf when
        he bleats.

    VERGES 'Tis very true.

    DOGBERRY This is the end of the charge: you, constable,
        are to present the prince's own person. If you meet
75   the prince in the night, you may stay him.

    VERGES Nay, by'r lady, that I think a cannot.

    DOGBERRY Five shillings to one on't, with any man that
        knows the statues, he may stay him: marry, not
        without the prince be willing, for indeed the watch
80   ought to offend no man, and it is an offence to stay a
        man against his will.

    VERGES By'r lady, I think it be so.

    DOGBERRY Ha, ah, ha! Well, masters, good night, an
        there be any matter of weight chances, call up me.

50 true honest   **55 by** according to   **56 pitch** black tar-like substance   **defiled** polluted, soiled   **62 by my will** out of choice   **63 more** Dogberry means 'less'   **65 still** quiet/calm   **74 present** represent   **75 stay** detain   **76 by'r lady** by Our Lady (the Virgin Mary)   **78 statues** malapropism for 'statutes'   **marry** by the Virgin Mary   **84 chances** i.e. chances to occur

85   Keep your fellows' counsels and your own, and good
      night. Come, neighbour.   *Starts to go*

      WATCHMAN Well, masters, we hear our charge. Let us go
      sit here upon the church-bench till two, and then all
      to bed.

90   **DOGBERRY** One word more, honest neighbours. I pray
      you watch about Signior Leonato's door, for the
      wedding being there tomorrow, there is a great coil
      tonight. Adieu. Be vigitant, I beseech you.

                            Exeunt [Dogberry and Verges]
      Enter Borachio and Conrad
      BORACHIO What, Conrad?

95   **WATCHMAN** Peace! Stir not.   *Aside*

      BORACHIO Conrad, I say!

      CONRAD Here, man, I am at thy elbow.

      BORACHIO Mass, and my elbow itched, I thought there
      would be a scab follow.

100   **CONRAD** I will owe thee an answer for that: and now
      forward with thy tale.

      BORACHIO Stand thee close then under this penthouse,
      for it drizzles rain, and I will, like a true drunkard,
      utter all to thee.

105   **WATCHMAN** Some treason, masters. Yet stand close.   *Aside*

      BORACHIO Therefore know, I have earned of Don John a
      thousand ducats.

      CONRAD Is it possible that any villainy should be so dear?

      BORACHIO Thou shouldst rather ask if it were possible

110   any villainy should be so rich, for when rich villains
      have need of poor ones, poor ones may make what
      price they will.

      CONRAD I wonder at it.

      BORACHIO That shows thou art unconfirmed. Thou

115   knowest that the fashion of a doublet, or a hat, or
      a cloak, is nothing to a man.

      CONRAD Yes, it is apparel.

      BORACHIO I mean the fashion.

      CONRAD Yes, the fashion is the fashion.

---

85 counsels confidences   **92 coil** bustle   **93 vigitant** malapropism for 'vigilant'   **98 Mass** by the Mass
99 scab scoundrel/skin disease characterized by a rash or scaliness and itching   **102 close** concealed
penthouse overhanging part of a building   **108 dear** costly   **114 unconfirmed** inexperienced
116 is ... man does not represent a man's true self (Conrad, however, understands 'is of no importance to a
man')   **118 fashion** i.e. the style as opposed to garments (**apparel**) themselves

120 **BORACHIO** Tush, I may as well say the fool's the fool. But
seest thou not what a deformed thief this fashion is?
WATCHMAN I know that Deformed: a has been a vile thief   *Aside*
this seven years, a goes up and down like a
gentleman. I remember his name.
125 **BORACHIO** Didst thou not hear somebody?
CONRAD No, 'twas the vane on the house.
BORACHIO Seest thou not, I say, what a deformed thief
this fashion is, how giddily a turns about all the hot
bloods   between   fourteen   and   five-and-thirty,
130 sometimes fashioning them like Pharaoh's soldiers
in the reechy painting, sometime like god Bel's priests
in the old church-window, sometime like the shaven
Hercules in the smirched worm-eaten tapestry,
where his codpiece seems as massy as his club?
135 **CONRAD** All this I see, and I see that the fashion wears
out more apparel than the man. But art not thou
thyself giddy with the fashion too, that thou hast
shifted out of thy tale into telling me of the fashion?
BORACHIO Not so, neither. But know that I have tonight
140 wooed Margaret, the Lady Hero's gentlewoman, by
the name of Hero. She leans me out at her mistress'
chamber-window, bids me a thousand times good
night — I tell this tale vilely — I should first tell thee
how the prince, Claudio and my master, planted and
145 placed and possessed by my master Don John, saw
afar off in the orchard this amiable encounter.
CONRAD And thought they Margaret was Hero?
BORACHIO Two of them did, the prince and Claudio, but
the devil my master knew she was Margaret, and
150 partly by his oaths, which first possessed them, partly
by the dark night, which did deceive them, but
chiefly by my villainy, which did confirm any slander
that Don John had made. Away went Claudio
enraged, swore he would meet her as he was

121 deformed i.e. as fashion is constantly changing   **123 up and down** all over the place   **128 hot
bloods** spirited, eager young men   **130 Pharaoh's soldiers** the soldiers of the Egyptian king who pursued
the fleeing Israelites and were drowned in the Red Sea   **131 reechy** smoky/grimy   **god Bel's priests** in
the apocryphal Book of Daniel, the priests of Bel were slain by the King of Persia when Daniel showed that
their god was false   **133 smirched** soiled/discoloured   **134 codpiece** a conspicuous attachment, often
ornamented, sewn onto the front of breeches over the crotch   **massy** massive/heavy   **138 shifted** moved
(puns on the senses of 'shift' as 'underclothing' and as 'a change of clothes')   **140 gentlewoman**
attendant   **141 leans me out** leans out   **145 possessed** informed (with connotations of demonic
possession, especially given that Don John is subsequently referred to as **the devil**)   **146 amiable** loving
150 oaths avowals

155 appointed next morning at the temple, and there,
before the whole congregation, shame her with what
he saw o'er-night, and send her home again without
a husband.

FIRST WATCHMAN We charge you in the prince's name,
160 stand!

SECOND WATCHMAN Call up the right master constable.
We have here recovered the most dangerous piece of
lechery that ever was known in the commonwealth.

FIRST WATCHMAN And one Deformed is one of them. I
165 know him, a wears a lock.

CONRAD Masters, masters—

SECOND WATCHMAN You'll be made bring Deformed
forth, I warrant you.

CONRAD Masters—

170 FIRST WATCHMAN Never speak, we charge you. Let us
obey you to go with us.

BORACHIO We are like to prove a goodly commodity,
being taken up of these men's bills.

CONRAD A commodity in question, I warrant you. Come,
175 we'll obey you.   *Exeunt*

Act 3 Scene 4   *running scene 8*

Enter Hero and Margaret and Ursula

HERO   Good Ursula, wake my cousin Beatrice, and
desire her to rise.

URSULA I will, lady.

HERO And bid her come hither.

5 URSULA Well.   [*Exit*]

MARGARET Troth, I think your other rabato were better.

HERO No, pray thee good Meg, I'll wear this.

MARGARET By my troth 's not so good, and I warrant
your cousin will say so.

10 HERO My cousin's a fool, and thou art another. I'll wear
none but this.

MARGARET I like the new tire within excellently, if the
hair were a thought browner, and your gown's a

162 **recovered** malapropism for 'discovered'   163 **lechery** malapropism for 'treachery'   165 **lock**
lovelock, a fashionable lock of curled hair   167 **made** made to   171 **obey** the First Watchman means
'command'   172 **commodity** product/goods bought on credit   173 **taken up** arrested/received on
credit   **bills** long-handled weapons/promissory notes   174 **in question** subject to legal procedures/sought
after/in doubt   **3.4   6 rabato** stiff linen collar, sometimes used to support a ruff   12 **tire** attire (i.e.
headdress)   **within** i.e. in an inner room   13 **hair** i.e. false hair on the head-dress

most rare fashion, i'faith. I saw the Duchess of
15   Milan's gown that they praise so.

HERO O, that exceeds, they say.

MARGARET By my troth 's but a night-gown in respect of
yours — cloth a gold, and cuts, and laced with silver,
set with pearls, down sleeves, side sleeves, and skirts,
20   round underborne with a bluish tinsel: but for a fine,
quaint, graceful and excellent fashion, yours is worth
ten on't.

HERO God give me joy to wear it, for my heart is
exceeding heavy.

25   **MARGARET** 'Twill be heavier soon by the weight of a
man.

HERO Fie upon thee, art not ashamed?

MARGARET Of what, lady? Of speaking honourably? Is
not marriage honourable in a beggar? Is not your
30   lord honourable without marriage? I think you
would have me say, saving your reverence, 'a
husband'. An bad thinking do not wrest true
speaking, I'll offend nobody. Is there any harm in
'the heavier for a husband'? None, I think, an it be
35   the right husband and the right wife, otherwise 'tis
light and not heavy. Ask my Lady Beatrice else, here
she comes.

Enter Beatrice

HERO Good morrow, coz.

BEATRICE Good morrow, sweet Hero.

40   **HERO** Why, how now? Do you speak in the sick tune?

BEATRICE I am out of all other tune, methinks.

MARGARET Clap's into 'Light o' love' — that goes
without a burden. Do you sing it, and I'll dance it.

---

14 **rare** splendid   16 **exceeds** excels/is beyond comparison   17 **respect of** comparison to   18 **cuts**
slashes in the fabric of a garment that reveal differently coloured material beneath   **laced** trimmed
19 **down sleeves** fitted sleeves that went down to the wrists   **side sleeves** secondary open sleeves
hanging from the shoulders   20 **round underborne** trimmed all the way round (this could refer either to
the skirt or to the visible hem of a petticoat)   **tinsel** silk shot with gold or silver thread   21 **quaint**
attractive/elegant/skilfully made   22 **on't** of it   24 **heavy** sorrowful (Ursula plays on the literal sense of
'weighed down')   27 **Fie upon thee** an expression of disgust or indignation   29 **in** even in   30 **I . . .
husband** i.e. at this rate, I must even apologize for mentioning the word 'husband'   32 **An** if   **wrest**
distort/misinterpret   34 **an** if   36 **light** puns on 'sexually loose'   **else** otherwise   38 **coz** cousin
42 **Clap's into** let us start singing   **'Light o' love'** a popular tune   43 **burden** a man's part, the bass
accompaniment (Ursula continues to play on the idea of the **weight of a man**)   **dance** playing on the sexual
connotations of dancing

BEATRICE Ye light o' love with your heels! Then, if your
45   husband have stables enough, you'll look he shall
    lack no barns.

MARGARET O illegitimate construction! I scorn that with
    my heels.

BEATRICE 'Tis almost five o'clock, cousin, 'tis time you
50   were ready. By my troth, I am exceeding ill. Hey-ho!

MARGARET For a hawk, a horse, or a husband?

BEATRICE For the letter that begins them all, H.

MARGARET Well, an you be not turned Turk, there's no
    more sailing by the star.

55 BEATRICE What means the fool, trow?

MARGARET Nothing I, but God send every one their
    heart's desire!

HERO These gloves the Count sent me, they are an
    excellent perfume.

60 BEATRICE I am stuffed, cousin, I cannot smell.

MARGARET A maid, and stuffed! There's goodly catching
    of cold.

BEATRICE O, God help me, God help me! How long have
    you professed apprehension?

65 MARGARET Even since you left it. Doth not my wit
    become me rarely?

BEATRICE It is not seen enough, you should wear it in
    your cap. By my troth, I am sick.

MARGARET Get you some of this distilled *carduus*
70   *benedictus*, and lay it to your heart: it is the only
    thing for a qualm.

HERO There thou prick'st her with a thistle.

BEATRICE *Benedictus*? Why *benedictus*? You have some
    moral in this *benedictus*.

75 MARGARET Moral? No, by my troth I have no moral
    meaning, I meant plain holy-thistle. You may think
    perchance that I think you are in love, nay, by'r lady,
    I am not such a fool to think what I list, nor I list not

44 Ye ... heels! You're a light-heeled (i.e. promiscuous) one!   46 barns puns on 'bairns' (i.e. children)
47 illegitimate construction incorrect interpretation (puns on the notion of illegitimate children)
scorn ... heels reject that by stamping on or kicking at it   50 Hey-ho! ... husband? Ursula plays on the
title of the well-known ballad   52 H puns on 'ache', which was pronounced in the same way as the letter
53 an if   be ... Turk have not rejected your faith (by rejecting your loathing of love)   54 star the North
Star, a reliable indicator for navigators   55 trow I wonder   60 stuffed with a cold (Ursula puns on the
senses of 'penetrated sexually' and 'pregnant')   64 professed apprehension claimed to be witty
66 rarely excellently (Beatrice plays on the sense of 'infrequently')   67 in your cap i.e. like a fool's coxcomb
(headgear resembling a cock's comb)   69 *carduus benedictus* the 'holy thistle', a plant often used in
medicine (with an obvious pun on 'Benedick')   71 qualm sudden sensation of faintness or nausea   78 list
please

to think what I can, nor indeed I cannot think, if I
80   would think my heart out of thinking, that you are in
love or that you will be in love or that you can be in
love. Yet Benedick was such another, and now is he
become a man: he swore he would never marry, and
yet now in despite of his heart, he eats his meat
85   without grudging. And how you may be converted I
know not, but methinks you look with your eyes as
other women do.

BEATRICE What pace is this that thy tongue keeps?
MARGARET Not a false gallop.

Enter Ursula

90   URSULA Madam, withdraw. The prince, the count,
Signior Benedick, Don John, and all the gallants of
the town are come to fetch you to church.

HERO Help to dress me, good coz, good Meg, good Ursula.

[*Exeunt*]

Act 3 Scene 5   *running scene 10*

*Enter Leonato, and the Constable [Dogberry] and the
Headborough [Verges]*

LEONATO What would you with me, honest neighbour?
DOGBERRY Marry, sir, I would have some confidence
with you that decerns you nearly.
LEONATO Brief, I pray you, for you see it is a busy time
5   with me.
DOGBERRY Marry, this it is, sir.
VERGES Yes, in truth it is, sir.
LEONATO What is it, my good friends?
DOGBERRY Goodman Verges, sir, speaks a little off the
10   matter — an old man, sir, and his wits are not so
blunt as, God help, I would desire they were, but, in
faith, honest as the skin between his brows.
VERGES Yes, I thank God, I am as honest as any man
living that is an old man, and no honester than I.
15   DOGBERRY Comparisons are odorous: *palabras*, neighbour
Verges.
LEONATO Neighbours, you are tedious.

82 such another i.e. a similar enemy to love   **84 eats ... grudging** i.e. accepts his lot without
complaining   **89 false gallop** literally, a canter, but Ursula means 'I speak the truth'
3.5   2 confidence private conference   **3 decerns** a malapropism for 'concerns'   **9 Goodman** title for a
person beneath the rank of gentleman   **11 blunt** Dogberry means 'sharp'   **15 odorous** malapropism for
'odious'   **palabras** short for *pocas palabras*, the Spanish for 'few words'

DOGBERRY It pleases your worship to say so, but we are
the poor duke's officers. But truly, for mine own part,
20 if I were as tedious as a king, I could find in my heart
to bestow it all of your worship.

LEONATO All thy tediousness on me, ah?

DOGBERRY Yea, an 'twere a thousand times more than
'tis, for I hear as good exclamation on your worship
25 as of any man in the city, and though I be but a poor
man, I am glad to hear it.

VERGES And so am I.

LEONATO I would fain know what you have to say.

VERGES Marry, sir, our watch tonight, excepting your
30 worship's presence, have ta'en a couple of as arrant
knaves as any in Messina.

DOGBERRY A good old man, sir, he will be talking. As
they say, 'When the age is in, the wit is out', God
help us, it is a world to see. Well said, i'faith,
35 neighbour Verges. Well, God's a good man, an two
men ride of a horse, one must ride behind. An honest
soul, i'faith, sir, by my troth he is, as ever broke
bread. But God is to be worshipped, all men are not
alike, alas, good neighbour.

40 **LEONATO** Indeed, neighbour, he comes too short of you.

DOGBERRY Gifts that God gives.

LEONATO I must leave you.

DOGBERRY One word, sir: our watch, sir, have indeed
comprehended two auspicious persons, and we
45 would have them this morning examined before
your worship.

LEONATO Take their examination yourself and bring it
me. I am now in great haste, as may appear unto
you.

50 **DOGBERRY** It shall be suffigance.

LEONATO Drink some wine ere you go. Fare you well.

[*Enter a Messenger*]

MESSENGER My lord, they stay for you to give your
daughter to her husband.

LEONATO I'll wait upon them. I am ready.

Exeunt [Leonato and Messenger]

---

19 poor duke's officers Dogberry means 'duke's poor officers'   **20 tedious** Dogberry thinks that the word
means something complimentary, such as 'rich'   **24 exclamation** public complaint, but Dogberry means
'acclamation'   **29 excepting** Dogberry means 'respecting'   **30 arrant** notorious/absolute   **34 a world** i.e.
wondrous   **35 a good man** i.e. good   **44 comprehended** malapropism for 'apprehended'   **auspicious**
malapropism for 'suspicious'   **50 suffigance** malapropism for 'sufficient'

55 **DOGBERRY** Go, good partner, go, get you to Francis
Seacole, bid him bring his pen and inkhorn to the jail.
We are now to examination those men.

VERGES And we must do it wisely.

DOGBERRY We will spare for no wit, I warrant you.
60 Here's that shall drive some of them to a non-come.
Only get the learned writer to set down our
excommunication and meet me at the jail. *Exeunt*

Act 4 Scene 1   *running scene 11*

*Enter Prince [Don Pedro, Don John the] Bastard, Leonato,
Friar [Francis], Claudio, Benedick, Hero and Beatrice [and
Attendants]*

LEONATO Come, Friar Francis, be brief: only to the plain
form of marriage, and you shall recount their
particular duties afterwards.

FRIAR FRANCIS You come hither, my lord, to marry this
5   lady.

CLAUDIO No.

LEONATO To be married to her. Friar, you come to marry
her.

FRIAR FRANCIS Lady, you come hither to be married to
10   this count.

HERO I do.

FRIAR FRANCIS If either of you know any inward
impediment why you should not be conjoined, I
charge you on your souls to utter it.

15 **CLAUDIO** Know you any, Hero?

HERO None, my lord.

FRIAR FRANCIS Know you any, Count?

LEONATO I dare make his answer, none.

CLAUDIO O, what men dare do! What men may do!
20   What men daily do, not knowing what they do!

BENEDICK How now? Interjections? Why then, some be
of laughing, as ha, ha, he!

CLAUDIO Stand thee by, friar. Father, by your leave:
Will you with free and unconstrainèd soul
25   Give me this maid, your daughter?

---

56 inkhorn ink-well   **60 non-come** Dogberry probably means 'nonplus' (i.e. state of perplexity), but the
phrase also suggests 'non compos mentis' (i.e. mad)   **62 excommunication** malapropism for 'commu-
nication' (i.e. discussion) or possibly 'examination'   **4.1   12 inward** secret   **23 Stand thee by** stand
aside   **by your leave** with your permission (i.e. to call you **Father**)

LEONATO As freely, son, as God did give her me.

CLAUDIO And what have I to give you back whose worth
    May counterpoise this rich and precious gift?

DON PEDRO Nothing, unless you render her again.

30 **CLAUDIO** Sweet prince, you learn me noble thankfulness.
    There, Leonato, take her back again.   *Hands Hero to Leonato*
    Give not this rotten orange to your friend.
    She's but the sign and semblance of her honour.
    Behold how like a maid she blushes here.

35   O, what authority and show of truth
    Can cunning sin cover itself withal!
    Comes not that blood as modest evidence
    To witness simple virtue? Would you not swear,
    All you that see her, that she were a maid,

40   By these exterior shows? But she is none.
    She knows the heat of a luxurious bed:
    Her blush is guiltiness, not modesty.

LEONATO What do you mean, my lord?

CLAUDIO Not to be married,

45   Not to knit my soul to an approvèd wanton.

LEONATO Dear my lord, if you, in your own proof,
    Have vanquished the resistance of her youth,
    And made defeat of her virginity—

CLAUDIO I know what you would say: if I have known
    her,

50   You will say she did embrace me as a husband,
    And so extenuate the 'forehand sin.
    No, Leonato,
    I never tempted her with word too large,
    But, as a brother to his sister, showed

55   Bashful sincerity and comely love.

HERO And seemed I ever otherwise to you?

CLAUDIO Out on thee, seeming! I will write against it.
    You seem to me as Dian in her orb,
    As chaste as is the bud ere it be blown.

60   But you are more intemperate in your blood

---

28 **counterpoise** balance, equal   29 **render her again** give her back   30 **learn** teach   33 **sign and semblance** outward appearance and mere image   36 **withal** with   37 **blood** i.e. blush   38 **witness** bear witness to   41 **luxurious** lecherous   45 **approvèd** proved   46 **in ... proof** your own test of her   49 **known** had sex with   51 **extenuate ... sin** lessen the sin of having sex before marriage   53 **large** unrestrained/licentious   55 **Bashful** modest/sensitive   **comely** becoming/proper   57 **write against it** i.e. denounce it publicly   58 **Dian ... orb** Diana, goddess of chastity and the moon (her **orb**)   59 **blown** in bloom   60 **intemperate** immoderate, unbridled   **blood** sexual desire

            Than Venus or those pampered animals
            That rage in savage sensuality.
    HERO Is my lord well that he doth speak so wide?
    LEONATO Sweet prince, why speak not you?
65 DON PEDRO What should I speak?
            I stand dishonoured, that have gone about
            To link my dear friend to a common stale.
    LEONATO Are these things spoken, or do I but dream?
    DON JOHN Sir, they are spoken, and these things are
            true.
70 BENEDICK This looks not like a nuptial.
    HERO 'True'? O God!
    CLAUDIO Leonato, stand I here?
            Is this the prince? Is this the prince's brother?
            Is this face Hero's? Are our eyes our own?
75 LEONATO All this is so, but what of this, my lord?
    CLAUDIO Let me but move one question to your
            daughter,
            And by that fatherly and kindly power
            That you have in her, bid her answer truly.
    LEONATO I charge thee do so, as thou art my child.   *To Hero*
80 HERO O, God defend me, how am I beset!
            What kind of catechizing call you this?
    CLAUDIO To make you answer truly to your name.
    HERO Is it not Hero? Who can blot that name
            With any just reproach?
85 CLAUDIO Marry, that can Hero:
            Hero itself can blot out Hero's virtue.
            What man was he talked with you yesternight,
            Out at your window betwixt twelve and one?
            Now if you are a maid, answer to this.
90 HERO I talked with no man at that hour, my lord.
    DON PEDRO Why, then you are no maiden. Leonato,
            I am sorry you must hear. Upon mine honour,
            Myself, my brother and this grievèd count
            Did see her, hear her, at that hour last night,
95   Talk with a ruffian at her chamber window,
            Who hath indeed, most like a liberal villain,

---

61 Venus goddess of love   **63 wide** wide of the mark   **67 stale** prostitute   **76 move** put   **77 kindly** natural   **80 beset** assailed, besieged   **81 catechizing** questioning, a form of instruction used by the Church in which a person answers a set of questions about the Christian faith   **82 answer ... name** the first question in the Anglican catechism asks the respondent his or her name   **93 grievèd** wronged/afflicted with sorrow   **96 liberal** licentious/unrestrained

Confessed the vile encounters they have had
A thousand times in secret.

DON JOHN Fie, fie, they are not to be named, my lord,
100   Not to be spoken of.
There is not chastity enough in language
Without offence to utter them. Thus, pretty lady,
I am sorry for thy much misgovernment.

CLAUDIO O Hero! What a Hero hadst thou been,
105   If half thy outward graces had been placed
About thy thoughts and counsels of thy heart!
But fare thee well, most foul, most fair! Farewell,
Thou pure impiety and impious purity!
For thee I'll lock up all the gates of love,
110   And on my eyelids shall conjecture hang,
To turn all beauty into thoughts of harm,
And never shall it more be gracious.

LEONATO Hath no man's dagger here a point for me?   *Hero swoons*

BEATRICE Why, how now, cousin! Wherefore sink you
        down?
115   **DON JOHN** Come, let us go. These things, come thus to
        light,
Smother her spirits up.
                [*Exeunt Don Pedro, Don John and Claudio*]

BENEDICK How doth the lady?

BEATRICE Dead, I think. Help, uncle!
Hero! Why, Hero! Uncle! Signior Benedick! Friar!

120   **LEONATO** O fate! Take not away thy heavy hand.
Death is the fairest cover for her shame
That may be wished for.

BEATRICE How now, cousin Hero!

FRIAR FRANCIS Have comfort, lady.

125   **LEONATO** Dost thou look up?

FRIAR FRANCIS Yea, wherefore should she not?

LEONATO Wherefore? Why, doth not every earthly thing
Cry shame upon her? Could she here deny
The story that is printed in her blood?
130   Do not live, Hero, do not ope thine eyes,
For did I think thou wouldst not quickly die,
Thought I thy spirits were stronger than thy shames,
Myself would on the rearward of reproaches

103 **much misgovernment** great misconduct   105 **graces** virtues/attractions   109 **For** because
of   110 **conjecture** suspicion   112 **gracious** attractive/joyful/virtuous   116 **spirits** vital energies
125 **look up** revive/look heavenwards   133 **on … reproaches** following this disgrace

Strike at thy life. Grieved I, I had but one?
135   Chid I for that at frugal nature's frame?
O, one too much by thee! Why had I one?
Why ever wast thou lovely in my eyes?
Why had I not with charitable hand
Took up a beggar's issue at my gates,
140   Who smearèd thus, and mired with infamy,
I might have said 'No part of it is mine:
This shame derives itself from unknown loins'?
But mine, and mine I loved, and mine I praised,
And mine that I was proud on, mine so much
145   That I myself was to myself not mine,
Valuing of her — why, she, O, she is fallen
Into a pit of ink, that the wide sea
Hath drops too few to wash her clean again,
And salt too little which may season give
150   To her foul-tainted flesh!
BENEDICK Sir, sir, be patient.
For my part, I am so attired in wonder,
I know not what to say.
BEATRICE O, on my soul my cousin is belied!
155   **BENEDICK** Lady, were you her bedfellow last night?
BEATRICE No, truly not: although until last night,
I have this twelvemonth been her bedfellow.
LEONATO Confirmed, confirmed! O, that is stronger made
Which was before barred up with ribs of iron.
160   Would the two princes lie, and Claudio lie,
Who loved her so that, speaking of her foulness,
Washed it with tears? Hence from her, let her die.
FRIAR FRANCIS Hear me a little:
For I have only been silent so long,
165   And given way unto this course of fortune,
By noting of the lady. I have marked
A thousand blushing apparitions
To start into her face, a thousand innocent shames
In angel whiteness beat away those blushes,
170   And in her eye there hath appeared a fire
To burn the errors that these princes hold
Against her maiden truth. Call me a fool,

---

134 Grieved … one? Did I once grieve that I only had one child?   **135 Chid** contended with/chastised
frame plan/scheme of things   **140 mired** soiled   **infamy** bad reputation/disgrace   **144 mine so … her**
I was so devoted to and proud of her that I cared nothing for myself   **149 season** preservative   **152 attired**
clothed   **154 belied** slandered   **165 given way** gone along with   **167 apparitions** appearances

Trust not my reading nor my observations,
Which with experimental seal doth warrant
175   The tenure of my book: trust not my age,
My reverence, calling, nor divinity,
If this sweet lady lie not guiltless here
Under some biting error.
LEONATO Friar, it cannot be.
180   Thou seest that all the grace that she hath left
Is that she will not add to her damnation
A sin of perjury: she not denies it.
Why seek'st thou then to cover with excuse
That which appears in proper nakedness?
185   **FRIAR FRANCIS** Lady, what man is he you are accused of?
HERO They know that do accuse me: I know none.
If I know more of any man alive
Than that which maiden modesty doth warrant,
Let all my sins lack mercy! O my father,   `
190   Prove you that any man with me conversed
At hours unmeet, or that I yesternight
Maintained the change of words with any creature,
Refuse me, hate me, torture me to death!
FRIAR FRANCIS There is some strange misprision in the
        princes.
195   **BENEDICK** Two of them have the very bent of honour,
And if their wisdoms be misled in this,
The practice of it lives in John the bastard,
Whose spirits toil in frame of villainies.
LEONATO I know not. If they speak but truth of her,
200   These hands shall tear her. If they wrong her honour,
The proudest of them shall well hear of it.
Time hath not yet so dried this blood of mine,
Nor age so eat up my invention,
Nor fortune made such havoc of my means,
205   Nor my bad life reft me so much of friends,
But they shall find, awaked in such a kind,
Both strength of limb and policy of mind,

---

174 Which ... book which validates, through the confirmation of experience, all that I have read in books   **176 reverence** respected state   **divinity** status as a clergyman/knowledge of theology   **178 biting** severe/painful   **182 perjury** swearing something false to be true   **184 proper** true   **188 warrant** sanction   **191 unmeet** unsuitable   **192 Maintained the change** engaged in the exchange   **193 Refuse** reject/disown   **194 misprision** mistake, misunderstanding   **195 very bent of** a total inclination for   **197 practice** scheming/carrying out   **198 frame** plotting/creating   **201 proudest** finest/most arrogant/most eminent/most vigorous   **203 eat** eaten   **invention** inventiveness (to plan revenge)   **204 means** resources/wealth   **205 reft** deprived   **206 kind** manner   **207 policy** shrewdness

Ability in means and choice of friends,
To quit me of them throughly.

210 **FRIAR FRANCIS** Pause awhile,
And let my counsel sway you in this case.
Your daughter here the princes left for dead:
Let her awhile be secretly kept in,
And publish it that she is dead indeed.

215 Maintain a mourning ostentation,
And on your family's old monument
Hang mournful epitaphs, and do all rites
That appertain unto a burial.

LEONATO What shall become of this? What will this do?

220 **FRIAR FRANCIS** Marry, this well carried shall on her
behalf
Change slander to remorse, that is some good.
But not for that dream I on this strange course,
But on this travail look for greater birth.
She dying, as it must so be maintained,

225 Upon the instant that she was accused,
Shall be lamented, pitied and excused
Of every hearer, for it so falls out
That what we have we prize not to the worth
Whiles we enjoy it; but, being lacked and lost,

230 Why, then we rack the value, then we find
The virtue that possession would not show us
Whiles it was ours. So will it fare with Claudio:
When he shall hear she died upon his words,
Th'idea of her life shall sweetly creep

235 Into his study of imagination,
And every lovely organ of her life
Shall come apparelled in more precious habit,
More moving-delicate and full of life,
Into the eye and prospect of his soul

240 Than when she lived indeed. Then shall he mourn —
If ever love had interest in his liver —
And wish he had not so accusèd her,
No, though he thought his accusation true.
Let this be so, and doubt not but success

---

209 **quit ... throughly** avenge myself on them thoroughly   214 **publish** proclaim/make public
215 **mourning ostentation** display of mourning   216 **monument** burial vault   220 **carried** carried out/
managed   222 **that** i.e. the changing of **slander to remorse**   223 **on this travail** as a result of this effort
(**travail** plays on the sense of 'pains of childbirth')   228 **prize ... worth** value not at its full worth
230 **rack** stretch   235 **study of imagination** introspective musings   236 **organ** aspect, feature
237 **apparelled** dressed   **habit** clothing   239 **prospect** field of view   241 **interest in** a claim over
liver believed to be the seat of love and passion   244 **success** succeeding events

245   Will fashion the event in better shape
        Than I can lay it down in likelihood.
        But if all aim but this be levelled false,
        The supposition of the lady's death
        Will quench the wonder of her infamy.
250   And if it sort not well, you may conceal her,
        As best befits her wounded reputation,
        In some reclusive and religious life,
        Out of all eyes, tongues, minds and injuries.
BENEDICK Signior Leonato, let the friar advise you.
255   And though you know my inwardness and love
        Is very much unto the prince and Claudio,
        Yet, by mine honour, I will deal in this
        As secretly and justly as your soul
        Should with your body.
260 **LEONATO** Being that I flow in grief,
        The smallest twine may lead me.
FRIAR FRANCIS 'Tis well consented. Presently away,
        For to strange sores strangely they strain the cure.
        Come, lady, die to live. This wedding day
265   Perhaps is but prolonged. Have patience and endure.
                        Exeunt [all but Benedick and Beatrice]
BENEDICK Lady Beatrice, have you wept all this while?
BEATRICE Yea, and I will weep a while longer.
BENEDICK I will not desire that.
BEATRICE You have no reason, I do it freely.
270 **BENEDICK** Surely I do believe your fair cousin is
        wronged.
BEATRICE Ah, how much might the man deserve of me
        that would right her.
BENEDICK Is there any way to show such friendship?
275 **BEATRICE** A very even way, but no such friend.
BENEDICK May a man do it?
BEATRICE It is a man's office, but not yours.
BENEDICK I do love nothing in the world so well as you.
        Is not that strange?
280 **BEATRICE** As strange as the thing I know not. It were as
        possible for me to say I loved nothing so well as you,
        but believe me not: and yet I lie not. I confess

---

245 event outcome   **246 lay ... likelihood** outline its probable outcome   **247 aim ... false** intentions except this one are confounded   **249 wonder of** amazement at/curiosity about   **250 sort** turn out   **253 injuries** insults   **255 inwardness** intimacy   **260 Being that** since   **flow in grief** overflow with grief/ am overcome with tears   **261 twine** thread   **263 For ... cure** for extreme/unusual ills require extreme/ unusual remedies   **275 even** direct   **friend** friend/lover nothing, nor I deny nothing. I am sorry for my cousin.

285 **BENEDICK** By my sword, Beatrice, thou lovest me.

BEATRICE Do not swear by it and eat it.

BENEDICK I will swear by it that you love me, and I will make him eat it that says I love not you.

BEATRICE Will you not eat your word?

290 **BENEDICK** With no sauce that can be devised to it. I protest I love thee.

BEATRICE Why then, God forgive me.

BENEDICK What offence, sweet Beatrice?

BEATRICE You have stayed me in a happy hour: I was
295 about to protest I loved you.

BENEDICK And do it with all thy heart.

BEATRICE I love you with so much of my heart that none is left to protest.

BENEDICK Come, bid me do anything for thee.

300 **BEATRICE** Kill Claudio.

BENEDICK Ha, not for the wide world.

BEATRICE You kill me to deny. Farewell.

BENEDICK Tarry, sweet Beatrice.

BEATRICE I am gone, though I am here. There is no love
305 in you. Nay I pray you let me go.

BENEDICK Beatrice—

BEATRICE In faith, I will go.

BENEDICK We'll be friends first.

BEATRICE You dare easier be friends with me than fight
310 with mine enemy.

BENEDICK Is Claudio thine enemy?

BEATRICE Is a not approved in the height a villain, that
hath slandered, scorned, dishonoured my
kinswoman? O that I were a man! What, bear her
315 in hand until they come to take hands, and then,
with public accusation, uncovered slander,
unmitigated rancour — O God, that I were a man!
I would eat his heart in the market-place.

BENEDICK Hear me, Beatrice—

320 **BEATRICE** Talk with a man out at a window! A proper
saying!

BENEDICK Nay, but Beatrice—

---

286 **eat it** eat your words   291 **protest** declare/avow/insist   294 **stayed** detained, halted   303 **Tarry**
stay/linger   314 **bear ... hand** delude her with false hopes   315 **take hands** i.e. in marriage
316 **uncovered** open, barefaced   320 **A proper saying!** A fine story!

BEATRICE Sweet Hero! She is wronged, she is slandered,
    she is undone.

325 BENEDICK Beat—

BEATRICE Princes and counties! Surely, a princely
    testimony, a goodly Count Comfit, a sweet gallant,
    surely! O that I were a man for his sake! Or that I had
    any friend would be a man for my sake! But
330   manhood is melted into curtsies, valour into
    compliment, and men are only turned into tongue,
    and trim ones too. He is now as valiant as Hercules
    that only tells a lie and swears it. I cannot be a man
    with wishing, therefore I will die a woman with
335   grieving.

BENEDICK Tarry, good Beatrice. By this hand I love thee.

BEATRICE Use it for my love some other way than
    swearing by it.

BENEDICK Think you in your soul the Count Claudio
340   hath wronged Hero?

BEATRICE Yea, as sure as I have a thought or a soul.

BENEDICK Enough: I am engaged, I will challenge him. I
    will kiss your hand, and so leave you. By this hand,
    Claudio shall render me a dear account. As you hear
345   of me, so think of me. Go comfort your cousin, I must
    say she is dead: and so farewell.   [*Exeunt separately*]

Act 4 Scene 2   *running scene 12*

Enter the Constables [Dogberry and Verges], Borachio and
[Sexton as] the Town Clerk in gowns [with Conrad, and the
Watch]

DOGBERRY Is our whole dissembly appeared?

VERGES O, a stool and a cushion for the sexton.

SEXTON Which be the malefactors?

DOGBERRY Marry, that am I and my partner.

5 VERGES Nay, that's certain, we have the exhibition to
    examine.

SEXTON But which are the offenders that are to be
    examined? Let them come before master constable.

---

324 undone ruined   **326 counties** counts   **327 testimony** evidence/condemnation of error   **Count** plays
on the sense of 'charge in an indictment'   **Comfit** candy/**sweet**   **331 compliment** etiquette/display
turned into tongue are all talk   **332 trim** fine/elegant   **333 swears it** merely swears that the **lie** is
true   **342 engaged** pledged/accepting of Beatrice's wish   **344 dear** costly/significant   **4.2** *Sexton* a
church officer   **1 dissembly** malapropism for 'assembly'   **3 malefactors** wrongdoers   **5 exhibition**
Dogberry means 'commission' (i.e. authority to **examine** the **offenders**)

DOGBERRY Yea, marry, let them come before me. What
10   is your name, friend?

*Borachio and
Conrad are
brought forward*

BORACHIO Borachio.

DOGBERRY Pray, write down 'Borachio'.— Yours,
sirrah?

CONRAD I am a gentleman, sir, and my name is Conrad.

15   **DOGBERRY** Write down 'master gentleman Conrad'.
Masters, do you serve God? Masters, it is proved
already that you are little better than false knaves,
and it will go near to be thought so shortly. How
answer you for yourselves?

20   **CONRAD** Marry, sir, we say we are none.

DOGBERRY A marvellous witty fellow, I assure you. But I
will go about with him. Come you hither, sirrah, a
word in your ear, sir: I say to you, it is thought you
are false knaves.

To Borachio

25   **BORACHIO** Sir, I say to you we are none.

DOGBERRY Well, stand aside. 'Fore God, they are both in
a tale. Have you writ down that they are none?

SEXTON Master constable, you go not the way to
examine. You must call forth the watch that are
30   their accusers.

DOGBERRY Yea, marry, that's the eftest way. Let the
watch come forth. Masters, I charge you, in the
prince's name, accuse these men.

FIRST WATCHMAN This man said, sir, that Don John, the
35   prince's brother, was a villain.

DOGBERRY Write down 'Prince John a villain'. Why, this
is flat perjury, to call a prince's brother villain.

BORACHIO Master constable—

DOGBERRY Pray thee fellow, peace: I do not like thy look,
40   I promise thee.

SEXTON What heard you him say else?

SECOND WATCHMAN Marry, that he had received a
thousand ducats of Don John for accusing the Lady
Hero wrongfully.

45   **DOGBERRY** Flat burglary as ever was committed.

VERGES Yea, by th'mass, that it is.

---

13 sirrah sir (contemptuous)   **16 do … God** the 1600 Quarto follows this with an exchange censored
from the Folio: Conrad and Borachio reply 'Yea, sir, we hope', to which Dogberry says 'Write down that they
hope they serve God. And write "God" first, for God defend but God should go before such villains.' He then
continues 'Masters …', as in Folio   **21 witty** clever/wily   **22 go about with** get the better of/handle
26 in a tale in agreement   **31 eftest** a nonsense word, which Dogberry intends to mean 'easiest/nearest'

SEXTON What else, fellow?

FIRST WATCHMAN And that Count Claudio did mean,
upon his words, to disgrace Hero before the whole
50   assembly, and not marry her.

DOGBERRY O villain! Thou wilt be condemned into
everlasting redemption for this.

SEXTON What else?

WATCHMEN This is all.

55 **SEXTON** And this is more, masters, than you can deny.
Prince John is this morning secretly stolen away.
Hero was in this manner accused, in this very
manner refused, and upon the grief of this suddenly
died. Master Constable, let these men be bound, and
60   brought to Leonato. I will go before and show him
their examination.   [*Exit*]

DOGBERRY Come, let them be opinioned.

VERGES Let them be in the hands—

CONRAD Off, coxcomb!

65 **DOGBERRY** God's my life, where's the sexton? Let him
write down 'the prince's officer coxcomb'. Come, bind
them.— Thou naughty varlet!

CONRAD Away! You are an ass, you are an ass.

DOGBERRY Dost thou not suspect my place? Dost thou
70   not suspect my years? O that he were here to write
me down an ass! But masters, remember that I am an
ass: though it be not written down, yet forget not
that I am an ass. No, thou villain, thou art full of
piety, as shall be proved upon thee by good witness. I
75   am a wise fellow, and which is more, an officer, and
which is more, a householder, and which is more, as
pretty a piece of flesh as any in Messina, and one that
knows the law, go to, and a rich fellow enough, go to,
and a fellow that hath had losses, and one that hath
80   two gowns and everything handsome about him.
Bring him away. O that I had been writ down an ass!
                                        Exeunt

---

52 redemption Dogberry means 'damnation'   **62 opinioned** malapropism for 'pinioned' (i.e. bound)
63 Let … hands let their hands be tied   **64 coxcomb** fool   **67 naughty** wicked   **69 suspect**
malapropism for 'respect'   **74 piety** Dogberry means 'impiety'   **79 had losses** i.e. he was formerly even
wealthier   **80 two gowns** cloaks were fairly costly, so Dogberry suggests he has reasonably good
finances   **handsome** fitting/comfortable

Act 5 Scene 1

Enter Leonato and his brother [Antonio]

ANTONIO If you go on thus, you will kill yourself,
And 'tis not wisdom thus to second grief
Against yourself.
LEONATO I pray thee, cease thy counsel,
5   Which falls into mine ears as profitless
As water in a sieve: give not me counsel,
Nor let no comforter delight mine ear
But such a one whose wrongs do suit with mine.
Bring me a father that so loved his child,
10   Whose joy of her is overwhelmed like mine,
And bid him speak of patience,
Measure his woe the length and breadth of mine,
And let it answer every strain for strain,
As thus for thus, and such a grief for such,
15   In every lineament, branch, shape and form.
If such a one will smile and stroke his beard,
Bid sorrow wag, cry 'Hem!' when he should groan,
Patch grief with proverbs, make misfortune drunk
With candle-wasters, bring him yet to me,
20   And I of him will gather patience.
But there is no such man: for, brother, men
Can counsel and speak comfort to that grief
Which they themselves not feel, but tasting it,
Their counsel turns to passion, which before
25   Would give preceptial medicine to rage,
Fetter strong madness in a silken thread,
Charm ache with air and agony with words.
No, no, 'tis all men's office to speak patience
To those that wring under the load of sorrow,
30   But no man's virtue nor sufficiency
To be so moral when he shall endure
The like himself: therefore give me no counsel.
My griefs cry louder than advertisement.
ANTONIO Therein do men from children nothing differ.

5.1   **2 second** support   **8 suit with** correspond to/fit   **13 answer** requite   **strain** emotional pang/
melody   **15 lineament** physical feature/characteristic   **branch** division/part   **17 wag** be off   **'Hem!'** i.e.
clear one's throat in preparation for speech   **19 candle-wasters** those who waste candles by staying up
late for study or drinking   **24 passion** powerful emotion/rage   **25 preceptial** of precepts (i.e. instructions
or rules)   **29 wring** writhe/are oppressed/weep   **30 sufficiency** ability   **31 moral** full of moralizing advice
and opinions   **33 advertisement** advice/admonition/public proclamation

35 LEONATO I pray thee peace. I will be flesh and blood,
        For there was never yet philosopher
        That could endure the toothache patiently,
        However they have writ the style of gods
        And made a push at chance and sufferance.
40 ANTONIO Yet bend not all the harm upon yourself,
        Make those that do offend you suffer too.
    LEONATO There thou speak'st reason. Nay, I will do so.
        My soul doth tell me Hero is belied,
        And that shall Claudio know, so shall the prince
45   And all of them that thus dishonour her.
    Enter Prince [Don Pedro] and Claudio
    ANTONIO Here comes the prince and Claudio hastily.
    DON PEDRO Good den, good den.
    CLAUDIO Good day to both of you.
    LEONATO Hear you, my lords—
50 DON PEDRO We have some haste, Leonato.
    LEONATO Some haste, my lord! Well, fare you well, my
            lord:
        Are you so hasty now? Well, all is one.
    DON PEDRO Nay, do not quarrel with us, good old man.
    ANTONIO If he could right himself with quarrelling,
55   Some of us would lie low.
    CLAUDIO Who wrongs him?
    LEONATO Marry, thou dost wrong me, thou dissembler,
            thou: *Claudio prepares to draw his sword*
        Nay, never lay thy hand upon thy sword,
        I fear thee not.
60 CLAUDIO Marry, beshrew my hand
        If it should give your age such cause of fear:
        In faith, my hand meant nothing to my sword.
    LEONATO Tush, tush, man, never fleer and jest at me:
        I speak not like a dotard nor a fool,
65   As under privilege of age to brag
        What I have done being young or what would do
        Were I not old. Know, Claudio, to thy head,
        Thou hast so wronged my innocent child and me
        That I am forced to lay my reverence by,
70   And with grey hairs and bruise of many days,

---

35 **peace** silence 38 **However** however much **writ ... of** written in the manner of/written as if with the authority of 39 **made ... at** scorned/attacked **sufferance** suffering/endurance (of misery) 50 **have are in** 52 **all is one** it's all one/it does not matter 55 **Some of us** i.e. Don Pedro and Claudio 57 **dissembler** deceiver/hypocrite 60 **beshrew** curse 62 **meant ... sword** had no intentions towards my sword 63 **fleer** mock, jeer 64 **dotard** old fool 67 **head** face 69 **reverence** respect due to an old man

Do challenge thee to trial of a man.
I say thou hast belied mine innocent child:
Thy slander hath gone through and through her
    heart,
And she lies buried with her ancestors —
75   O, in a tomb where never scandal slept,
Save this of hers, framed by thy villainy!

CLAUDIO My villainy?

LEONATO Thine, Claudio, thine, I say.

DON PEDRO You say not right, old man.

80   **LEONATO** My lord, my lord,
I'll prove it on his body if he dare,
Despite his nice fence and his active practice,
His May of youth and bloom of lustihood.

CLAUDIO Away! I will not have to do with you.

85   **LEONATO** Canst thou so daff me? Thou hast killed my
        child:
If thou kill'st me, boy, thou shalt kill a man.

ANTONIO He shall kill two of us, and men indeed:
But that's no matter, let him kill one first.
Win me and wear me, let him answer me.
90   Come follow me, boy, come, sir boy, come follow me:
Sir boy, I'll whip you from your foining fence,
Nay, as I am a gentleman, I will.

LEONATO Brother—

ANTONIO Content yourself. God knows I loved my niece,
95   And she is dead, slandered to death by villains,
That dare as well answer a man indeed
As I dare take a serpent by the tongue.
Boys, apes, braggarts, Jacks, milksops!

LEONATO Brother Antony—

100   **ANTONIO** Hold you content. What, man! I know them,
        yea,
And what they weigh, even to the utmost scruple,
Scrambling, out-facing, fashion-monging boys,
That lie and cog and flout, deprave and slander,
Go anticly, and show outward hideousness,
105   And speak off half a dozen dang'rous words,

---

71 **trial … man** i.e. a duel   82 **nice fence** refined and skilful swordsmanship/defensive action
(contemptuous)   83 **lustihood** vigour   85 **daff** cast aside   89 **Win … me** overcome me and then brag
about it, flaunt your prize   91 **foining fence** thrusting swordsmanship   98 **braggarts** boasters   **Jacks**
rascals/louts   **milksops** effeminate/cowardly men   101 **weigh** i.e. are worth   **scruple** very small
measurement of weight   102 **Scrambling** contentious/uncouth   **out-facing** defiant/confrontational/
bullying   **fashion-monging** preoccupied with fashion/dandies   103 **cog** cheat   **flout** insult/mock
deprave defame/deride   104 **anticly** grotesquely   105 **speak off** throw out

How they might hurt their enemies, if they durst,
And this is all.

LEONATO But, brother Antony—

ANTONIO Come, 'tis no matter:

110   Do not you meddle, let me deal in this.

DON PEDRO Gentlemen both, we will not wake your
      patience.
      My heart is sorry for your daughter's death.
      But on my honour, she was charged with nothing
      But what was true, and very full of proof.

115   **LEONATO** My lord, my lord—

DON PEDRO I will not hear you.

Enter Benedick

LEONATO No? Come, brother, away! I will be heard.

ANTONIO And shall, or some of us will smart for it.

                    Exeunt both [Leonato and Antonio]

DON PEDRO See, see, here comes the man we went to
120   seek.

CLAUDIO Now, signior, what news?

BENEDICK Good day, my lord.

DON PEDRO Welcome, signior: you are almost come to
      part almost a fray.

125   **CLAUDIO** We had like to have had our two noses snapped
      off with two old men without teeth.

DON PEDRO Leonato and his brother. What think'st
      thou? Had we fought, I doubt we should have been
      too young for them.

130   **BENEDICK** In a false quarrel there is no true valour. I
      came to seek you both.

CLAUDIO We have been up and down to seek thee, for
      we are high-proof melancholy and would fain have it
      beaten away. Wilt thou use thy wit?

135   **BENEDICK** It is in my scabbard: shall I draw it?

DON PEDRO Dost thou wear thy wit by thy side?

CLAUDIO Never any did so, though very many have been
      beside their wit. I will bid thee draw, as we do the
      minstrels, draw to pleasure us.

140   **DON PEDRO** As I am an honest man, he looks pale. Art
      thou sick, or angry?

---

106 durst dared   **111 wake your patience** disturb your patience further   **125 had ... have** nearly
126 with by   **128 doubt** fear (said with irony)   **133 high-proof** in the highest degree   **135 draw** as one
draws a sword   **138 beside their wit** out of their minds (plays on **by thy side**)   **draw ... minstrels** draw it
as a musician (**minstrel**) would draw out his instrument from its case or draw a bow across strings

CLAUDIO What, courage, man! What though care killed
a cat, thou hast mettle enough in thee to kill care.

BENEDICK Sir, I shall meet your wit in the career, an you
145   charge it against me. I pray you choose another
subject.

CLAUDIO Nay then, give him another staff: this last was
broke cross.

DON PEDRO By this light, he changes more and more: I
150   think he be angry indeed.

CLAUDIO If he be, he knows how to turn his girdle.

BENEDICK Shall I speak a word in your ear?

CLAUDIO God bless me from a challenge!

BENEDICK You are a villain. I jest not: I will make it good   *Aside to Claudio*
155   how you dare, with what you dare, and when you
dare. Do me right, or I will protest your cowardice.
You have killed a sweet lady, and her death shall fall
heavy on you. Let me hear from you.

CLAUDIO Well, I will meet you, so I may have good
160   cheer.

DON PEDRO What? A feast, a feast?

CLAUDIO I'faith, I thank him: he hath bid me to a calf's
head and a capon, the which if I do not carve most
curiously, say my knife's naught. Shall I not find a
165   woodcock too?

BENEDICK Sir, your wit ambles well, it goes easily.

DON PEDRO I'll tell thee how Beatrice praised thy wit the
other day: I said, thou hadst a fine wit. 'True,' says
she, 'a fine little one.' 'No,' said I, 'a great wit.'
170   'Right,' says she, 'a great gross one.' 'Nay,' said I, 'a
good wit.' 'Just,' said she, 'it hurts nobody.' 'Nay,'
said I, 'the gentleman is wise.' 'Certain,' said she, 'a
wise gentleman.' 'Nay,' said I, 'he hath the tongues.'
'That I believe,' said she, 'for he swore a thing to me
175   on Monday night, which he forswore on Tuesday

142 care ... cat a common proverb   care anxiety/sorrow   143 mettle spirit, vigour   144 in the career
at full gallop, as in a jousting tournament   an if   145 charge level/advance in attack   147 staff
lance   148 cross crosswise, in the middle (an indication of clumsiness)   151 turn his girdle a common
proverb referring to the turning of one's belt (girdle) so that the buckle is at the back, and meaning 'put up
with it'   156 Do me right give me satisfaction   protest declare   159 so provided   160 cheer
entertainment   162 calf's ... capon animals associated with foolishness (the calf) and cowardice (the
capon, a castrated cockerel)   164 curiously skilfully   165 woodcock a bird associated with stupidity
166 ambles strolls (as opposed to moving rapidly)   easily in a state of ease/unhurriedly   168 fine
excellent (Beatrice's response plays on the senses of 'marvellously' and 'slender')   wit plays on the sense of
'penis'   173 wise gentleman either said with irony or meaning 'old fool'   hath the tongues can speak
foreign languages   175 forswore swore against/denied

morning: there's a double tongue, there's two
tongues.' Thus did she, an hour together,
transshape thy particular virtues: yet at last she
concluded with a sigh, thou wast the properest man
180   in Italy.

CLAUDIO For the which she wept heartily and said she
cared not.

DON PEDRO Yea, that she did: but yet for all that, an if
she did not hate him deadly, she would love him
185   dearly. The old man's daughter told us all.

CLAUDIO All, all, and moreover, God saw him when he
was hid in the garden.

DON PEDRO But when shall we set the savage bull's
horns on the sensible Benedick's head?

190   CLAUDIO Yea, and text underneath, 'Here dwells
Benedick the married man'?

BENEDICK Fare you well, boy, you know my mind. I will
leave you now to your gossip-like humour. You
break jests as braggarts do their blades, which God be
195   thanked, hurt not. My lord, for your many courtesies
I thank you. I must discontinue your company. Your
brother the bastard is fled from Messina: you have
among you killed a sweet and innocent lady. For my
Lord Lackbeard there, he and I shall meet: and till
200   then, peace be with him.   [*Exit*]

DON PEDRO He is in earnest.

CLAUDIO In most profound earnest, and I'll warrant you,
for the love of Beatrice.

DON PEDRO And hath challenged thee.

205   CLAUDIO Most sincerely.

DON PEDRO What a pretty thing man is when he goes in
his doublet and hose and leaves off his wit!

Enter Constable [*Dogberry, Verges and the Watch, with*]
Conrad and Borachio

CLAUDIO He is then a giant to an ape, but then is an ape
a doctor to such a man.

---

176 **double** twofold/duplicitous   178 **transshape** transform   179 **properest** most handsome/finest
185 **old man's daughter** i.e. Hero   186 **God … garden** an allusion both to Benedick hiding in the arbour
and to Adam, after his transgression, hiding from God in the Garden of Eden   188 **But … man** Don Pedro
and Claudio recall Benedick's earlier statement that this is to be his fate if he marries   194 **braggarts …**
blades i.e. as boasters damage or break their swords themselves to make it look as if they have been
fighting   195 **My lord** i.e. Don Pedro   207 **hose** breeches   208 **He … man** he (i.e. one who has left **off**
his wit) is then a hero (**giant**) in the eyes of a fool (**ape**), but in fact the fool is a learned person (**doctor**) in
comparison to him

210   DON PEDRO But, soft you, let me be: pluck up, my heart,
       and be sad. Did he not say my brother was fled?

       DOGBERRY Come you, sir: if justice cannot tame you, she
       shall ne'er weigh more reasons in her balance. Nay,
       an you be a cursing hypocrite once, you must be
215   looked to.

       DON PEDRO How now? Two of my brother's men bound?
       Borachio one!

       CLAUDIO Hearken after their offence, my lord.

       DON PEDRO Officers, what offence have these men done?
220   DOGBERRY Marry, sir, they have committed false report,
       moreover, they have spoken untruths, secondarily,
       they are slanders, sixth and lastly, they have belied a
       lady, thirdly, they have verified unjust things, and to
       conclude, they are lying knaves.

225   DON PEDRO First, I ask thee what they have done,
       thirdly, I ask thee what's their offence, sixth and
       lastly, why they are committed, and to conclude,
       what you lay to their charge.

       CLAUDIO Rightly reasoned, and in his own division. And
230   by my troth, there's one meaning well suited.

       DON PEDRO Who have you offended, masters, that you
       are thus bound to your answer? This learned
       constable is too cunning to be understood. What's
       your offence?

235   BORACHIO Sweet prince, let me go no farther to mine
       answer. Do you hear me, and let this count kill me. I
       have deceived even your very eyes. What your
       wisdoms could not discover, these shallow fools have
       brought to light, who in the night overheard me
240   confessing to this man, how Don John your brother
       incensed me to slander the Lady Hero, how you were
       brought into the orchard and saw me court Margaret
       in Hero's garments, how you disgraced her when you
       should marry her. My villainy they have upon
245   record, which I had rather seal with my death than
       repeat over to my shame. The lady is dead upon mine

---

210 **soft you** wait a moment   **pluck up** rouse/collect yourself   211 **sad** serious   213 **reasons** plays on
'raisins', then pronounced in a similar manner   **balance** scales, which Justice is traditionally depicted as
carrying   214 **cursing** swearing, or Dogberry may mean 'accursed'   218 **Hearken** inquire   220 **false
report** slander/untruths   222 **slanders** Dogberry means 'slanderers'   229 **division** logical order
232 **bound** on the way/tied up   **answer** trial   233 **cunning** ingenious/knowledgeable   241 **incensed**
incited

and my master's false accusation, and briefly, I desire
nothing but the reward of a villain.
DON PEDRO Runs not this speech like iron through your   *To Claudio*
250 blood?
CLAUDIO I have drunk poison whiles he uttered it.
DON PEDRO But did my brother set thee on to this?   *To Borachio*
BORACHIO Yea, and paid me richly for the practice of it.
DON PEDRO He is composed and framed of treachery,
And fled he is upon this villainy.
255 CLAUDIO Sweet Hero! Now thy image doth appear
In the rare semblance that I loved it first.
DOGBERRY Come, bring away the plaintiffs. By this time
our sexton hath reformed Signior Leonato of the
matter. And masters, do not forget to specify, when
260 time and place shall serve, that I am an ass.
VERGES Here, here comes master Signior Leonato, and
the sexton too.
Enter Leonato [and Antonio, with the Sexton]
LEONATO Which is the villain? Let me see his eyes,
That, when I note another man like him,
265 I may avoid him. Which of these is he?
BORACHIO If you would know your wronger, look on
me.
LEONATO Art thou the slave that with thy breath hast
killed
Mine innocent child?
BORACHIO Yea, even I alone.
270 LEONATO No, not so, villain, thou beliest thyself:
Here stand a pair of honourable men,
A third is fled, that had a hand in it.
I thank you, princes, for my daughter's death.
Record it with your high and worthy deeds,
275 'Twas bravely done, if you bethink you of it.
CLAUDIO I know not how to pray your patience,
Yet I must speak. Choose your revenge yourself,
Impose me to what penance your invention
Can lay upon my sin. Yet sinned I not
280 But in mistaking.
DON PEDRO By my soul, nor I.
And yet, to satisfy this good old man,

256 **semblance** image   257 **plaintiffs** Dogberry means 'defendants' (a plaintiff is a complainant)
258 **reformed** malapropism for 'informed'   271 **honourable men** i.e. Don Pedro and Claudio
278 **Impose me to** impose on me

           I would bend under any heavy weight
           That he'll enjoin me to.
285   **LEONATO** I cannot bid you bid my daughter live —
           That were impossible — but I pray you both,
           Possess the people in Messina here
           How innocent she died, and if your love
           Can labour aught in sad invention,
290   Hang her an epitaph upon her tomb,
           And sing it to her bones, sing it tonight:
           Tomorrow morning come you to my house,
           And since you could not be my son-in-law,
           Be yet my nephew. My brother hath a daughter,
295   Almost the copy of my child that's dead,
           And she alone is heir to both of us:
           Give her the right you should have giv'n her cousin,
           And so dies my revenge.
       CLAUDIO O noble sir,
300   Your over-kindness doth wring tears from me!
           I do embrace your offer and dispose
           For henceforth of poor Claudio.
       LEONATO Tomorrow then I will expect your coming,
           Tonight I take my leave. This naughty man
305   Shall face to face be brought to Margaret,
           Who I believe was packed in all this wrong,
           Hired to it by your brother.
       BORACHIO No, by my soul, she was not,
           Nor knew not what she did when she spoke to me,
310   But always hath been just and virtuous
           In anything that I do know by her.
       DOGBERRY Moreover, sir, which indeed is not under
           white and black, this plaintiff here, the offender, did
           call me ass. I beseech you let it be remembered in his
315   punishment. And also the watch heard them talk of
           one Deformed: they say he wears a key in his ear and
           a lock hanging by it, and borrows money in God's
           name, the which he hath used so long and never paid
           that now men grow hard-hearted and will lend
320   nothing for God's sake. Pray you examine him upon
           that point.
       LEONATO I thank thee for thy care and honest pains.

---

287 **Possess** inform   289 **aught** at all, to any extent   **invention** inventiveness/imagination   297 **right** puns on 'rite'   301 **dispose** you may dispose   306 **packed** implicated/acting as an accomplice 312 **under ... black** in writing   316 **they ... it** Dogberry's misunderstanding of the First Watchman's claim that Deformed **wears a lock**   317 **in God's name** the usual plea of a beggar

DOGBERRY Your worship speaks like a most thankful
and reverend youth, and I praise God for you.

325 **LEONATO** There's for thy pains.   *Gives money*

DOGBERRY God save the foundation!

LEONATO Go, I discharge thee of thy prisoner, and I
thank thee.

DOGBERRY I leave an arrant knave with your worship,

330 which I beseech your worship to correct yourself, for
the example of others. God keep your worship! I wish
your worship well. God restore you to health! I
humbly give you leave to depart, and if a merry
meeting may be wished, God prohibit it! Come,

335 neighbour.

LEONATO Until tomorrow morning, lords, farewell.

Exeunt [Dogberry and Verges]

ANTONIO Farewell, my lords: we look for you tomorrow.

DON PEDRO We will not fail.

CLAUDIO Tonight I'll mourn with Hero.

340 **LEONATO** Bring you these fellows on.— We'll talk with
Margaret,

How her acquaintance grew with this lewd fellow.   *To the Watch*

Exeunt [separately]

Act 5 Scene 2   *running scene 14*

Enter Benedick and Margaret [meeting]

BENEDICK Pray thee, sweet Mistress Margaret, deserve
well at my hands by helping me to the speech of
Beatrice.

MARGARET Will you then write me a sonnet in praise of

5 my beauty?

BENEDICK In so high a style, Margaret, that no man
living shall come over it, for in most comely truth
thou deservest it.

MARGARET To have no man come over me? Why, shall I

10 always keep below stairs?

BENEDICK Thy wit is as quick as the greyhound's mouth,
it catches.

326 **God … foundation!** the usual response of one receiving alms from a charitable foundation   333 **give you** Dogberry means 'ask your'   334 **prohibit** Dogberry means 'permit'   337 **look for** expect   341 **lewd** wicked/base   **5.2   2 the speech of** speak with   6 **style** poetic style (puns on 'stile')   7 **come over** surpass/surmount (Margaret plays on the sense of 'mount sexually')   **comely** proper/pleasing   10 **keep below stairs** remain (unmarried) in the servants' quarters   12 **catches** seizes (its prey)

MARGARET And yours as blunt as the fencer's foils,
which hit but hurt not.

15 BENEDICK A most manly wit, Margaret, it will not hurt a
woman: and so, I pray thee call Beatrice, I give thee
the bucklers.

MARGARET Give us the swords, we have bucklers of our
own.

20 BENEDICK If you use them, Margaret, you must put in
the pikes with a vice, and they are dangerous
weapons for maids.

MARGARET Well, I will call Beatrice to you, who I think
hath legs.   *Exit Margaret*

25 BENEDICK And therefore will come.
        The god of love,   *Sings*
        That sits above,
        And knows me, and knows me,
        How pitiful I deserve—

30 I mean in singing: but in loving, Leander the good
swimmer, Troilus the first employer of panders, and a
whole bookful of these quondam carpet-mongers,
whose names yet run smoothly in the even road of a
blank verse, why, they were never so truly turned

35 over and over as my poor self in love. Marry, I cannot
show it in rhyme, I have tried: I can find out no
rhyme to 'lady' but 'baby' — an innocent rhyme: for
'scorn,' 'horn' — a hard rhyme: for 'school,' 'fool' —
a babbling rhyme: very ominous endings. No, I was

40 not born under a rhyming planet, for I cannot woo in
festival terms.

Enter Beatrice

        Sweet Beatrice, wouldst thou come when I called
        thee?

BEATRICE Yea, signior, and depart when you bid me.

45 BENEDICK O, stay but till then!

---

13 foils swords with blunt edges   **16 give … bucklers** surrender   **18 swords** with phallic connotations   **bucklers** small shields with spikes in their centres/vaginas   **21 pikes** the shield's spikes/penises   **vice** screw (with sexual connotations)   **25 come** a possible pun on 'orgasm'   **26 The … deserve** the lyrics to a well-known Elizabethan song   **29 How … singing** how much pity I deserve for my poor singing   **30 Leander … swimmer** Leander regularly swam across the Hellespont to see his lover Hero, until one night he drowned   **31 Troilus … panders** Troilus was helped in his love affair with Cressida by the go-between (**pander**) Pandarus, though Cressida eventually rejected him   **32 quondam carpet-mongers** former ladies' men   **37 innocent** simple/foolish   **38 hard** poor/erect (playing on the phallic connotations of **horn**)   **41 festival** merry/light-hearted/celebratory

BEATRICE 'Then' is spoken: fare you well now. And yet
    ere I go, let me go with that I came, which is, with
    knowing what hath passed between you and
    Claudio.

50 BENEDICK Only foul words: and thereupon I will kiss
    thee.

BEATRICE Foul words is but foul wind, and foul wind is
    but foul breath, and foul breath is noisome: therefore
    I will depart unkissed.

55 BENEDICK Thou hast frighted the word out of his right
    sense, so forcible is thy wit. But I must tell thee
    plainly, Claudio undergoes my challenge, and either I
    must shortly hear from him, or I will subscribe him a
    coward. And I pray thee now tell me, for which of my
60   bad parts didst thou first fall in love with me?

BEATRICE For them all together, which maintained so
    politic a state of evil that they will not admit any
    good part to intermingle with them. But for which of
    my good parts did you first suffer love for me?

65 BENEDICK 'Suffer love'! A good epithet! I do suffer love
    indeed, for I love thee against my will.

BEATRICE In spite of your heart, I think. Alas, poor heart!
    If you spite it for my sake, I will spite it for yours, for I
    will never love that which my friend hates.

70 BENEDICK Thou and I are too wise to woo peaceably.

BEATRICE It appears not in this confession. There's not
    one wise man among twenty that will praise himself.

BENEDICK An old, an old instance, Beatrice, that lived in
    the time of good neighbours. If a man do not erect in
75   this age his own tomb ere he dies, he shall live no
    longer in monuments than the bells ring, and the
    widow weeps.

BEATRICE And how long is that, think you?

BENEDICK Question: why, an hour in clamour and a
80   quarter in rheum. Therefore is it most expedient for
    the wise, if Don Worm, his conscience, find no
    impediment to the contrary, to be the trumpet of his
    own virtues, as I am to myself. So much for praising

---

47 **that I came** that which I came for   53 **noisome** noxious   58 **subscribe** state/declare in writing
62 **politic** prudent   64 **suffer** experience/permit (Benedick puns on the senses of 'feel pain' and 'endure')
69 **friend** lover   71 **confession** statement/declaration/admission   73 **instance** saying/argument
74 **time ... neighbours** good old days (when neighbours were friendly)   75 **tomb** i.e. memorial
76 **monuments** memory   **bells ... weeps** i.e. the duration of the funeral and mourning period
79 **Question** you have asked a question, here follows the answer   **clamour** noise of the bells   80 **rheum**
tears   81 **Don ... conscience** conscience was often imaged as a gnawing worm

myself, who I myself will bear witness is
85   praiseworthy. And now tell me, how doth your
cousin?

BEATRICE Very ill.

BENEDICK And how do you?

BEATRICE Very ill too.

Enter Ursula

90   **BENEDICK** Serve God, love me and mend. There will I
leave you too, for here comes one in haste.

URSULA Madam, you must come to your uncle —
yonder's old coil at home: it is proved my Lady
Hero hath been falsely accused, the prince and
95   Claudio mightily abused, and Don John is the author
of all, who is fled and gone. Will you come presently?

BEATRICE Will you go hear this news, signior?

BENEDICK I will live in thy heart, die in thy lap, and be
buried in thy eyes. And moreover, I will go with thee
100   to thy uncle's.   *Exeunt*

Act 5 Scene 3   *running scene 15*

*Enter Claudio, Prince [Don Pedro] and three or four with
tapers [followed by Balthasar and Musicians]*

CLAUDIO Is this the monument of Leonato?

LORD It is, my lord.

CLAUDIO [*Reads the*] *epitaph*
        'Done to death by slanderous tongues
        Was the Hero that here lies:
5   Death, in guerdon of her wrongs,
        Gives her fame which never dies.
        So the life that died with shame
        Lives in death with glorious fame.'
    Hang thou there upon the tomb,
10   Praising her when I am dumb.
    Now, music, sound, and sing your solemn hymn.

BALTHASAR [*Sings the*] *song*
        Pardon, goddess of the night,
        Those that slew thy virgin knight,
        For the which, with songs of woe,
15   Round about her tomb they go.

93 **old coil** great turmoil   98 **die** puns on the sense of 'orgasm'   99 **eyes** puns on the sense of 'vagina'
5.3   5 guerdon recompense   **6 fame** renown/reputation   **12 goddess ... night** Diana, goddess of the moon and of chastity   **13 virgin knight** i.e. her follower, Hero

Midnight, assist our moan,
Help us to sigh and groan,
Heavily, heavily:
Graves, yawn and yield your dead,
20   Till death be utterèd,
Heavily, heavily.
CLAUDIO Now, unto thy bones good night!
Yearly will I do this rite.
DON PEDRO Good morrow, masters, put your torches
out.
25   The wolves have preyed, and look, the gentle day
Before the wheels of Phoebus round about
Dapples the drowsy east with spots of grey.
Thanks to you all, and leave us. Fare you well.
CLAUDIO Good morrow, masters: each his several way.
30 DON PEDRO Come, let us hence, and put on other weeds,
And then to Leonato's we will go.
CLAUDIO And Hymen now with luckier issue speed's
Than this for whom we rendered up this woe. *Exeunt*

Act 5 Scene 4   *running scene 16*

*Enter Leonato, Benedick, [Beatrice,] Margaret, Ursula, old
man [Antonio], Friar [Francis and] Hero*
FRIAR FRANCIS Did I not tell you she was innocent?
LEONATO So are the prince and Claudio, who accused
her
Upon the error that you heard debated.
But Margaret was in some fault for this,
5   Although against her will, as it appears
In the true course of all the question.
ANTONIO Well, I am glad that all things sort so well.
BENEDICK And so am I, being else by faith enforced
To call young Claudio to a reckoning for it.
10 LEONATO Well, daughter, and you gentlewomen all,
Withdraw into a chamber by yourselves,
And when I send for you, come hither masked.
The prince and Claudio promised by this hour
To visit me. You know your office, brother:

---

26 **wheels of Phoebus** wheels of the chariot of Phoebus, the sun god   30 **weeds** clothes   32 **Hymen** god
of marriage   **speed's** speed us (i.e. make us prosper)   **5.4**   3 **Upon** as a result of   **debated** discussed
5 **against her will** unintentionally   6 **question** questioning/investigation   8 **else** otherwise   **faith** i.e. his
promise to Beatrice   9 **reckoning** settling of accounts (i.e. a duel)

15   You must be father to your brother's daughter,
        And give her to young Claudio.   *Exeunt Ladies*
ANTONIO Which I will do with confirmed countenance.
BENEDICK Friar, I must entreat your pains, I think.
FRIAR FRANCIS To do what, signior?
20   **BENEDICK** To bind me, or undo me — one of them.
        Signior Leonato, truth it is, good signior,
        Your niece regards me with an eye of favour.
LEONATO That eye my daughter lent her: 'tis most true.
BENEDICK And I do with an eye of love requite her.
25   **LEONATO** The sight whereof I think you had from me,
        From Claudio and the prince: but what's your will?
BENEDICK Your answer, sir, is enigmatical.
        But for my will, my will is your good will
        May stand with ours, this day to be conjoined
30   In the state of honourable marriage,
        In which, good friar, I shall desire your help.
LEONATO My heart is with your liking.
FRIAR FRANCIS And my help.
Enter Prince [Don Pedro] and Claudio, with Attendants
DON PEDRO Good morrow to this fair assembly.
35   **LEONATO** Good morrow, prince, good morrow, Claudio:
        We here attend you. Are you yet determined
        Today to marry with my brother's daughter?
CLAUDIO I'll hold my mind, were she an Ethiope.
LEONATO Call her forth, brother: here's the friar ready.
                                                    [Exit Antonio]
40   **DON PEDRO** Good morrow, Benedick. Why, what's the
            matter,
        That you have such a February face,
        So full of frost, of storm and cloudiness?
CLAUDIO I think he thinks upon the savage bull.
        Tush, fear not, man: we'll tip thy horns with gold,
45   And all Europa shall rejoice at thee,
        As once Europa did at lusty Jove,
        When he would play the noble beast in love.
BENEDICK Bull Jove, sir, had an amiable low,
        And some such strange bull leaped your father's cow,
50   And got a calf in that same noble feat
        Much like to you, for you have just his bleat.

---

17 confirmed countenance resolute appearance/demeanour   **20 undo** ruin/untie   **28 for** as for   **is** is
that   **38 Ethiope** Ethiopian   **45 Europa** Europe   **46 Europa … love** in the form of a bull Jove carried off
the princess Europa

Enter brother [Antonio], Hero, Beatrice, Margaret, [and]
Ursula [the ladies all masked]

CLAUDIO For this I owe you: here comes other
  reck'nings.
 Which is the lady I must seize upon?

ANTONIO This same is she, and I do give you her.

55 **CLAUDIO** Why, then she's mine. Sweet, let me see your
  face.

LEONATO No, that you shall not, till you take her hand
 Before this friar and swear to marry her.

CLAUDIO Give me your hand before this holy friar.
 I am your husband, if you like of me.

60 **HERO** And when I lived, I was your other wife:
 And when you loved, you were my other husband.   *Unmasks*

CLAUDIO Another Hero?

HERO Nothing certainer.
 One Hero died defiled, but I do live,

65 And surely as I live, I am a maid.

DON PEDRO The former Hero! Hero that is dead!

LEONATO She died, my lord, but whiles her slander lived.

FRIAR FRANCIS All this amazement can I qualify,
 When after that the holy rites are ended,

70 I'll tell you largely of fair Hero's death.
 Meantime let wonder seem familiar,
 And to the chapel let us presently.

BENEDICK Soft and fair, friar. Which is Beatrice?

BEATRICE I answer to that name. What is your will?   *Unmasks*

75 **BENEDICK** Do not you love me?

BEATRICE Why, no, no more than reason.

BENEDICK Why then, your uncle, and the prince, and
  Claudio
 Have been deceived: they swore you did.

BEATRICE Do not you love me?

80 **BENEDICK** Troth, no, no more than reason.

BEATRICE Why then, my cousin, Margaret and Ursula
 Are much deceived, for they did swear you did.

BENEDICK They swore you were almost sick for me.

BEATRICE They swore you were well-nigh dead for me.

85 **BENEDICK** 'Tis no matter. Then you do not love me?

BEATRICE No, truly, but in friendly recompense.

---

52 owe you i.e. owe you a response **68 qualify** moderate **70 largely** in full **73 soft and fair** hold on a
moment **81 cousin** i.e. Hero

LEONATO Come, cousin, I am sure you love the
    gentleman.
CLAUDIO And I'll be sworn upon't that he loves her,
    For here's a paper written in his hand,   *Shows a paper*
90   A halting sonnet of his own pure brain,
    Fashioned to Beatrice.
HERO And here's another   *Shows another paper*
    Writ in my cousin's hand, stolen from her pocket,
    Containing her affection unto Benedick.
95 BENEDICK A miracle! Here's our own hands against our
    hearts. Come, I will have thee, but by this light I take
    thee for pity.
BEATRICE I would not deny you, but by this good day I
    yield upon great persuasion, and partly to save your
100   life, for I was told you were in a consumption.
LEONATO Peace! I will stop your mouth. *Makes Beatrice and Benedick kiss*
DON PEDRO How dost thou, 'Benedick, the married
    man'?
BENEDICK I'll tell thee what, prince: a college of wit-
105   crackers cannot flout me out of my humour. Dost
    thou think I care for a satire or an epigram? No. If a
    man will be beaten with brains, a shall wear nothing
    handsome about him. In brief, since I do purpose to
    marry, I will think nothing to any purpose that the
110   world can say against it, and therefore never flout at
    me for what I have said against it, for man is a giddy
    thing, and this is my conclusion. For thy part,
    Claudio, I did think to have beaten thee, but in that
    thou art like to be my kinsman, live unbruised and
115   love my cousin.
CLAUDIO I had well hoped thou wouldst have denied
    Beatrice, that I might have cudgelled thee out of thy
    single life to make thee a double-dealer, which out of
    question thou wilt be, if my cousin do not look
120   exceeding narrowly to thee.
BENEDICK Come, come, we are friends. Let's have a
    dance ere we are married, that we may lighten our
    own hearts and our wives' heels.
LEONATO We'll have dancing afterward.

87 cousin Beatrice is his niece but cousin could refer to any relative   100 in a consumption wasting
away   104 college assembly/fellowship   105 flout mock   107 shall ... him i.e. for fear of attracting
attention or having his dress sense mocked   111 giddy unstable/flighty   114 like likely   117 cudgelled
beaten   118 double-dealer married man/unfaithful husband   122 lighten ... heels make our wives'
heels nimble through dancing/make our wives sexually eager

125 **BENEDICK** First, of my word: therefore play, music.
Prince, thou art sad: get thee a wife, get thee a
wife. There is no staff more reverend than one tipped
with horn.

Enter a Messenger

MESSENGER My lord, your brother John is ta'en in flight,
130 And brought with armèd men back to Messina.

BENEDICK Think not on him till tomorrow.
I'll devise thee brave punishments for him.
Strike up, pipers!   *Dance [and exeunt]*

126 sad grave/mournful   **127 no ... horn** another reference to cuckoldry   **132 brave** fine

TEXTUAL NOTES

Q = First Quarto text of 1600
F = First Folio text of 1623
F2 = a correction introduced in the Second Folio text of 1632
Ed = a correction introduced by a later editor
SD = stage direction
SH = speech heading (i.e. speaker's name)

List of parts = Ed

1.1.40 bird-bolt *spelled* Burbolt *in* F **49 eat** = Q. F = ease **92 are you come** = Q. F = you are come **102 sir** = Q. *Not in* F **136 yours** = Q. F = your **142 That** = Q. F = This **217 spoke** = Q. F = speake **297–8 and ... her** = Q. *Not in* F **300 you do** = Q. F = doe you

1.2.3 SH ANTONIO = Ed. F = *Old. (throughout scene)* **4 strange** = Q. *Not in* F **6 event** = F2. F = events **9 my** = F. Q = mine **thus** = F. Q = thus much

1.3.7 bringeth = F. Q = brings **8 yet** = F. Q = at least **22 true root** = Q. F = root **37 will make** = F. Q = make **59 me behind** = Q. F = behind

2.1.31 upon = F. Q = on **39 bearward** *spelled* Berrord *in* F **52 Father** = Q. F *omits* **61 account** = F. Q = an account **77 sinks** = F. Q = sincke **82 SD [*Don*] *John*** = Ed. F = *or dumbe Iohn* **83 a bout** = Ed. F = about **93 Jove** = Q. F = Loue **96, 99, 101 SH BALTHASAR** = Ed. F = *Bene.* **137 pleaseth** = F. Q = pleases **182 count** = F. Q = county **183 of** = Q. F = off **207 think I told** = Q. F = thinke, told **208 good will** = Q. F = will **211 a rod** = F. Q = vp a rod **234 and** = F. *Not in* Q **239 her terminations** = Q. F = terminations **264 this** = F. Q = my **268 his single** = Q. F = a single **283 a jealous** = F. Q = that iealous **303 her heart** = Q. F = my heart **346 my mind** = Q. F = mind

2.2.33 Don = Q. F = on **48 truths** = F. Q = truth **53 thou** = F. Q = you

2.3.33 I for = Q. F = for **36 SD *Balthasar*** = Ed. F = *Iacke Wilson (apparently the actor who played Balthasar)* **45–6 To ... excellency** *mistakenly printed twice in* F **48 woo** = Q. F = woe **64 SH BALTHASAR** = Ed. *Not in* F **75 was** = Q. F = were **136 told us of** = F. Q = told of vs **156 but make** = F. Q = make but **185 SH LEONATO** = F. Q = *Claudio* **187 see** = F. Q = say **189 Christian-like** = F. Q = most christianlike **196 seek** = Q. F = see **204 to ... good** = F. Q = so good **210 gentlewoman** = F. Q = gentlewomen **218 the full** = F. Q = their full

3.1.0 *gentlewomen* = Q. F = *Gentlemen* **60 she make** = F. Q = sheele make **81 than** = Q. F = to **106 ta'en** = F. Q = limed

3.2.31 Frenchman tomorrow = F. Q *continues* or in the shape of two countries at once, as a Germaine from the waste downward, all slops, and a Spaniard from the hip upward, no dublet: unlesse ... you would have it appeare he is **55 Conclude** = F. Q = conclude, conclude

3.3.35 talk = F. Q = to talke **37 SH WATCHMAN** F's *Watch. does not distinguish between the first and second watchmen* **43 bid them** = F. Q = bid those **78 statues** = F. Q = statutes

123 years = F. Q = yeere **135 and I see** = Q. F = and see **147 they** = Q. F = thy **170 SH FIRST WATCHMAN** = Ed. F *gives the speech to Conrad*

3.4.45 look = F. Q = see

3.5.7 SH VERGES = Ed. F = *Headb. (throughout scene)* **9 off** *spelled* of *in* F **23 times** = F. Q = pound **48 as may** = F. Q = as it may **57 examination** = Q. F = examine **those men** = F. Q = these men

4.1.20 not … do = Q. *Not in* F **79 do so** = Q. F = do **91 you are** = F. Q = are you **100 spoken** = F. Q = spoke **133 rearward** = Q. F = reward **140 smearèd** = F. Q = smirched **160 two princes** = Q. F = princes **169 beat** = Q. F = beare **212 princes** = Ed. F = Princesse **286 swear by it** = F. Q = sweare **302 deny** = F. Q = deny it **343 leave** = F. Q = I leave

4.2.1 SH DOGBERRY = Ed. F = *Keeper.* **2 SH VERGES** = Ed. F = *Cowley (apparently the actor who played Verges)* **4 SH DOGBERRY** = Ed. F = *Andrew.* **9 SH DOGBERRY** = Ed. F = *Kemp. (throughout rest of scene) (Will Kempe was apparently the actor who played Dogberry)* **16 serve God? Masters** = F. Q = serue God? *Both* Yea sir we hope. *Kem [i.e. Kemp]* Write downe, that they hope they serue God: and write God first, for God defend but God shoulde go before such villaines: maisters **60 Leonato** = F. Q = Leonatoes **63 SH VERGES** = Ed. F = *Sex*[ton]. Q = *Couley (actor playing Verges)* **64 SH CONRAD Off** = Ed. Q/F *continue previous speech of Coxcombe* **70 O that** = Q. F = Of that **77 any in** = F. Q = anie is in

5.1.7 comforter = Q. F = comfort **8 do** = Q. F = doth **17 Bid** = Ed. Q/F = And **68 my** = F. Q = mine **105 off** = Ed. F = of **168 says** = F. Q = said **267 thou** = Q. F = thou thou

5.2.33 names = Q. F = name **36 in** = Q. *Not in* F **38 hard rhyme** = Q. F = hard time **40 for** = F. Q = nor **76 monuments** = F. Q = monument

5.3.3 SH CLAUDIO = Ed. *Not in* F **10 dumb** = F. Q = dead **11 SH BALTHASAR** = Ed. *Not in* F **21 Heavily, heavily** = Q. F = Heavenly, heavenly **22 SH CLAUDIO** = Ed. F = *Lo.*

5.4.7 sort = F. Q = sorts **33 my help.** = F. Q = my helpe. Heere comes the Prince and Claudio, **50 And got** = Q. F = A got **54 SH ANTONIO** = Ed. F = *Leo.* **64 died defiled** = Q. F = died **83 swore you** = F. Q = swore that you **84 swore you** = Q. F = swore that you **85 no matter** = F. Q = no such matter **101 SH LEONATO** = F. *Most eds assign to* BENEDICK **111 what I have** = Q. F = I have

SCENE-BY-SCENE ANALYSIS

ACT 1 SCENE 1

The play opens at the house of Leonato, Governor of Messina. A Messenger arrives to inform Leonato, Hero and Beatrice that Don Pedro, Prince of Aragon, is to arrive there from a recent war, accompanied by his illegitimate brother, Don John, and two young noblemen, Claudio and Benedick. We are introduced to all of the main characters and essential information is conveyed about events prior to the action of the play. Several key themes, such as love, marriage, deception and secrecy, are established, as are the recurrent motifs concerning fashion, value/'worth' and images of animals and cuckolding.

Lines 1–91: The Messenger brings the news of Don Pedro's imminent arrival and Beatrice inquires after 'Signior Mountanto', meaning Benedick. She continues to criticize him to the Messenger, who is confused by her attitude. Leonato explains that there is a long-standing battle of wits between Beatrice and Benedick.

Lines 92–155: Don Pedro and his party arrive. Initial pleasantries are exchanged and, while Leonato and Don Pedro talk aside, Beatrice and Benedick insult each other in a fast-paced, witty exchange in which they both assert their dislike of the opposite sex. The simultaneous antagonism and attraction that exists between these two characters is clearly established in their first 'skirmish of wit', and forms the basis for much of the verbal, 'high' comedy in the play. Don Pedro then announces that Leonato has invited himself, Claudio and Benedick to stay for at least a month. Leonato extends this invitation to Don John and we learn that there has previously been conflict between the two brothers, although they are now 'reconciled'.

Lines 156–195: When they are alone, Claudio asks Benedick his opinion of Hero. Benedick dismisses her and compares her to Beatrice who 'exceeds her in beauty'. Although he qualifies this with a comment on Beatrice's temper, it suggests that he may feel some attraction. Claudio praises Hero as 'sweet', 'modest' and 'worthy'. The ambiguity of the term 'worth' is sustained throughout the remainder of the scene.

Lines 196–316: Don Pedro returns and Claudio confesses that he loves Hero. Benedick continues to reject marriage and women and asserts his intention to remain a bachelor. He leaves with a message for Leonato. Don Pedro meanwhile confirms that Hero is Leonato's heir, reminding the audience that marriage is also a financial contract, and offers to woo her on Claudio's behalf, 'in some disguise'.

ACT 1 SCENE 2

Antonio reveals that his servant overheard Don Pedro and Claudio discussing Hero, introducing the device of concealed overhearing or observation that runs throughout the play. It also establishes the ongoing theme of misunderstanding, as Antonio's servant has reported that it is Don Pedro, not Claudio, who is in love with Hero. Leonato resolves to tell Hero of the prince's intentions so that she may give him the right answer.

ACT 1 SCENE 3

Lines 1–38: Don John discusses his mood and his situation with Conrad, who encourages him to conceal his true feelings towards Don Pedro and wait for an opportunity to act against him. Don John claims that he cannot hide what he is, 'a plain-dealing villain', and refuses to alter his sour appearance.

Lines 39–71: Borachio arrives with the news of Claudio's intention to marry Hero. As before, this information has been obtained by eavesdropping, but this time it has been correctly understood. We learn that Claudio was instrumental in Don John's downfall. Conrad and Borachio pledge to help Don John prevent the marriage.

ACT 2 SCENE 1

The setting of the dance allows several smaller scenes-within-a-scene as different pairs or groups of characters are focused on in turn. These exchanges use dramatic irony to present comic situations, misunderstandings, and further the progress of the plots that have emerged so far. The masking of the characters allows for visual comedy in addition to the witty dialogue, and serves as a physical representation of the themes of deception and secrecy.

Lines 1–82: Leonato, Antonio, Hero and Beatrice wait for the prince and his party to arrive. They discuss Don John's bitter temperament, and Beatrice jokes that the ideal man would be a combination of Don John and Benedick – one says too little and the other too much. This leads to a more general discussion of men and marriage, with Beatrice demonstrating her wit and professing similar opinions to those of Benedick in Act 1 scene 1, asserting that she will not marry. Leonato reminds Hero of her duty to accept Don Pedro if he should propose, reinforcing the differences between the two cousins: Beatrice appears relatively free in terms of both speech and decision but Hero is subject to her father's authority and, in fact, says nothing throughout the whole exchange.

Lines 83–95: Don Pedro asks Hero to dance with him. Their conversation is romantic, but Hero tells him she cannot give him an answer until she knows who he is.

Lines 96–107: Margaret rebuffs Balthasar's advances.

Lines 108–120: Antonio denies his true identity to Ursula who claims she knows him by the marks of his old age, such as his 'dry hand', but then gives a more tactful reason – he cannot hide his 'excellent wit'.

Lines 121–149: Benedick use his anonymity to verbally abuse Beatrice, pretending to report an insult by someone else. Beatrice pretends not to know she is talking to Benedick and criticizes him at length, suggesting that he overestimates his own wit and that others find him 'a very dull fool'.

Lines 150–165: Don John and Borachio pretend to believe that Claudio is Benedick and ask to speak to him as a friend of Don Pedro's. They tell him that Don Pedro is in love with Hero and means to marry her, and ask 'Benedick' to warn the prince against this as she is not his equal.

Lines 166–202: Claudio's soliloquy reveals that he believes that Don Pedro has won Hero for himself. This reveals a gullible and jealous side to his personality. Benedick enters, and, apparently labouring under the same misconception as Claudio, offers to fashion him a willow garland – the emblem of a forsaken lover. Claudio leaves and Benedick reflects on Beatrice's earlier criticism.

Lines 203–264: Don Pedro, Leonato and Hero enter, looking for Claudio. Benedick tells them that Claudio believes that the prince has wooed Hero for himself, and is told that this is not true: Hero is intended for Claudio. Don Pedro reports that the gentleman that danced with Beatrice told her that she is 'much wronged' by Benedick, who makes a furious speech about how, conversely, she 'misused' him and how much he dislikes her. As Beatrice enters, bringing Claudio, he begs Don Pedro to send him on an errand 'to the world's end', so that he may avoid her. The prince refuses, but Benedick leaves anyway.

Lines 265–327: Don Pedro comments to Beatrice that she has lost Benedick's heart, and she comments that in the past 'he lent it' to her, suggesting a previous attachment between them. Beatrice says that she has brought Claudio, commenting on his jealous disposition. Don Pedro explains that he has Leonato's consent to Claudio marrying Hero, and the lovers exchange vows, although, again, Hero is silent – Beatrice supplies her words. Beatrice then claims to regret her single status, and Don Pedro makes her a half-joking offer of marriage. Beatrice refuses on the grounds that, like a good suit of clothes, he is too expensive to 'wear every day'. She then apologizes to him for being 'all mirth and no matter', before Leonato sends her off on an errand.

Lines 328–372: The assembled characters discuss Beatrice's lively disposition and her single state. Don Pedro comments that she would be 'an excellent wife for Benedick'. Claudio states his intention to marry Hero the next day, but Leonato says that they must wait a week. Don Pedro suggests that they pass this time by making Benedick and Beatrice fall in love. Everyone agrees to help.

ACT 2 SCENE 2

Borachio shows Don John how he can prevent Claudio's marriage to Hero and injure Don Pedro and Leonato. Don John will tell Claudio and Don Pedro that Hero is unfaithful and show them a scene that Borachio will stage at Hero's window, in which he will play out a lovers' encounter with Margaret, calling her 'Hero' throughout. Hero's honour will be ruined, as will that of her father, Claudio and Don Pedro.

ACT 2 SCENE 3

Theatrical self-awareness is sustained through the next three scenes, as different characters are set up to observe the 'dramas' that are being played to deceive them. The first of these is the duping of Benedick in the garden of Leonato's house. The dramatic irony and Benedick's asides add to the comedy, and the theme of deception is reinforced by the sustained trapping imagery.

Lines 1–36: Benedick's soliloquy focuses on the change in Claudio since he fell in love. He contemplates whether he himself will ever be 'converted', dwelling on the virtues that his ideal woman would have. He sees the other men and hides in the arbour.

Lines 37–92: Don Pedro and Claudio establish that Benedick is listening, then talk of love and request Balthasar to play a love song, the words of which reinforce the theme of deception. Benedick's asides are cynical and prosaic.

Lines 93–215: After Balthasar has left, Don Pedro, Claudio and Leonato discuss the fact that Beatrice is in love with Benedick and cannot tell him. They agree that he should not know because he would only 'torment' Beatrice. They discuss Beatrice's many virtues, and Benedick's unworthiness. There are asides between the characters as they gauge Benedick's response, and from Benedick, who suspects it is a 'gull', but decides it cannot be because Leonato is a part of the conversation.

Lines 216–240: In one short soliloquy Benedick undergoes a rapidly-changing array of emotions and self-analysis, and a complete reversal of opinion with regard to Beatrice. Believing that Beatrice loves him, he resolves to bear the mockery he will receive after having 'railed so long against marriage' and to return her love.

Lines 241–257: Beatrice comes to call Benedick for dinner. Her responses to his pleasantries are ill-tempered, but he persists in reading non-existent double meanings into her words, and finding evidence of her love.

ACT 3 SCENE 1

Lines 1–23: Hero directs Margaret to go and tell Beatrice that she and Ursula are discussing her in the orchard. She then primes Ursula as to what their conversation must be about – praising Benedick and discussing his love for Beatrice. They see Beatrice enter and conceal herself, and move so that she can overhear them. They use similar images of trapping to those in the previous scene.

Lines 24–108: They discuss Benedick's love for Beatrice and the fact that Hero has supposedly refused to tell Beatrice because 'she cannot love' and her response would be to 'make sport' of Benedick. They list Benedick's virtues and Hero resolves to tell Benedick to 'fight against his passion'. They leave to choose a wedding outfit for Hero.

Lines 109–118: Beatrice declares she will 'requite' Benedick's love in a speech that, like his in Act 2 scene 3, shows change and increased self-awareness.

ACT 3 SCENE 2

We do not watch the deceptive performance staged by Borachio. Instead, we see Don John prepare Don Pedro and Claudio to witness it.

Lines 1–65: Don Pedro intends to leave for Aragon once Claudio's marriage is accomplished, taking Benedick with him for company. Benedick enters, claiming to have toothache. Don Pedro, Claudio and Leonato tease him, saying he shows all the signs of being in love – changing his clothes, shaving his beard, using perfume and, above all, being melancholy. Benedick asks to speak to Leonato in private and they leave.

Lines 66–123: Don John approaches and, having acknowledged that Claudio distrusts him, tells them that Hero is 'disloyal' and offers to show them the evidence that night at Hero's window. Claudio and Don Pedro seem reluctant to believe him at first, but by the end of the scene they have vowed to publicly disgrace her if they see proof that Don John is telling the truth.

ACT 3 SCENE 3

Lines 1–93: The master constable, Dogberry, and parish officer, Verges, issue instructions to the Watch. The Watchmen are revealed to be incompetent and stupid, and the nonsensical comedy that is created is compounded by Dogberry's hyperbolic and inaccurate vocabulary, in particular his use of malapropisms. Dogberry's final instruction is to keep an eye on Leonato's house, because of all the wedding preparations.

Lines 94–175: Borachio and Conrad enter, drunk, and the Watch overhear their conversation as Borachio recounts to Conrad his part in the deception of Don Pedro and Claudio. He describes how Don John incited Don Pedro and Claudio with 'oaths', and then how his own performance in leaving Hero's window convinced them. He reports that Claudio has sworn to shame Hero in church the next day. The Watch arrest them, despite not understanding all that they have heard.

ACT 3 SCENE 4

Margaret helps Hero to dress for her wedding, while Ursula goes to wake Beatrice. As they discuss clothes, and Margaret makes innuendoes about Hero's impending loss of virginity, Beatrice enters. Like Benedick in Act 3 scene 2, she puts her melancholy down to illness. Margaret teases her, suggesting that she is in love, and dropping hints about Benedick. Ursula tells them that the men have come to take Hero to church and they withdraw to help her finish dressing.

ACT 3 SCENE 5

Dogberry and Verges go to inform Leonato of the arrest of Borachio and Conrad and the revelation of Don John's plot. Leonato is impatient and too busy to listen to their 'tedious', long-winded beginning and is called away to the wedding before they can tell him.

ACT 4 SCENE 1

Lines 1–116: All the characters assemble for the marriage of Hero and Claudio, and Leonato tells the Friar to keep the service brief.

Claudio asks if Leonato gives Hero freely to him and, reinforcing the theme of 'worth' from earlier, asks what he can give in return for 'this rich and precious gift'. Don Pedro suggests that all he can do is return the gift. Claudio does so, denouncing Hero as an 'approvèd wanton', who has only the appearance of modesty and chastity. Initially, Leonato thinks that Claudio himself has taken Hero's virginity, but Claudio denies this. Hero suggests that Claudio must be ill to speak so falsely. Leonato appeals to Don Pedro, who claims that he has been dishonoured by helping to link Claudio to 'a common stale'.

Claudio asks Hero what man she spoke with at her window the previous night. Hero answers 'no man', in one of the few lines she speaks in the whole scene. Claudio, believing what he saw, recounts it to the assembled company, adding that the man has confessed to many previous sexual encounters with Hero. He rejects Hero once more and declares that he will never love again. Hero faints and Don Pedro, Claudio and Don John leave.

Lines 117–265: Beatrice tries to help Hero, fearing she may be dead. Leonato says that it would be better if she was and prays that she does not wake up, regretting that he ever had a child. At this point, he is torn between the public and domestic elements of his life: his social position and honour, and his love for his only child. Beatrice insists that Hero is 'belied'. The Friar intervenes, saying that he observed Hero's expressions throughout and that he believes her to be innocent and that Claudio and Don Pedro are deceived. He questions Hero, who denies everything. Benedick suggests that Don John may be responsible. Leonato threatens to kill those who have wronged Hero, but the Friar suggests that they pretend she has died as a result of the slander while they find out the truth. Failing this, Hero can be placed quietly in a convent. He argues that Hero's 'death' will create remorse in Claudio and, even if they cannot prove her innocence, pity 'will quench the wonder of her infamy'. Leonato agrees and Benedick vows to keep the secret.

Lines 266–346: Once alone, Benedick attempts to comfort Beatrice and reassure her that be believes Hero is innocent. She wishes that there was a man who could help, but when Benedick offers, she says it is not his 'office'. He then declares his love for her, and after some procrastination, she returns it. He asks her to bid him to do anything for her, but when she tells him to 'Kill Claudio', he refuses. She threatens to leave and insists again that Hero is wronged and that Claudio is a villain, wishing she were a man so that she might be revenged. Benedick is torn between the bond of male friendship and his love for Beatrice, but eventually agrees to challenge Claudio.

ACT 4 SCENE 2

Borachio and Conrad are interrogated before the Sexton. Again, the process is prolonged by Dogberry's comic self-importance and long-windedness. He selects nonsensical extracts from the proceedings and insists that they are written down, including Conrad's insult that he is 'an ass'. The Sexton gets to the truth, reporting that the public disgrace of Hero has taken place, that Hero has died as a result, and that Don John has left in secrecy. He states his intention to show Leonato the evidence of the interrogation, and instructs the constable to bring Borachio and Conrad.

ACT 5 SCENE 1

Lines 1–45: Leonato rejects Antonio's attempts to comfort him, and resolves to tell Claudio and Don Pedro that they have slandered Hero.

Lines 46–207: Don Pedro and Claudio are in a hurry and do not wish to quarrel with Leonato, but he accuses them of 'villainy' and threatens to fight Claudio. Claudio dismisses his challenge, but Antonio then joins in. Don Pedro refuses to fight two old men and will not listen to Leonato, who leaves with Antonio as Benedick arrives. Don Pedro and Claudio attempt to joke with Benedick as before about love and Beatrice, but he will not respond, and the male camaraderie that previously existed between the three men is awkwardly absent. He quietly challenges Claudio to a duel, and then leaves, telling them that they have 'killed a sweet and innocent lady' and that Don John has left Messina.

Lines 208–341: Dogberry and Verges enter, leading Borachio and Conrad. Don Pedro and Claudio inquire why they are bound, and Borachio interrupts Dogberry's confused response and confesses. The revelation of the truth affects Claudio as though he had 'drunk poison', as he simultaneously experiences shame, grief, and love for Hero. Leonato returns with the Sexton and demands to see the villain. Borachio owns up, but Leonato points out that Don Pedro and Claudio had a part in it as well. Claudio asks that Leonato choose his punishment. Leonato says that he must tell everyone of Hero's innocence, hang an epitaph on Hero's tomb, and marry his niece in place of Hero the next day. Claudio agrees. Borachio establishes Margaret's innocence of her part in the plot and is taken away.

ACT 5 SCENE 2

Benedick tells Margaret to send Beatrice to him and, while he waits, attempts to compose a love song. As he laments his inability to do so, Beatrice enters and asks what has happened between him and Claudio. When he replies 'Only foul words', she refuses to kiss him and starts to leave. He tells her that he has challenged Claudio and they talk in romantic terms but conclude they are 'too wise to woo peaceably', as they cannot avoid jibing at each other. Ursula comes to tell them that Hero is proved innocent and that they are to go to Leonato.

ACT 5 SCENE 3

Claudio hangs the epitaph on Hero's tomb, declaring her innocence. Balthasar sings a 'solemn hymn' and Claudio vows to perform the same rite every year. They leave to prepare for Claudio's wedding to Leonato's 'niece'.

ACT 5 SCENE 4

The lovers are united in marriage, a symbol of order restored. Masks are used again, but the removal of the masks represents the revelation of truths and the end of deception. The only question we may be left with is whether Claudio deserves Hero.

Lines 1–33: Leonato sends the women to mask themselves and consents to Benedick's request to marry Beatrice. The Friar agrees to perform the ceremony.

Lines 34–51: Don Pedro and Claudio arrive and Claudio declares his intention to go through with the marriage.

Lines 52–133: The women enter, masked, and Claudio asks to see the face of the one he is to marry. Leonato insists he must swear to marry her before he sees her. He does so and Hero reveals her face. Claudio and Don Pedro are amazed and Leonato briefly tells of the deception, which the Friar says can be explained after the ceremony. Benedick asks Beatrice if she loves him. She denies it, and he says that Leonato, Don Pedro and Claudio swore she did. She asks him the same question and he also denies it. They begin to argue, but Claudio produces a sonnet that Benedick has written for Beatrice, and Hero a love letter that Beatrice has written to Benedick. Beatrice continues to wrangle but Leonato says he will stop her mouth by making her and Benedick kiss. Don Pedro teases Benedick for going back on his word and choosing to marry, but Benedick just recommends that he get himself a wife, adding that he will devise 'brave punishments' for Don John later. They all dance.

MUCH ADO ABOUT NOTHING IN PERFORMANCE: THE RSC AND BEYOND

The best way to understand a Shakespeare play is to see it or ideally to participate in it. By examining a range of productions, we may gain a sense of the extraordinary variety of approaches and interpretations that are possible – a variety that gives Shakespeare his unique capacity to be reinvented and made 'our contemporary' four centuries after his death.

We begin with a brief overview of the play's theatrical and cinematic life, offering historical perspectives on how it has been performed. We then analyse in more detail a series of productions staged over the last half-century by the Royal Shakespeare Company. The sense of dialogue between productions that can only occur when a company is dedicated to the revival and investigation of the Shakespeare canon over a long period, together with the uniquely comprehensive archival resource of promptbooks, programme notes, reviews and interviews held on behalf of the RSC at the Shakespeare Birthplace Trust in Stratford-upon-Avon, allows an 'RSC stage history' to become a crucible in which the chemistry of the play can be explored.

We then go to the horse's mouth. Modern theatre is dominated by the figure of the director. He or she must hold together the whole play, whereas the actor must concentrate on his or her part. The director's viewpoint is therefore especially valuable. Shakespeare's plasticity is wonderfully revealed when we hear the directors of two highly successful productions answering the same questions in very different ways. And finally, we offer the actor's perspective: a view of the play through the eyes of Beatrice.

FOUR CENTURIES OF *MUCH ADO*: AN OVERVIEW

Much Ado has been popular since it was first written around 1598. The title page of the 1600 Quarto announces it had been '*sundrie times publikely* acted by the right honourable, the Lord Chamberlaine his seruants'. The substitution of 'Kemp' for Dogberry and 'Cowley' for Verges in speech headings help date the play[1] and also tell us that the leading comedian with Shakespeare's company, the Chamberlain's (subsequently the King's) Men, William Kempe, played the part of Dogberry and another comic actor, Richard Cowley, played Verges. The next references suggest the reason for its popularity. It was one of twenty plays performed at court to celebrate the marriage of James I's daughter Elizabeth to Frederick V, Elector of Palatine, in 1613 which included not only *Much ado abowte nothinge* but also *Benedicte and Betteris*, both titles assumed to refer to Shakespeare's play. Charles I scribbled 'Bennedike and Betrice' against *Much Ado* in his copy of the 1632 Second Folio of Shakespeare's plays, and the poet Leonard Digges wrote in the prefatory poem to his 1640 edition of Shakespeare's poems:

> ... let but Beatrice
> And *Benedicke* be seene, loe in a trice
> The Cockpit, Galleries, Boxes, all are full.

After the closure of the theatres in 1642 and their reopening in 1660 at the Restoration, the play was assigned to Sir William Davenant's company. Davenant incorporated the ever-popular Beatrice and Benedick into his improbable adaptation of *Measure for Measure*, *The Law Against Lovers* (1662), in which Benedick becomes Angelo's younger brother and leads an insurrection against the prison to free Claudio. Beatrice, now a wealthy heiress, is sister to Juliet, and Angelo's ward. A younger sister, Viola, dances a sarabande with castanets. Angelo, disgusted by the low morals of women in his society, claims to have been merely testing Isabella, whom he finally marries. Benedick marries Beatrice, and the duke retires to a monastery. Samuel Pepys records he thought it 'a good play and well performed'.[2] Charles Johnson subsequently incorporated a number of Benedick's lines into his 1723 adaptation of *As You Like It, Love in a Forest*. In 1737 James Miller also amalgamated *Much Ado* with Molière's *Princess d'Elide* in his comedy, *The Universal Passion*, in which Benedick and Beatrice become Lord Proteus and Delia.

There were a handful of productions of Shakespeare's play in the early eighteenth century, but it was David Garrick's Drury Lane production of 1748 that re-established it firmly in the popular repertoire, a place it has retained ever since. Garrick continued to play Benedick in frequent revivals to great popular acclaim until his retirement from the stage in 1776; Arthur Murphy, actor, writer and Garrick's biographer, called it 'one of Mr Garrick's best Parts in Comedy'.[3] His most celebrated Beatrice was Hannah Pritchard, whose performance was 'so fine that every scene between her and the great Garrick was a continued struggle for superiority, in which the spectators could not award preference'.[4] Garrick was still charming audiences in the part the year before his retirement:

> In the dance in *Much Ado about Nothing*, he excels all the rest by the agility of his springs ... In his face all can observe, without any refinement of feature, the happy intellect in his unruffled brow, and the alert observer and wit in the lively eye, often bright with roguishness. His gestures are so clear and vivacious as to arouse in one similar emotions.[5]

Garrick's lively performance contrasted with John Philip Kemble's more serious production and stately Benedick. Using a bowdlerized text, Kemble was partnered by a number of successful Beatrices including the future King William's mistress, Dorothea Jordan. His brother, Charles Kemble, had more success in the part which he, too, played for over thirty years from 1803 to 1836 in productions which featured a number of distinguished Beatrices, including Anne Brunton, Helen Faucit and his own daughter, Fanny

Kemble. William Charles Macready also produced the play and played Benedick. Charles Kean's spectacular staging at the Princess' Theatre in 1858 included 'a sunset view of the port of Messina, the sun gradually disappearing in the west, casting its declining rays on the houses and ships. Then the moon rose on a brilliant masquerade scene with variegated lights from garden and bridge lamps that shone through the arches of the palace'.[6]

The most successful nineteenth-century production, however, was Henry Irving's at the Lyceum with Ellen Terry as Beatrice. It was universally admired:

> The sumptuous revival by Mr Henry Irving of this wise and witty comedy has, at any rate, proved to the public satisfaction that Shakespeare, if properly understood, is an evergreen.[7]

> The settings were the most sumptuous and picturesque. I can remember none more beautiful even at the Lyceum; the Bay of Messina with Leonato's Marble Palace; the Garden; the Church; the Ballroom – never was mounting more appropriate and helpful, and the result was triumphant. As I have heard others say, and as I have always myself maintained: 'The most completely satisfying entertainment I have ever known in the theatre.'[8]

It was the central performances of Terry and Irving that captivated audiences though. Irving was credited with a new reading of Benedick: 'He conceived the character on completely new lines and gave the play a new vitality. His Benedick was an eccentric, a fantastic, an oddity, but *preux chevalier* [valiant knight] always.'[9] But as Bram Stoker, Irving's dresser, observed, Terry 'was born for the part' of Beatrice. Praise of her performance was unstinting:

> Merriment is the abiding quality of Miss Ellen Terry's Beatrice. She is Shakespeare's 'pleasant-spirited lady'; she was born in a 'merry hour'; we know that a 'star danced, and under that was she born'; she has a 'merry heart', and the actress leans charmingly on this view of the character. All the people about

the court love Beatrice, as well they may. They know her antipathy to the rougher sex is only skin deep, and they trick her into matrimony. She is no virago or vixen, but a smiling, chaffing, madcap girl, whose laughter and high spirits are next door to tears.[10]

Terry herself was more critical: 'there was very much to admire in Henry Irving's Benedick. But he gave me little help. Beatrice must be swift, swift, swift! Owing to Henry's rather finicking, deliberate method as Benedick, I could never put the right pace into my part.'[11] She also objected to a number of the traditional gags Irving continued to employ, but was impressed by the young Johnston Forbes-Robertson's Claudio in which she thought he revealed 'a touch of Leontes'.[12] She was happier with the 1891 revival: 'Henry has vastly improved upon his old rendering . . . acts larger now.'

Terry reprised the role in 1903 with Oscar Ashe as Benedick in a production by her son Edward Gordon Craig. Its 'bare and impressionistic setting'[13] contrasted with the lavish spectacle of previous productions. The critic J. C. Trewin describes how 'Gordon Craig indicated the church simply by the widening light that illuminated the many colours of a huge cross. Otherwise he used only curtains that hung in folds and were painted with pillars.'[14] Even the acerbic George Bernard Shaw was impressed as he confided in a letter to Terry: 'I went to see Much Adoodle-do yesterday evening. It is a shocking bad play . . . ', but he admits: 'I have never seen the church scene go before – didnt [sic] think it *could* go, in fact.'[15] The production recouped the losses Terry and Gordon Craig made on their other production – Ibsen's *The Vikings*. The advent of modernist writers such as Ibsen and the theatrical experiments of William Poel's Elizabethan Stage Society, which attempted to produce Shakespeare's plays under something approaching original staging conditions, suggest a new theatrical mood. Nevertheless, initial response to Poel's production at the Royal Court was cool: *The Times* thought it 'owed more to . . . antiquarian interest than to the histrionic talents of the players', and was 'painfully slow'.[16]

Herbert Beerbohm Tree staged a lavish Victorian-style spectacular at His Majesty's the following year. Of Beerbohm Tree's Benedick, George Bernard Shaw said: 'I defy anybody not to be amused by him. When he is not amusingly good from Mr Tree's point of view he is amusingly bad from the classical Shakespearian point of view...It is, in its way colossal.' He admired Winifred Emery's Beatrice though, clearly conceived in reaction to Terry's charm in the part: 'she was clever enough to play Lady Disdain instead of playing for sentimental sympathy; and the effect was keenly good and original'. This is his ironic judgement:

> All the lovely things Shakespear [sic] dispensed with are there in bounteous plenty. Fair ladies, Sicilian landscapes, Italian gardens, summer nights and dawns (compressed into five minutes), Renascential splendours, dancing, singing, masquerading, architecture, orchestration carefully culled from Wagner, Bizet, and German, and endless larks in the way of stage business devised by Mr Tree, and carried out with much innocent enjoyment, which is fairly infectious on the other side of the footlights...On the whole, my advice is, go and see it: you will never again have the chance of enjoying such an entertainment.[17]

Shaw was correct in his assessment of modern theatrical trends, and the numerous productions of the early twentieth century employed the pared-down style advocated by Poel and Harley Granville Barker which eliminated many of the traditional gags and stage business that Ellen Terry had complained of and allowed for a faster-paced, fluid acting style using a fuller text.

The play was regularly produced in London and Stratford under directors such as Ben Greet, Harcourt Williams, William Bridges-Adams, Iden Payne and Hugh Hunt, with a variety of distinguished actors including Sybil Thorndike, Lewis Casson, Edith Evans, Baliol Holloway, Fabia Drake, Alec Clunes, Robert Donat, George Hayes and Margaretta Scott, and including a post-war production with William Devlin's Dogberry as an air raid warden on a bicycle.

1. John Gielgud's 1949 Stratford production with Diana Wynyard as Beatrice and Anthony Quayle as Benedick was the most successful post-war production: Gielgud himself took over the role of Benedick two years later with Peggy Ashcroft as Beatrice.

The most successful post-war production was undoubtedly John Gielgud's in 1949 which was still enjoying critical acclaim five years later:

> This production by Sir John Gielgud, with sets and dresses by Mr Mariano Andreu, is attaining to a sort of classic status. Five years ago it delighted Stratford, happily introducing Miss Peggy Ashcroft to the festival; two years later, coming to the Phoenix theatre with Miss Diana Wynyard as Beatrice, it delighted London; and now it brings Miss Ashcroft and Sir John Gielgud together again ... The producer, who is also the principal actor, has had to reckon with many different actors; but his production somehow has a perennial freshness.[18]

Gielgud's unequivocally romantic production set in the Renaissance continued touring successfully until 1959. Gielgud stated his personal preference for productions set in their original period,[19] but nevertheless, since then many of the most successful productions of *Much Ado* have been updated and moved around geographically, partly at least as a response to the greater attention which has been focused on the Claudio–Hero plot and the need to find a cultural ambience which might explain if not excuse Claudio's callous treatment of Hero and Leonato's response to her slander. These productions have attracted a mixed critical reception. John Houseman and Jack Landau transported their 1957 American Shakespeare Festival production, which starred Katharine Hepburn and Alfred Drake, to 'the American-Spanish Southwest about a hundred years ago'. The well-known critic Brooks Atkinson continued: 'It is a brisk idea for one excellent reason. Katharine Hepburn is very much the modern actress. The hard surface of modern wit, the brittle remarks, the sophisticated eyes become her, as do the flowing costumes and the Spanish headdresses with which Rouben Ter-Arutinian has draped her.'[20] While Atkinson thought it all worked except Dogberry as a Western sheriff, Henry Hewes thought the opposite: 'The nicest performance in the show comes from Larry Gates as Dogberry, the muddled Western Sheriff.'[21]

Critics were similarly divided about Douglas Seale's 1958 Shakespeare Memorial Theatre production which V. S. Pritchett argued 'impudently twitches the Bard into light opera' and moves the play forward to 1850 and the Italy of Verdi and Rossini: 'This is to the advantage of the comedy which gains Romantic verve and settles for the picturesque; but a disadvantage to the melodramatic conspiracy.'[22] *The Times'* critic, however, came to precisely the opposite conclusion: 'The period chosen was a source of profit to the more serious scenes. It was easier than usual to take Don John's conspiracy at its face value when Don John looked and behaved as he did, as Mr Richard Johnson did, as though he had walked straight out of a portrait by Delacroix.'[23] And while Pritchett admired the performances of Googie Withers as Beatrice and Michael Redgrave as Benedick, Alan Brien complained that they were 'almost buried

2. Rachel Kempson as Ursula, Geraldine McEwan as Hero and Zoe Caldwell as Margaret 'almost buried beneath all this meringue' in Douglas Seale's 1958 'light opera' production at Stratford.

beneath all this meringue . . . Beatrice becomes a rattling bore whose spinsterhood is only too understandable. Michael Redgrave, too, seems uneasy inside this nineteenth-century Italian joker.'[24]

Michael Langham's production for the Stratford Festival, Ontario, of 1958, also set in 'the Europe of the last century in a sort of Viennese-operetta style',[25] was warmly reviewed, especially the performances of Christopher Plummer as Benedick and Eileen Herlie as Beatrice, but less well received when it transferred to the Royal Shakespeare Theatre in 1961 with Geraldine McEwan as Beatrice. In his 1965 National Theatre production, Franco Zeffirelli had

the dazzlingly simple idea of placing it exactly where Shakespeare laid it himself: not in an elocutory limbo, which is where it usually happens, but in Messina . . . the moment the play is localized, it meshes as precisely as a watch. Instead of being the proponent of a distant love ethic that now lies pickled in troubadour poetry, Hero becomes a wretchedly believable girl trapped in perfectly recognizable Sicily where the same ferocious code of chastity endures to this day.[26]

Not everyone was convinced. *The Times*' critic complained that

Zeffirelli's Sicily has enormous charm. A nattily uniformed town band parades its streets blaring forth crudely harmonized marches: the troops swagger back from the war in dress swords and plumed pill-box hats and are mobbed by a welcoming crowd of frock-coated civilians. And as for the civic statuary, Zeffirelli has provided it in the shape of self-assembling monuments – ethereal girls who drift on and freeze into Ondines at the base of a fountain, and an unearthly warrior who clambers onto a pedestal and takes up a martial stance as a local hero covered in bird droppings . . . But where, meanwhile, is the play?[27]

There were also criticisms of Robert Graves' textual revisions aimed at clarifying some of the denser language. B. A. Young, however, found it

full of superb comic acting. I am no longer able to write with restraint about Maggie Smith; I can only say that the part of Beatrice might have been written for her. Robert Stephens makes Benedick a provincial Italian wide boy, who soon exchanges his uniform for a variety of sharp suits; he plays the part with sensitivity and wit, and speaks his lines most musically. Albert Finney's Don Pedro . . . is a gorgeous comic creation.[28]

A. J. Antoon set his 1972 New York Shakespeare Festival production in small-town Middle America:

This is a pre-World War I America – marked by chauvinism, self-confidence and suddenly requited love. The gentlemen wear spats and carry pocket flasks. The ladies sneak a shared cigarette, and clear the smoke away before the father of the house enters. Almost everyone is inhibited by social conventions – yet everyone is having a glorious time. As sparklers flare, the couples dance Donald Saddler [ballroom] dances by the light of

Japanese lanterns – and the Central Park moon could be part of the set.[29]

Some critics admired the updating and performances of Sam Waterston as Benedick and Kathleen Widdoes as Beatrice, with Dogberry and the Watch played as Keystone Kops. Stanley Kauffman thought it changed 'the Beatrice and Benedick backchat into very recognizable Yankee sass, without altering a word', as well as enabling him to use 'American actors as Americans instead of as fake Britishers and failed classicists'.[30] Others, such as H. R. Coursen, were unconvinced:

> For some incomprehensible reason, this *Much Ado* is set in 1910 America. The production is defeated at the outset by its conception. Aristocratic love and Italianate intrigue collide in mid-air with small-town America, bands, balloons, and Blue Ribbon Beer. Language, 'By my troth,' clashes with spats and gramophones, turkey trots, and Keystone Cops.[31]

John Barton's successful 1976 RSC production, discussed in detail below, meanwhile set the play in the India of the British Raj, creating a similarly removed, claustrophobic environment. Jerry Turner transported the play to seventeenth-century Holland in his 1977 American Conservatory Theatre production, while John Bell's production with the Nimrod Theatre Company in Adelaide, Australia, used a circus atmosphere. Terrence Knapp's Tokyo production set the play in late nineteenth-century Japan and employed a cultural vocabulary of Japanese references, while Dana Larson Evans offered a futuristic, space-age vision at California's Grove Shakespeare Festival in 1980.

Terry Hands' 1982 production for the RSC marked a revival of the play's lush romanticism, in contrast to Gerald Freedman's 1988 New York Shakespeare Festival production, described as:

> A high-spirited romp from beginning to end, this 'Much Ado' opens with a mock sword fight; ferociously engaged with his soldierly colleague Claudio, Mr [Kevin] Kline's Benedick immediately displays the dazzling physical virtuosity that has so

often characterized his performances... his Benedick may be brilliant, but he is also vain and hilariously foolish. As he whirls about the stage, Blythe Danner's Beatrice pointedly refuses to look up from her book – but even before she and Benedick commence their verbal volleys, the potential heat of their ultimate destiny is obvious.[32]

In the same year, Judi Dench directed a warmly-received production for Kenneth Branagh's newly-formed Renaissance Theatre Company, with Branagh himself as Benedick and Samantha Bond as Beatrice. The simplicity of its staging and conception was in marked contrast to Di Trevis' production at the RSC. Since then *Much Ado* has continued its merry war in countless theatres all over the world, including Richard Monette's modern, cosmopolitan 1998 Stratford Ontario production. Peter Meineck directed Robert Richmond's version of the play for New York's Aquila Theater in 2001, turning it 'into a spoof of 1960s–70s TV and film secret agents'.[33] Greg Doran's brilliant Sicilian RSC production was staged in 2002, the same year as Mark Lamos' Hartford Stage/ Shakespeare Theater production set 'mostly in the garden of an English country house in the 1920s'.[34] Daniela Varon's 2003 production at the Founders' Theater in Lenox, Massachusetts, again set the play in a Messina 'inspired by popular images of Sicily in the 1950s,... steeped in the culture of violence and family loyalty associated with the Mafia'.[35]

A play that has enjoyed such continuous popularity in the theatre would seem an obvious candidate for screen treatment. The earliest was Phillips Smalley's 1913 American silent version. There was an East German version in 1963 and two Russian films in 1956 and 1973. A number of successful stage productions were filmed, including Zeffirelli's 1965 National Theatre production with Maggie Smith and Robert Stephens, as well as Joseph Papp's 1973 New York Shakespeare Festival production. Musical adaptations include Hector Berlioz's acclaimed *Béatrice et Bénédict* (1862) and the 2006 American musical adaptation *The Boys are Coming Home*, set in the Second World War. The most successful film adaptation, though, is undoubtedly Kenneth Branagh's 1993 film set, as Branagh describes in his introduction to the screenplay, in an 'imaginary world [which] could have existed almost anytime between 1700 and 1900':

> It was distant enough to allow the language to work without the clash of period anachronisms and for a certain fairy tale quality to emerge. This fairy tale idea seemed to spring naturally out of the countryside in which we were working. We were in Tuscany, central Italy, a magical landscape of vines and olives that seemed untouched by modern life. Lusher and more verdant than Sicily (Shakespeare's setting), it allowed us to create a visual idyll in which this cautionary tale might be told.[36]

AT THE RSC

Much Ado about Nothing is among the most performed of Shakespeare's plays and regarded as a 'banker' by theatre managers. Critical, as well as popular, focus is invariably on the performances of the actors playing Beatrice and Benedick, on the nature of their relationship and the quality of their repartee. *Much Ado* was chosen as the opening production at the freshly named Royal Shakespeare Theatre (RST) under the new management of Peter Hall as Artistic Director, and Trevor Nunn made it his first production when he took over as Artistic Director in 1968. The RSC has mounted twelve productions since 1961: two touring productions, nine at the RST and one at the Swan Theatre – Marianne Elliott's production for the 2006/07 Complete Works season was widely regarded as one of the season's jewels, as well as being a strong box-office success.

When and Where Messina?

Much Ado has the highest prose content of all the plays except *The Merry Wives of Windsor* and it is, perhaps, the immediacy, freshness and informality of the dialogue that has led directors, for the most part, to move the play away from its Elizabethan origins to later periods. RSC productions have been set in the Regency and

Victorian periods, during the British Raj in India, in the 1930s, 1940s and 1950s. Sets have rarely made much of the specifically Sicilian location of Messina, though Stephen Brimson Lewis designed a sun-baked piazza for Gregory Doran's 2002 production at the RST.

Regency and Victorian Settings

Michael Langham's 1961 production, designed by Desmond Heeley, was played against a backdrop of a towering Italian house of honeydew-coloured stone and set in the early nineteenth century, with the women dressed in graceful, high-waisted, neo-classical dresses and the men dashing in immaculately-tailored Napoleonic War uniforms. Although the production touched only lightly on the play's darker elements, they were suggested in the autumnal leaves on the creeper climbing the house front and in the rainstorm that had the guests at Hero and Claudio's wedding arriving with dripping umbrellas. Perhaps unsurprisingly at the start of a decade that was to see such radical social changes in Britain, W. A. Darlington in the *Daily Telegraph* was conscious that Leonato and his family had been made well-to-do middle class, in contrast to the young noblemen who were their house guests.[37]

In 1971, Ronald Eyre directed a production unequivocally set in Victorian England. The action in Leonato's house took place in an elegant conservatory with a view of immaculate green lawns beyond and costumes described by several critics as 'Ruritanian comic opera'. The effect, as critic Michael Billington described it, was of a 'Betjemanesque' world, where 'everything conspires to suggest a leisurely, sunlit, aristocratic society'. Lighting 'miraculously transformed' the conservatory into entrance hall, courtyard and church.[38]

John Barton's 1976 setting of the play in late nineteenth-century British India was generally regarded as a triumph: 'an ideal background for the play about the prankish practical jokes of a bored officer class and about the liberation of long-suppressed emotion'.[39] A garrison town was suggested by a double tier of timber

3. Helen Mirren as Hero, Janet Suzman as Beatrice and Rowena Cooper as Ursula in Trevor Nunn's 1968 Stratford production, with its emphasis on the spying and eavesdropping that pervade the play.

balconies, draped with beaded or cheesecloth curtains and sunblinds. Cricket could be heard being played offstage.

Sixteenth- and Seventeenth-Century Settings

For Trevor Nunn's 1968 production, Christopher Morley designed Elizabethan costumes with a twentieth-century twist: many of the fabrics suggested military camouflage in their colour and pattern. The militarism of the men was emphasized, and their dance at the party at Leonato's house was an aggressive sword-dance performed in threatening visors. There was a sombre and sinister air to the production, with an emphasis on the spying and eavesdropping that pervade the play. The acting area was enclosed by a severe rectangular box of translucent gauze that could be lit in a variety of ways to suggest interior and exterior locations but was always slightly sinister: 'Comedy and the sinister were continually in tension.'[40] Nunn is quoted as saying: 'I have yet to see the play done with sufficient seriousness; "Kill Claudio" is for real.'[41]

For Terry Hands' 1982 production, designer Ralph Koltai also enclosed the stage in a box, but this time it had a mirrored floor and walls constructed of perspex screens imprinted with stylized trees. The effect was not sinister but 'achingly beautiful',[42] magical and romantic. The mirrored setting suggested a self-regarding, self-loving, narcissistic society, and the Cavalier-style costumes gave the production an elegant courtliness while implying that this world was about to come to an end – Michael Billington in the *Guardian* felt that Hands had missed a trick: 'Surely if Don Pedro and his chums are Cavaliers, Don John should be a Roundhead?'[43] The overall effect, however, was not elegiac but romantic – joy just tinged with melancholy. This was a highly successful production, acclaimed by critics and enjoyed by audiences. It had a long afterlife following its season at the RST: it went to Newcastle and The Barbican in 1983 and spent 1984 touring, culminating in performances in New York and Washington.

Of Bill Alexander's 1990 production it was suggested:

Two years ago, the RSC bombed badly with a vogue-ish *Much Ado About Nothing* set in some 50's no-man's-land. They now make amends with a visually seductive, socially consistent Bill Alexander production that aroused the audience to ecstasy.[44]

The production's designer, Kit Surrey, returned to the seventeenth century with an elegantly-hedged English garden which 'neatly suggests a hierarchical world in which everyone knows his or her place'.[45] Lighting cast a golden glow: 'it bathed the cast's faces in wonderful amalgams of amber, bronze, flame, white and creamy pink. It gave the evening its enchanted atmosphere – and its meaning.'[46]

In 1996, Michael Boyd's production was staged in another enclosed courtyard, but its eclectic nature failed to please: 'The costumes are Elizabethan enough but Tom Piper's set is decidedly odd, a mixture of 18th-century drawing-room, Guildford Cathedral and de Chirico piazza that comes complete with a tree splintering up through varnished floorboards.'[47] Like the 1982 production, the set also featured mirrors and portraits, but here they were disturbing; the whole production was dark in tone, focusing on the Hero‐Claudio–Don John plot as the core of the play. Even the final dance 'was accompanied by music to slit your wrists to'.[48] Many of the critics disliked the air of gloom, although Nicholas de Jongh found it exhilarating: 'It makes it feel as if an early Shakespeare comedy is being transformed into one of his dark problem plays or late romances.'[49] He alone commented on the ending of the play: the roof of the courtyard rose to reveal blue sky and the audience saw the mirrored reflection of a small boy standing beside a sapling tree – signs that the future was assured. It was, he suggested, '*Much Ado* turned vividly inside out'.[50]

1930s, 1940s and 1950s Settings

In 1988 Di Trevis turned a materialist-feminist light on the play. Messina was a Mediterranean playground for the rich and idle; the set (designed by Mark Thompson) a pillared white-marble patio complete with swimming pools. The costumes were 1950s couture, but the decade glanced at was the materialistic 1980s. At the opening of the play, the lazy luxury of Messina was disrupted by the sound of a helicopter overhead from which a wounded soldier was winched down before the other men appeared. The gender attitudes of a patriarchal society were made very clear, and the 'happy ending' of the double wedding was subverted by dressing Beatrice and Hero in black with black confetti fluttering down on them. Critics and audiences, for the most part, found this a problematic interpretation; Robert Smallwood commented: 'It is difficult to go on disliking the whole of Messina's high society as much as the production seems to want us to.'[51]

For Gregory Doran's 2002 production, Stephen Brimson Lewis designed a set which let the audience know instantly that it was in Sicily – 'a sun-baked Sicilian piazza, which glows like a ripe tomato',[52] with a great wall on wooden shutters and wrought-iron balconies. For some critics the opening moments were too crowd-pleasing: 'an appallingly saccharine start – wheeling in a brass band, a cute schoolboy and the predictable jolly local on a bike',[53] but the men returning from the war were black-shirted – Mussolini's troops, back from the Ethiopian campaign – and the scene was set firmly in 1930s fascist Sicily. Though the sun shone and the comedy flourished, the dark underbelly of the play was never hidden for long.

For Marianne Elliott's 2006 production, Lez Brotherston transformed the Swan Theatre into Havana. Multicoloured lights were strung across the auditorium and the audience entered a Cuban nightclub alive with salsa music and cigar smoke. Smiles broke out in expectation of fun. This was early 1950s, pre-Castro Cuba: 'You half expect Sky Masterson and Sarah Brown, on their whirlwind trip to Havana, to wander in from *Guys and Dolls*.'[54] Elliott had chosen a Latin country for the play's hot blood and macho honour code and an era just before the changes in western sexual mores of the 1960s which would make the Hero–Claudio plot implausible. In addition, as Michael Billington suggested, 'What it offers is a plausible military context, a raffish glamour and endless opportunities, gloriously seized by Olly Fox's score, for rumbas, sambas and congas.'[55] On the darker side, 'The reflex sexism of this Catholic society suits the sobering aspects of a play in which an innocent girl is slandered at the altar by credulous barrack-room misogynists.'[56] The change in mood in the play's second half was strongly signalled: the audience returned from the interval to find the strings of lights turned off.

Beatrice and Benedick

These roles dominate performances and productions are remembered more for the actors who played them than for their directors or design features or for the playing of any of the other roles. Since the second half of the twentieth century was a period during which gender issues were of unprecedented interest, a variety of constructions of the gender politics of this play have been reflected in the playing of these central roles, and the role of Beatrice in particular.

1961 – A New Kind of Beatrice

The actors in the 1961 production must have felt a huge weight of expectation on their shoulders: not only were they starring in the RST's opening production, but critics and audiences brought with them the golden memory of a very popular 1955 production starring Peggy Ashcroft and John Gielgud. This romantic, lyrical staging, in which Beatrice and Benedick were clearly in love from the outset, had been hugely popular – and Peggy Ashcroft was in the audience for the 1961 opening night. Geraldine McEwan and Christopher Plummer, as Beatrice and Benedick, could hardly have been more different from these earlier models. McEwan's Beatrice bore resemblances to Jane Austen's Elizabeth Bennet: she was 'crackling' and 'fiery'. Oddly, she was criticized for a lack of poetry when the only verse Beatrice speaks is her 'What fire is in mine ears?' soliloquy, but perhaps it was an absence of lyricism that troubled the critics. *The Times'* reviewer commented that 'she dispenses with the airs and graces of the traditional Beatrice'; she was 'hoydenish' and 'a modern young woman who thoroughly enjoys the Elizabethan notion of repartee'.[57] These are significant comments: the 'airs and graces' had only accrued to actresses playing Beatrice from the Victorian period onwards. Seventeenth- and eighteenth-century audiences, to judge from the critics' comments, had enjoyed a forceful, fiery, combative performance from their Beatrices: 'every word stabbed', the critics observed approvingly, and praised the actresses' 'spirit' and 'vigour'. In the nineteenth century, however, we find actresses in the role beings extolled as 'feminine', 'womanly', 'refined' and 'well-bred' and their raillery had become 'pleasant archness'.[58] Actresses were being required to tone down Beatrice's combativeness, and went on doing so, it seems, through to the 1950s. Again, 1961 was a significant date.

Christopher Plummer, a Canadian actor making his English debut, was an energetic, virile Benedick, in the young Olivier mould, according to Bernard Levin in the *Daily Express*. Where Gielgud had played a sophisticated, poised, rather intellectual Benedick, Plummer gave a far more physical, soldierly performance which some critics found charmless.

1971, 1976, 1988, 2002 – Middle-Aged Lovers

In the sunlit Victorian 1971 production Elizabeth Spriggs and Derek Godfrey played Beatrice and Benedick approaching middle age. Elizabeth Spriggs had made a career in comic supporting roles and was a surprising choice for Beatrice. She created a cheerful, bustling forty-something spinster, constantly busy early on with small household tasks but growing visibly younger from the moment when she believed herself to be loved; he was a hearty public school type, still indulging in schoolboy behaviour (at one point, Benedick's pants were thrown around by his friends). Their early verbal battles were good-natured but sad, freighted with disappointing experience; in place of the brittle exchange of barbs, they fell into comforting, familiar routines. Audiences found them very appealing.

In John Barton's 1976 production, set in late nineteenth-century India under the British Raj, Judi Dench and Donald Sinden played a couple on the brink of a lonely middle age, both slight outsiders in their social milieu. One critic wrote: 'They make no attempt to be archly charming nor to hold tennis rallies . . . They swap their insults with a sort of desiccated desperation.'[59] Dench, in an unbecoming wig, was 'an intelligent spinster who knows she is edging towards the status of maiden aunt',[60] while beneath Sinden's plummy mannerisms was a man who knew he was heading for the role of eccentric uncle. In Sinden's performance, 'swagger and buffoonery are a camouflage for easily wounded private feelings';[61] he had moments of acute shyness. As her key to playing Beatrice, Dench took the revelation that Benedick had once won Beatrice's heart 'with false dice'. She played a sad, spinsterish woman who had once believed that Benedick loved her but felt she had been deceived; when she 'overheard' Hero talking of Benedick's love for her, she literally skipped for joy.

In 1988 in Di Trevis' opulent, cold, materialistic 1950s Messina, Maggie Steed and Clive Merrison played another ageing couple. Steed was 'a brassily-painted maypole',[62] 'an acid-tongued spinster'[63] who

> is on the point of settling into the role of eccentric maiden aunt. Everything about her, from her swooping movement and exaggerated handling of long, swishing costumes, to her advance on the mocking girls with a bared hatpin and her trick of winding up each anti-marital fusillade with a dazzling mirthless grin, comes over as a mocking parody of the feminine arts.[64]

Steed has said that she saw Beatrice as the poor relation in the household (where Hero is the heiress), who 'sings for her supper' by playing the joker.[65] Merrison, too, was a joker, balding and knobbly-kneed in his Bermuda shorts, once he had taken off his military uniform, physically dominated by the taller Steed.

In Gregory Doran's acclaimed 2002 production, set in Mussolini's Sicily, Harriet Walter and Nicholas le Prévost played a couple well into middle age. Le Prévost was 'a shabby roué', 'a lank-haired, unshaven old louche, for whom even the plink and fizz of a soluble aspirin proves too vexatious the morning after the night before'.[66] Walter, on the other hand, was an intensely glamorous older woman, 'dazzlingly attractive in her Thirties outfits', with 'the thoroughbred wit and presence of a Katherine Hepburn'.[67] The critics were unanimous in praise of her performance:

> Walter exudes the kind of sophisticated Thirties sassiness one associates with comedies featuring cocktails and Cole Porter. Her Beatrice can switch winningly between headgirl surliness and heartfelt hurt, and even hints at a deeply pained past with her old sparring partner Benedick.[68]

In the first scene, elegantly trousered, she jumped onto the dispatch rider's motor-bike and 'thereafter remained the play's moral engine'.[69]

She and Gregory Doran solved the problem that very 'sassy', controlled Beatrices have of her sudden melt into girly helplessness at the end of the eavesdropping scene: 'And, Benedick, love on, I will requite thee, / Taming my wild heart to thy loving hand' (3.1.113–14). Hero deliberately doused her with water while watering the hedge behind which she was hiding so that she emerged unglamorously dripping and dishevelled, her physical disarray mirroring her emotional confusion. (This piece of business also provided a reason for the cold she is suffering from on the morning of Hero's wedding – an idea used in the 1988 production where Maggie Steed hid in the swimming pool during the eavesdropping scene.) Walter and le Prévost were a couple who grew into an extraordinary and touching emotional closeness in the dark second half of the play.

1968, 1982 – The Rebels

When Trevor Nunn directed the play in 1968 he was only twenty-eight, though he had just taken over as Artistic Director at the RSC. He directed Janet Suzman and Alan Howard as a very young, almost adolescent Beatrice and Benedick, boisterous, frivolous and cynical, in rebellion against the match-making society around them, denying their evident attraction to one another. In spite of the Elizabethan costume, there was a suggestion of 1960s' disaffection in their attitudes. Suzman was a zany Beatrice, her hair and clothes often in disarray; B. A. Young, in the *Financial Times*, thought she seemed 'not altogether to have got over her Katherine in last year's *Shrew*'.[70]

Sinead Cusack's Beatrice in 1982 also evoked comparisons with Katherine: one critic stated: 'when she says "I would eat his heart in the market place" you'd better believe it', before going on to suggest she was a 'self-taming shrew', who comes to emotional equilibrium through love.[71] Cusack herself has said that she had some conflict with her director, Terry Hands, over her interpretation. Young, blonde and beautiful, she had been cast for her femininity: 'That's what he cast. That's what he used in his direction of me. But . . . I showed him other areas of her character. A Beatrice who is very angry. A woman who has been damaged by society.'[72] Her Benedick, Derek Jacobi, played a 'skittish, larky, life-and-soul-of-the-party bachelor'[73] with some camp mannerisms, who sobered up and grew up under the influence of love. The play ended on an unashamedly romantic note, with the pair left alone, dancing together and talking – the beginning of a lifelong conversation – as a red sun set behind them.

4. Derek Jacobi as Benedick and Sinead Cusack as Beatrice in Terry Hands' 1982 RSC production. Cusack played her as 'A Beatrice who is very angry. A woman who has been damaged by society.'

1996 – Lovers in Dark Times

The dark tone of Michael Boyd's 1996 production was a challenge to Siobhan Redmond and Alex Jennings in their early exchanges: audiences expect fun from Beatrice and Benedick, and this production was not about fun. Alex Jennings played the part with 'sardonic and urbane wit', 'elegant nobility' and, later, 'sober gravity';[74] his performance was widely regarded as the play's 'one unqualified success...[he] seems to be taking part in a different play from everyone else – the real play. He is unashamedly charming, a smoothie who is also engagingly ridiculous.'[75] Siobhan Redmond played a 'restless babbling Beatrice, lightweight but intense';[76] she burst into wretched tears on hearing that Benedick loved her.

1990, 2006 – Sexual Attraction

Before the opening of Bill Alexander's 1990 production, Susan Fleetwood, who was to play Beatrice, was interviewed with her Benedick, Roger Allam. Of Beatrice she said:

> She is delicious – a wonderful, eruptive person, an oddball, like Benedick. The two don't fit into their society. Beatrice is quick, sharp, vulnerable, then there are moments when she is pure joy, when she wants to just fly for the hell of it...I've never worked with Roger before but we'll buzz one another up and be a treat...You've got to play...for sex – opposite Roger you couldn't do anything else.[77]

Behind her cutting one-liners, Fleetwood always suggested her intense feelings for Allam's relaxed, charming, intelligent Benedick.

Tamsin Greig came as the star name to the 2006 1950s Cuba production in The Swan. Well-known as a comedienne in her television work, she found much more in the role than the comedy. A striking figure in black and white, in contrast to the sweet-pea frocks of Hero and the other young women, she dominated the stage early on. Critics reached out for comparisons to convey her style: 'Greig brings to Beatrice the caustic wit and pencil-skirted style of a wise-cracking Hollywood dame like Eve Arden';[78] 'Tamsin Greig makes a handsome Beatrice, who with her slit skirt, pointy shoes, cigarette holder and hands on hips has something of the tart grandeur of a down-market Princess Margaret.'[79] What she also suggested was the barely-controlled frustration of a woman who was faster and brighter than anyone else around. The scene of her eavesdropping was quite as funny as Benedick's, where it is often less so, but faced with the news that Benedick loved her, she was filled with an aching vulnerability. Joseph Millson as Benedick was not overshadowed though: 'Joseph Millson's performance . . . strikes me as definitive. Handsome in voice and in person, he can carry the audience on his roar and draw it into his hush. The elements of wit, anger and vulnerability are thrillingly mixed in this actor.'[80] Together they made a funny, intelligent, passionate pairing.

'Kill Claudio'

The delivery of this notoriously difficult line is often singled out for comment by the critics. In 1968, Janet Suzman yelled the line with tigerish intensity and Alan Howard yelled back 'Not for the wide world!' One critic felt that they 'solved the problem' of the line.[81] Many thought that Judi Dench, in 1976, delivered it beautifully (with a smothered giggle) but others complained that the line raised a laugh. Michael Billington wrote of Susan Fleetwood in 1990 that she 'delivers that death-trap injunction to Benedick, "Kill Claudio", with such intensity that not a titter runs through the house. This is real acting.'[82] Billington commented on Harriet Walter's delivery of the line too: 'the exchanges (in the Church scene) between Harriet Walter's Beatrice and Nicholas le Prévost's Benedick are charged with a heady mix of eroticism and violence. Walter's demand that he "Kill Claudio" springs out of an incandescent fury that leads her to kick over the church pews.'[83] Tamsin Greig in the 2006 production spilled out the line amidst a torrent of tears and kisses, sometimes evoking a laugh from the audience and sometimes an awed hush.

Claudio and Hero

Technically, the Claudio–Hero plot is the play's main plot, but they are invariably overshadowed. Finding the balance between the pleasure of the Beatrice–Benedick plot and the pain of the Hero–Claudio one emerges as more of an issue in later productions. In 1961, Michael Langham made little of the pain and Michael Billington noted the difficulties created for this part of the play by the very English setting of Ronald Eyre's 1971 production, lacking as it did 'Italian ardour'. The golden glow of the English garden in Bill Alexander's 1992 production similarly marginalized Hero's suffering, though Alex Kingston was a touching Hero.

In 1968, Trevor Nunn took the Hero–Claudio–Don John plot as its dark focus, and though the Claudio was generally felt by critics to be under-cast, Helen Mirren was a moving Hero, playing her as barely more than a child, wide-eyed and excited at the prospect of marriage, a true lamb to the slaughter. In Barton's 1976 production, Cherie Lunghi played an appealing Hero and Richard Durden a heartless Claudio who was as 'coldly frivolous' after the disgrace of Hero as he had been before. Billington observed that the two plots melded unusually well because Don John's plot against Claudio and Hero was a particularly vicious extension of the practical jokes indulged in by a heartless officer class.[84]

The cruelty of Hero's treatment, not only by Don John and Claudio but by her own father, was strongly emphasized in Di Trevis' 1988 production. Ralph Fiennes played a particularly unpleasant, smug, sycophantic Claudio, and Irving Wardle noted: 'There is perhaps more substance in the production's feminist angle: as where Hero (Julia Ford) collapses in church and is immediately surrounded by a flock of sympathetic girls, while the men all retire to nurse their personal grievances.'[85]

In Gregory Doran's 2002 production, the Sicilian setting supported the play's masculine honour code and the mood shifted

5. In Di Trevis' 1988 RSC production, when Julia Ford as Hero collapsed, she was 'immediately surrounded by a flock of sympathetic girls, while the men all retire[d] to nurse their personal grievances'.

successfully from sun-drenched comedy to the darkness of Hero's betrayal:

> Doran also captures the darkness which casts such threatening shadows over this golden comedy. The great scene in which that callow gold-digger Claudio (excellent John Hopkins) accuses Hero of being a whore during their wedding ceremony is played with real psychological perception and packs a devastating and painful dramatic punch. When even Hero's loving father viciously turns on her, the eggshell surface of the comedy cracks to reveal the possibility of real tragedy.[86]

John Hopkins played Claudio as a man genuinely hurt as well as wounded in his pride, and Kirsten Parker was a deeply affecting Hero, 'who, in the rejection scene, retains all the dignity of a princess'.[87] With a skilled director's touch, Doran later had the wan face of Hero, immured indoors, look down from an upstairs window to see her now penitent father cradling her bridal veil.

In the salsa-filled Cuban setting of 2006, director Marianne Elliott made no attempt to keep the mood light in the second half: the bright lights went out in the interval, literally darkening the atmosphere: 'The pain of the wedding scene in which Morven Christie's sweet young Hero is so vilely traduced by Adam Rayner's cruel, callow Claudio achieves a bruising tragic intensity.'[88]

Of all the productions, Michael Boyd's in 1996 went furthest in giving main-plot status to this thread in the play. Emily Bruni as Hero was withdrawn and unsmiling, passive in her acquiescence to an arranged marriage and traumatized by what followed.

Minor Roles

The role of Don John has been a jumping-off point for several young actors who would go on to highly successful careers both in the RSC and outside it. Several critics noted a 'cankerous' performance in 1961 by a young Ian Richardson, who played Don John with a 'sinister stammer',[89] and in 1971, Richard Pasco, too, was a 'canker' in the otherwise sunny Victorian garden, playing Don John as a viciously repressed homosexual. In 1996, reviewing the production which strikingly foregrounded Don John's plot against Claudio, Alastair Macaulay comments: 'a very impressive young actor brings Don John to life with a nervous, laughing loutishness that is both dangerous and naïve',[90] while de Jongh writes: 'The remarkable Damian Lewis plays this villain as a suave but passionate malcontent, who puts a disarming face upon sheer evil.'[91] In 1968, Don John's lieutenants, Conrad and Borachio, were played with villainous perfection by two young actors, Ben Kingsley and Patrick Stewart.

In Bill Alexander's 1990 production, critics singled out John Carlisle:

The most complete performance of the evening comes from John Carlisle as Don Pedro. This is no princely cipher but an ageing

Cavalier, shrouded in solitude, hungry for emotional contact. Mr Carlisle enters into the proxy wooing of Hero with suspicious enthusiasm and proposes to Beatrice with direct urgency. He creates a character where on the page one barely exists.[92]

The Dogberry–Verges–Watch scenes are difficult to pull off, and actors and directors often seem to be trying too hard. 'Frenziedly overpitched', says Billington of Terry Hands' 1982 production.[93] David Waller played a richly comic, pompous, bucolic Dogberry in Nunn's 1968 production, in fine contrast to Clifford Rose's delicate Verges; John Woodvine's Sikh Dogberry in Barton's 1976 production was generally praised as bringing fresh comedy to Dogberry's malapropisms and self-importance. Audiences would be less comfortable with the implied racial attitudes now, and even then, as one critic commented cuttingly, 'You only need to raise a finger and a Paki accent and you're home.'[94] Marianne Elliott in 2006 tried to inject humour into Dogberry by casting Bette Bourne as an outrageously camp officer, accessorizing his uniform with a pink suspender belt and lipstick, making him appear like 'a slightly scary low-rent drag queen'.[95]

THE DIRECTOR'S CUT: INTERVIEWS WITH MARIANNE ELLIOTT AND NICHOLAS HYTNER

Marianne Elliott was born in 1967 into a distinguished theatrical family and brought up in Manchester where her father was co-founder of the Manchester Royal Exchange. She studied drama at Hull University, but spent some years working in a variety of jobs unconnected with the theatre before working as a casting director and then setting up her own company, Small Talk. She was subsequently appointed Artistic Director at the Manchester Royal Exchange. Her production of Lillian Hellman's *The Little Foxes* with Penelope Wilton at the Donmar Warehouse in 2001 was highly praised, and she went on to become an Associate Director at London's Royal Court. She has directed numerous successful productions as an Associate Director at the National, including an adaptation of Emile Zola's *Thérèse Raquin*, Michael Morpurgo's *War Horse*, Shaw's *St Joan* and Samuel Adamson's *Mrs Affleck*. She was nominated for an Evening Standard theatre award for her 2005 production of Ibsen's *Pillars of the Community*. Marianne directed the highly acclaimed 2006 production of *Much Ado about Nothing* in the Swan Theatre for the RSC Complete Works Festival with Tamsin Greig as Beatrice and Joseph Millson as Benedick.

Nicholas Hytner was appointed Director of the National Theatre in 2003. He was born in Manchester in 1956 and, after attending Manchester Grammar School, read English at Cambridge. He was Associate Director of Manchester's Royal Exchange Theatre from 1985 to 1989 and at the National from 1989 to 1997. He was a Visiting Professor of Contemporary Theatre at Oxford University in 2000–01, and is an Honorary Fellow of Trinity Hall, Cambridge. He is credited with revolutionizing the National Theatre artistically and with attracting large new audiences by producing bold, original work. He has directed many plays from the classical repertoire, including *King Lear* and *The Tempest* at the RSC and *The Winter's Tale*, *Henry V*, *The Alchemist* and *Phedre* at the National. His long-standing collaboration with the playwright Alan Bennett includes *The Madness of George III* and *The History Boys* at the National. His films include *The Madness of King George*, *The Crucible* and *The History Boys*. He directed Zoë Wanamaker and Simon Russell Beale in *Much Ado about Nothing* in 2007–08.

What sort of a world was your Messina? Did you give particular attention to the element of soldiers returning from the war, the transition from the battlefield to the battle of the sexes?

ME: Our Messina was Cuba around 1953, just after a rebel uprising had been crushed. The soldiers are victorious and ready to celebrate, get drunk, meet girls, etc. It's party time.

I felt the setting needed to be an imperialistic and patriarchal society. Men and women are viewed and treated very differently, hence their battling. It is also a society that is rather exotic and glamorous; like Italy was viewed by the English when Shakespeare wrote the play. Hence Cuba felt right. It's a place where there's a merging between public and private places, between street and house. This helped the in and out scenes: the outside party/festival feel and the more private family scenes. Cuba is a place that can hum to the beat of music. We used the rhythms of the time which had a feel like the Buena Vista Social Club. Ours was a world where music was very much part of the soul of the people; the atmosphere was hot, sexy and sweaty with an air of machismo. It's tropical, it's possibly a bit wild, and it's nothing like England! Cuba is somewhere we recognize as a sophisticated, glamorous, Latino place with a holiday feel, but at that time it had a darker side. In 1953, just before the revolution, it was in a flux of change, just like the characters in the play.

NH: Leonato's household is made up of many women and a couple of old men. It's very deliberately a testosterone-free zone. Its femininity is more interesting, and more unusual, than the locker-room machismo of the army. An army which isn't returning home incidentally – it's a mercenary army, presumably recruited from all over Italy, commanded by a Spaniard on behalf of the Spanish crown, billeting itself temporarily before further action. It's more like the army in *Three Sisters* – disrupting a sleepy backwater – but there's no suspicion that Messina is dead without it. We took care to create an easy-going, hospitable household, very Sicilian. Its first instinct is to throw a party. You don't get the impression that it is in any way incomplete before the army arrives. On the contrary, it seems content and at ease with itself. It's quite hard to negotiate through the first forty-five minutes without repeated gales of cheesy stage laughter.

The battle between Beatrice and Benedick seems to me to be less a battle between the sexes than a painful, and very funny, mutual baptism. They have in common a refusal to take the plunge: they cast themselves instead in the same roles in relation to the largely single-sex worlds to which they have resigned themselves. They are both their respective 'prince's fool', and there is in both an underlying unhappiness with the corner they've painted themselves into. Their banter is a front for their emotional dishonesty; the 'mountain of affection' is the elephant in the room and Don Pedro's therapeutic trick makes it impossible for them to ignore it. We played our gulling scene around a pool. Both jumped in it to hide. They took the plunge, literally.

The real battle is between unthinking patriarchy and the apparently irrational, instinctive female loyalty embodied by Beatrice. The evidence of their own eyes seems to favour Claudio and Don Pedro. Leonato impulsively takes their side against his daughter. Beatrice's instinctive refusal to believe them is based on something truer than the evidence: she has a genuine capacity to know – to note – those around her. She knows Hero. When Benedick joins her, it's not so much a resolution of a battle between the sexes as a union between two people who, through allowing themselves to be genuinely and fully known by each other, have the capacity to know those around them.

There is clearly a history between Beatrice and Benedick that has taken place before the play starts. Is that something you explored in rehearsal?

ME: We were interested in all the characters wearing metaphorical masks and creating unrealistic images of themselves, but Beatrice and Benedick specifically seemed to exist under a very polished veneer. They live carefully guarded lives, which they have cultivated – always resorting to making people laugh rather than letting anyone in. Of course, this changes during the play through the power of their love and the shock of what happens to Hero. As for their history, we felt there would be no reason for them to hate each other unless they've been burnt by each other before. There would be no reason for them to keep touting their rather vain 'joker' images of themselves if they weren't trying to cover up something vulnerable inside – and/or trying to control everyone and everything around them.

NH: It's essential to create a past for Beatrice and Benedick. We agreed on a very specific history – not something that we intended to be legible to the audience, but a foundation for the palpable pain that they cause each other by being in each other's presence. Our assumption was that at some stage Beatrice read their deepening friendship as blossoming love; that she pushed too hard and that Benedick did a runner. Benedick, we assumed, was a greater coward than Beatrice. And the memory is still raw. These secret histories are essential actors' tools. They played their first exchange in Act 1 scene 1 ('nobody marks you'; 'Are you yet living?') not as a public performance but away from the crowd, a private acknowledgement of the disdain that masks deep hurt.

It's a commonplace that Shakespeare's marriages seem very often to be built on shaky foundations, and that Beatrice and Benedick make the marriage most likely to succeed in all of his plays. Essential, therefore, that both actors convey that they know the worst about each other and marry because of it, not in spite of it. Zoë Wanamaker and Simon Russell Beale were in an established tradition of middle-aged Beatrices and Benedicks: people who have lived, failed, resigned themselves to loneliness and, through a genuine sense of each other in the round (prompted admittedly by a trick), become capable of the compromise that long-lasting relationships require.

Did you find there were some key shifts in the balance of power between them? The 'Kill Claudio' moment's a crucial one, isn't it?

ME: Yes, it is a crucial moment. It's difficult to do nowadays as it can engender a giggly, slightly embarrassed reaction in the audience because it is so surprising and so extreme. But Beatrice is very much a product of where she comes from. She's an incredibly strong, strident woman, but she is living in a patriarchal, war-like world where the men are fighters and their enemies are very real and immediate. She wants Benedick to be a man of action, to stop all his talk and do something about the horrendous situation.

6. Simon Russell Beale as Benedick and Zoë Wanamaker as Beatrice argue as intellectual equals in Nicholas Hytner's 2007 National Theatre production.

It's also a test, of course, because although she really does believe that Claudio should be exterminated Mafia-style, she is pushing Benedick to the limit, to see how far and how deep this newly professed love for her is. She's been hurt by him before, don't forget. Of course, in this moment the lady takes all the power. Benedick has to perform a very difficult (nearly impossible) task to win her.

Generally, we found that Benedick and Beatrice were constantly looking for the upper hand. We explored that in our production by having them always playing to the crowd. Whichever of them had the joke that got the biggest reaction had the power and the control. That reinforced their image, their veneer of being the sophisticated, witty one who could bring the other down with a damning look or word. Beatrice won these subtle little wars quite a lot, we found! But this habit of theirs is a hard one to crack, even at the end of the play!

NH: We were less interested in shifts in the balance of power than in their uncovering of themselves to each other. Beatrice is plainly wittier than Benedick – she gets the better of him through most of the banter. But they share a way of looking at the world even before they declare themselves to each other. The banter is a way of avoiding the truth.

'Kill Claudio' is so shockingly truthful that it always gets a laugh – in recognition, I think, of how desperately helpless a man like Benedick is bound to be in the face of such raw hatred. It's tricky (and critically de trop) to make these sorts of judgement about fictional characters, but it's worth saying that Benedick is a man of unusual integrity, a good man. Beatrice is also good – a loyal cousin and a caring niece. Her murderousness is the consequence of her love for Hero – evidence, if any were needed, of how deeply she is capable of loving. Audiences laugh because they expect Benedick to be comically wrong-footed. (There's a need to release tension too.) The play's most striking reversal of expectation is Benedick's agreement to challenge Claudio. He must know that he hasn't got a chance. Claudio is set up from the start of the play as a demon soldier. Opinions vary about Benedick, but you're inclined to believe Don Pedro when he accuses him of 'Christian-like fear'. So, for love of Beatrice, and out of an altruistic dismay at the injustice done to Hero, Benedick embarks on a journey that could end in his death. Simon Russell Beale took this entirely seriously. Zoë Wanamaker slowly realized the magnitude of his sacrifice.

The Hero–Claudio storyline is often overshadowed by the Beatrice–Benedick one, isn't it? Berlioz left it out of his operatic version altogether! Did you find ways of keeping it whole, giving due weight to the 'romantic' lovers? Especially tough with Hero, maybe, since she has so few lines?

ME: It's crucial to the story that Hero is a virginal, pure, straightforward, obedient girl but, of course, this does not have the same meaning for a modern audience. It's also crucial that Claudio's character undergoes a *massive* turnaround on just a couple of lines. His sense of 'honour' (a very important theme in the whole play) is upturned. His cruel and shocking behaviour towards Hero in the church when he tries to protect his 'honour' is finally seen as the most dishonourable thing of all. Again, a man's honour and reputation doesn't mean the same thing now. Hence the importance of setting the production in a place and period where all this is still very much alive.

We tried to serve the through-lines of Hero and Claudio honestly. While Hero does have quite a wicked sense of humour – because Beatrice is her mate she can have moments where her sense of humour is quite sharp – she also has to truly believe that being a virgin and being a young, pure, inexperienced woman who obeys her father and then her husband is what you should aspire to. I think Beatrice has slightly different opinions about that! Beatrice was older than Hero in our production. As Hero was very young we tried to show how she starts to learn about men as things happen to her. Claudio's repentance is a genuine one, or so we tried to convey; it is so deeply felt that, in a play where the gift of articulacy is rewarded, he simply can't find the words to express his shame.

The main characters are definitely Beatrice and Benedick; they're the most complex characters. Claudio and Hero are much more straightforward because they haven't had the experience of life that the other two have had. Shakespeare has less fun with them!

NH: But isn't that the point? Hero and Claudio are barely allowed by the playwright to talk to each other. They plainly don't get to know each other. Claudio gets an unfairly bad rap for making sure that Hero is Leonato's heir before he proposes. But he's making a conventional, sensible marriage. The problem is that although they're clearly attracted to each other, neither he nor Hero bother to note each other.

I'm very taken by the puns in the title of the play. 'Nothing' – no thing (slang for 'vagina'). 'Noting' – the Elizabethan pronunciation of 'nothing'. The third is the most important. The failure to note properly, to look properly, to listen properly is what the play's about. It's there from the start: Antonio, Borachio, Leonato, Benedick, Beatrice, Don Pedro and, most disastrously, Claudio (at Hero's window) are among those who get it wrong. The main plot (Hero–Claudio) is about the terrible consequences of not looking, not engaging. It's about the folly of an attraction that is conventional and skin-deep. The Beatrice–Benedick plot is about two people who love, warts and all. The great heart-stopper ('I do love nothing in the world so well as you. Is not that strange?') is moving because it acknowledges both an evident truth and the genuine strangeness not of a *coup de foudre* (happens all the time, rarely meaningful, not particularly strange) but of their capacity to love without narcissism. They have discovered how to look, to know, to note the other and love the other, not as a projection of romantic perfection, but for who the other actually is. And how strange for Benedick to find himself not ambushed by passion but overwhelmed by the gradual realization that he's found the courage to love, and to say it. Hero and Claudio are age-appropriate, class-appropriate and good-looking. It's not enough. Beatrice and Benedick are more than intellectual equals. They become capable of being truly vulnerable to each other (Benedick: 'And how do you?' Beatrice: 'Very ill too.' Benedick: 'Serve God, love me and mend'). Claudio and Hero never get beyond conventional pleasantries ('Lady, as you are mine, I am yours').

Their relative callowness is the point. That doesn't mean that the actors playing them should patronize them. Nor is it good enough to write Claudio off as irredeemable. He falls for a stupid trick and he behaves with naked aggression at the wedding. But so do all the other men on stage apart from Benedick. Claudio isn't alone in his failure to note properly, and although it's Hero who suffers the worst consequences of an arrogant impulsiveness that seems to be the hallmark of masculinity, Claudio is at least given an opening to grow up.

Berlioz wasn't the first (or last) great artist to love Shakespeare to death. He wrote about Shakespeare better than he set him to music. *Béatrice et Bénédict* isn't the worst Shakespeare opera (far too much competition), but he blundered badly by cutting the main plot. There is terrific satisfaction in watching an unsatisfactory relationship fall apart, and it's tantalizing to sniff the possibility that they may be able to start again on a firmer footing.

Your actresses must have particularly enjoyed the women-only scenes, such as the one with Margaret and Ursula before the wedding?

ME: No, they found them really difficult! Particularly the gulling scene that comes after the mens' and has so much pressure on it to be funny. The scene before the wedding is quite fun, though, as the women get a chance to shine a little because they're alone and Beatrice is ill. But there aren't long and interesting through-lines for Margaret and Ursula in the play. They generally have very little to say.

NH: You're right. They did.

Are Don John and Borachio simply machiavellian characters, or did you find a different explanation for their actions?

ME: I thought Don John was understandably bereaved. For me he was a Che Guevara-type figure, which fitted with our setting the play in 1950s Cuba. He was absolutely anti-establishment and therefore unfairly treated. I did feel very passionately that in our production Don John and Borachio should have reasons for doing the things that they were doing. On a larger level, this society needs to change, and if it weren't for characters like Don John and Borachio then there would be nothing to unsettle the status quo. We had Borachio be in love with Hero. When he sees Claudio, the new young celebrity of the war, suddenly win Hero, with everyone's vocal approval, then he wants to exact revenge on him. He takes his plan to Don John, who would do anything to hurt his brother's regime.

NH: It's not unusual for Shakespeare to be compact in his writing of a character and to leave the actors to fill in the gaps. Imagine a draft of the play that fleshed out Don John, explored his inner life, and spent valuable stage time providing him with a history that motivated his malevolence. A decent director would reach immediately for the blue pencil. Shakespeare always knows where his plays give off heat and where they don't, where it's worth hanging around and where it's best to move on. There's too much else of interest in *Much Ado* to make more space for Don John.

So he gives the actors the responsibility to ground Don John and Borachio in emotional reality. A convincing performance gives an impression of psychological truth that may be missing in the text. Don John is plainly jealous of Claudio, resentful of his relationship with Don Pedro, and as Iago hates Cassio for the daily beauty in his life, so Don John hates Claudio for being the most popular officer in the mess. Andrew Woodall decided that Don John had once made a pass at Claudio, and that Claudio had brusquely rejected it. That appealed to me: it felt right that Don John was eaten up with self-loathing and fury that he'd allowed Claudio to note him. There's no particular textual evidence for this – but it allowed the actor to give emotional flesh where the playwright has provided a functional theatrical skeleton.

Dogberry: a difficult balancing act between, on the one hand, the plodding mind and the mixed-up words, and, on the other hand, the goodness of heart and the part played in exposing the plot?

ME: He's meant to be a funny character and funny characters in Shakespeare have their pressures, because there are often a lot of colloquialisms or period references that don't mean anything today. He's muddled and probably uneducated but trying to create an important image of himself. Because he gets it wrong, it's recognizably comical – hopefully. But in other ways he's the play's true hero. His actions again subvert the idea of what is 'honourable'. He has a clear sense of right and wrong.

NH: So find a good actor.

Seventy per cent prose and only 30 per cent verse: unusual proportions for Shakespeare. Did that make a difference to your language work with the actors?

ME: Shakespeare chooses such amazing words and creates such extraordinary images that unless you get behind exactly what they are, it can seem senseless. He does, however, give you little clues all the time; in the alliteration, in the sound of a word when spoken, in the metre, in the visualization of the image – all things that take a bit of time to really understand. Each word is like its own delectable sweet! But you can't stress everything. Working at the RSC, you have a lot of experts on hand to help you. We had about two weeks at the beginning of rehearsal just exploring Shakespeare's writing before we even started on the play.

NH: Not really. The rhetorical patterns of Shakespeare's prose are often tricky. Prose is generally longer-winded than verse, and sometimes knotted and obscure. But the intellectual, emotional and imaginative challenges are the same.

Hero's return: a neat trick for which we're well prepared, and yet isn't there some element of magical resurrection about it – one thinks back to the Alcestis of Euripides and forward to the revival of Hermione's statue in *The Winter's Tale?* The problem, though, is Claudio's rather grudging participation?

ME: We didn't treat it as particularly magical because the audience are told beforehand that it's going to happen. Because they are better informed than Claudio, you don't see it as a piece of magic but more as a trick on him. What I was interested in doing was subverting what the society was about. Claudio started to understand that women weren't necessarily either icons or whores; he started to understand that there was much more complexity to it, and that what he had done was a horrific crime that had led to somebody's death. When Hero returned, I brought out all the girls wearing Virgin Mary masks, so that every time he saw one of them appear he was literally confronted with the Virgin Mary iconography, and had to question quite fundamentally a few things in his culture and religion. He *should* be grudging at the idea of taking a new wife – if he truly loves his dead Hero. When he discovered that it was Hero resurrected to him, then we tried to make his reaction very celebratory. He picked her up and swung her round. But he's still learnt a very salutary lesson.

7. Adam Rayner as Claudio confronted by 'all the girls wearing Virgin Mary masks' in Marianne Elliott's 2006 Cuban *Much Ado* for the RSC.

NH: The question rather overlooks the scene at Hero's fake tomb. Nobody could deny that Claudio's repentance is under-written. But whenever Shakespeare calls for music, you know that he recognizes its insidious communicative power. The theatrical potential of the tomb scene is less in its text than in ritual and music. It's possible to create an event that gives Claudio space for genuine repentance. If Hero witnesses an act of true contrition (Leonato can bring her to watch surreptitiously), the resolution comes more easily.

Admittedly, Claudio in Act 5 seems to revert (at least with Benedick) to the locker room. But in nearly all of his romantic comedies, Shakespeare insists on the possibility of repentance and forgiveness. He thinks people can change. He's realistic about how hard it is, but he believes in a second chance. We're less inclined to, nowadays. Our loss.

If you were to direct the play again, would you consider following the early Quarto and Folio texts – and this edition – and giving the line 'Peace! I will stop your mouth' (5.4.101) to Leonato, rather than assigning it to Benedick, as most productions have done? How might that alter this moment of resolution?

ME: When we rehearsed it, we were constantly chopping and changing between the different versions. If I did it again? Difficult to say, as I don't know what kind of production that would be. But I love that moment. I wanted to show they were genuinely in love and quips wouldn't serve them any more. Benedick is stopping Beatrice gabbing away again at her usual game of verbal wit by just cutting it short with a kiss. At last! The resolution is one of love.

When you direct a play it becomes very personal. It's hard to explain how. It's not just personal to you, it's personal to everybody involved in the rehearsal room: the creative team and the actors. If I did it again I would probably, at that time of my life, be interested in different things, as I'm sure everyone else in the room would be, so we would do it with a slightly different slant. At the time I really wanted to explore the character of Beatrice, and who she was. I was fascinated by Benedick too, but really very interested in Beatrice; in the way she lived within the world, as described above, but still with a sense of her own individuality. And given that she had to fight to be so different to everyone else, how does she fall in love? And with whom? And what does that do to change her? And if it changes her, how does that change the world around her? And what does it mean anyway that the world changes? That's what I wanted to explore. Maybe if I did it again I'd be much more interested in Benedick, or the fact that Benedick and Beatrice were much older and perhaps felt they were past it, and then re-found their sexiness and allure – which Nick Hytner's production portrayed so brilliantly.

I'd be interested in other things. That's why theatre is so alive, isn't it? It's ephemeral, of the moment. Productions shouldn't be compared. They are their own entities, produced by a particular group of people, at a particular time in history, who relate to the material as products of their time and place.

NH: I would consider it briefly and decide that we were right first time. There are all sorts of reasons to give the line to Leonato that look good in the study. Leonato has spent the play trying (often ineffectually) to exert control – particularly over Beatrice. By silencing Beatrice, Benedick might be in danger of coming across as a crypto-Petruchio – better to leave Leonato with the line and allow them to end the play in perfect equality. And so on.

But in the theatre, it's blindingly obvious that the line is Benedick's and that the Quarto compositor got it wrong. It's about a kiss. It's about a marriage. It's about a man and a woman. That old thing. Therefore play, music.

HARRIET WALTER ON PLAYING BEATRICE

Harriet Walter was born in 1950 and trained at the London Academy of Music and Dramatic Art. Her early experience included work with the Joint Stock touring theatre company, Paines Plough touring company and the Dukes playhouse, Lancaster. She has worked with the RSC many times during her career and was made an Associate Artist in 1987. She has numerous television and film roles to her credit, including DI Natalie Chandler in *Law and Order: UK*, *Sense and Sensibility*, and *Atonement*. Apart from Beatrice in Gregory Doran's successful 2002 production of *Much Ado about Nothing*, she has played Helena in Trevor Nunn's 1981 production of *All's Well that Ends Well* and Imogen in Bill Alexander's 1987 production of *Cymbeline* at The Other Place, as well as Lady Macbeth in Doran's 1999 production of *Macbeth*, chronicling the experience in her book *Macbeth* in Faber and Faber's 'Actors on Shakespeare' series, and a much-acclaimed Cleopatra in his 2006 production of *Antony and Cleopatra*.

There is clearly a history between Beatrice and Benedick that has taken place before the play starts. Is that something you explored in rehearsal?

We certainly discussed this, yes. We found quite a few possible scenarios, but the most helpful thought was that at some point in the past when they were letting their guard down and verging on a loving relationship, there had been a misunderstanding whereby Beatrice and Benedick had each interpreted the other as having rejected them. Both pretend to the world and to themselves that they were the dumper, not the dumpee. Both are too proud to admit their pain, so they revert to raillery and public scorn or teasing.

This 'performance' not only acts as a much-needed shield to protect each of their egos, but it also becomes so publicly entertaining that they feel obliged to please the crowd and keep it up. They are trapped by the success of their posturing into a habit of mutual dislike. Everyone expects it of them and they have got to a point where each privately expects it of him/herself.

It is doubtful that Benedick ever got so far as to consciously think he was ever in love with Beatrice, while Beatrice, who is a little more in touch with her heart, probably did admit to loving Benedick, though by the beginning of the play this has long since been converted to strong dislike. Her comment 'I know you of old' was interesting to play with an awareness of hurt inside. She skates near the edge, teasing her audience with hints. For example, in Act 2 scene 1:

> **DON PEDRO** Come, lady, come, you have lost the heart of Signior Benedick.
> **BEATRICE** Indeed, my lord, he lent it me awhile, and I gave him use for it, a double heart for his single one: marry, once before he won it of me with false dice, therefore your Grace may well say I have lost it.

It felt to me as though she both wanted to be found out, and was, at the same time, absolutely loath to be found out. Her jokes are a brilliant mask and also a trap.

It takes the two eavesdropping scenes to reveal Beatrice and Benedick's true feelings to themselves. It is their private shock (and relief in a way) on discovering they love deep down, the bit they 'privately' confess to the audience, that is moving and funny. It is

8. Harriet Walter as Beatrice in Gregory Doran's Sicilian *Much Ado* for the RSC in 2002.

also important, for all the actors involved in those duping scenes in the garden, to remember that each group *thinks* they are tricking each of the lovers into believing a lie that the other is in love with them, and neither group realizes till much later that they have in fact revealed the truth.

Did you find there were some key shifts in the balance of power between them? The 'Kill Claudio' moment's a crucial one, isn't it?

I think both Beatrice and Benedick are sticklers for equality, which is what makes their relationship at the end so sympathetic to a modern audience. The Hero–Claudio plot takes over so quickly after Beatrice and Benedick discover their love for one another that Shakespeare denies the latter couple the happy payoff scene, or at least he postpones it until Act 5 scene 2. Instead they have to admit their love in the urgent and stressed circumstances of Hero's humiliation at the wedding. Just as Beatrice was beginning to unfurl and put her trust in Benedick, she is reminded of all that she mistrusts about the male species. There is Claudio willing to believe so quickly that his betrothed has been sleeping with another man, and Hero's own father is shockingly quick to believe hearsay above a lifetime's knowledge of his daughter. Both men love their own honour better than they ever love Hero. This is the Sicilian climate of macho honour, of *omerta*.

By setting the play in a recognizable Sicily and stressing this male code so strongly, [director] Gregory Doran helped me enormously. It justified Beatrice's defensive bloody-mindedness. It comes from a deep place of fear, however humorously expressed. In such a culture, the bonds between men are stronger than any bond between a man and a woman, and while women will bond together in mutual protection against this fact, once they marry they are expected to switch their primary loyalty to their man and children. For a mature marriage to work, a man must prove himself capable of doing the same and leaving his boyish comrades behind. This is essentially what Beatrice is demanding of Benedick when she says 'Kill Claudio'. I believe it is not so much that she wants to see Claudio dead, as that she wants proof that Benedick is capable of rejecting and criticizing this worst aspect of male behaviour. She needs to know that he can distance himself from his past allegiances and truly commit to her.

The Hero–Claudio storyline is often overshadowed by the Beatrice–Benedick one, isn't it? Berlioz left it out of his operatic version altogether! Did you find ways of helping your director to keep it whole, to give due weight to the 'romantic' lovers? Especially tough with Hero, maybe, since she has so few lines?

The distinctive and very modern aspect of the relationship between Beatrice and Benedick is that from the moment they admit their love to one another they are free to respect one another's strength of character. In each of them, submitting to love was linked with an idea of loss of power and control. But having had such a long drawn-out and often antagonistic courtship, they can be said to really know one another and to have seen the worst of one another. This is very different from the untested and idealistic love between Claudio and Hero, who have really only fallen in love with one another's image and social suitability. Shakespeare deliberately contrasts these two types of relationship and each plot elucidates the other.

Was it a particular pleasure to play the women-only scenes?

This is an interesting question. In fact the women-only scenes are quite difficult to find the tone for. Aside from a general ease of atmosphere, the plotting is less obviously funny than in the all-male scenes. Dare I wonder whether it has something to do with Shakespeare himself not quite knowing what women get up to or talk about when men aren't around? Aside from the delightful scene between Katherine and Alice in *Henry V*, most of Shakespeare's successful all-female scenes either have a girl posing as a boy, as in *Twelfth Night*, or they are between a wiser older woman and a younger (*Othello*, *All's Well*). All-girlie scenes are harder for him to write and therefore harder to play. Having said that, it was very noticeable that the hierarchy changes distinctly in Hero's household when there are no men about. Hero becomes the dominant female.

She has the highest social status and the actress gets a chance to play a sparky character, very different from the subdued trophy bride and favourite daughter she is forced to play in public.

Seventy per cent prose and only 30 per cent verse: unusual proportions for Shakespeare. Did that make a difference to your language work on this play?

Yes. Beatrice only speaks in verse at the end of Act 3 scene 1. It is also her only soliloquy. I therefore took it that this was a moment to reveal her deepest feelings and romantic aspirations – things she wouldn't dream of revealing to anyone 'inside' the play. As actors we are always asked to note where the language changes from verse to prose or to rhyming. There are no hard-and-fast rules as to what Shakespeare means by these changes, but if an actor observes them, a kind of reason is revealed inside us via the different rhythms and notes that are sounded in our subconscious. We note the changes and try and justify or explain them later. It is better that way round.

Hero's return: a neat trick for which we're well prepared, and yet isn't there some element of magical resurrection about it – one thinks back to the Alcestis of Euripides and forward to the revival of Hermione's statue in *The Winter's Tale?* The problem, though, is Claudio's rather grudging participation?

Yes. In each of these cases what is required is a solemnity, an almost religious ritual to match the scale of the conversion of the wrongdoer and to earn the audience's forgiveness. In our production, Gregory Doran recognized that Claudio's rehabilitation can seem very glib and speedy, and wanted to make his contrition at Hero's supposed graveside as true and as heartfelt as possible. He gave the scene more time and gravity than usual, and Claudio's grief was played (by John Hopkins) with moving sincerity. Despite these best efforts, I think the play leaves us all with a big worry for the future of Claudio and Hero's partnership, in contrast to our pleasure in the coming together of the less romantic, less deluded Beatrice and Benedick.

If you were to play the part again, how would you feel if the director followed the early Quarto and Folio texts – and this edition – and gave the line 'Peace! I will stop your mouth' (5.4.101) to Leonato, rather than assigning it to Benedick, as most productions have done? If Leonato more or less forces Benedick to stop Beatrice's mouth with a kiss, how might that alter the moment of resolution? Might it get round the problem you have when Benedick speaks the line, whereby Beatrice is effectively, if only momentarily, suffocated with the kiss (something that seems more *Othello* than *Much Ado*)?

I am convinced that it is better to give the line to Benedick, and I don't find it is a sinister suffocation at all. Rather, it seems to be a restoration of their usual banter but with love behind it now. Their power struggles are over. Beatrice no longer feels the need to have the last word. They have a wonderful confidence in one another. It is playable the other way, of course, but is not so dramatically compact or eloquent. I am glad most productions have disobeyed the early Quarto and Folio texts.

What interesting connections and contrasts did you discover in the process of playing this Shakespearean lead, as opposed to others such as Innogen in *Cymbeline*, Helen in *All's Well that Ends Well*, and Cleopatra or even Lady Macbeth?

I have a tendency to seek dissimilarities rather than similarities between the characters I have played, so I haven't given much thought to the links. The most obvious thing that springs to mind in retrospect is that Beatrice does not drive the plot to the extent of Lady Macbeth or Cleopatra or Imogen or Helena. This is partly to do with her position in the household as a sort of poor relation, and partly because she reveals herself through a lot of prose banter rather than arias of great poetry. The great soliloquies give an actor a special sort of command of the stage and of the audience. Beatrice, as befits her place in the community, has to win her points through wit, through ducking and diving and dancing and then, when

Benedick offers her first taste of unfettered power – 'Come, bid me do anything for thee' – she surprises everyone (including herself) with the depth of passion she feels; 'Kill Claudio'. Cleopatra or Lady Macbeth would probably have been instantly obeyed. Beatrice gets a greater reward than obedience. Benedick goes as far as his integrity will allow and challenges Claudio to a duel. The play, being a comedy, lets us all off the hook, but Beatrice has found an ally who loves her but is still his own man. Perfect.

SHAKESPEARE'S CAREER IN THE THEATRE

BEGINNINGS

William Shakespeare was an extraordinarily intelligent man who was born and died in an ordinary market town in the English Midlands. He lived an uneventful life in an eventful age. Born in April 1564, he was the eldest son of John Shakespeare, a glove-maker who was prominent on the town council until he fell into financial difficulties. Young William was educated at the local grammar in Stratford-upon-Avon, Warwickshire, where he gained a thorough grounding in the Latin language, the art of rhetoric and classical poetry. He married Ann Hathaway and had three children (Susanna, then the twins Hamnet and Judith) before his twenty-first birthday: an exceptionally young age for the period. We do not know how he supported his family in the mid-1580s.

Like many clever country boys, he moved to the city in order to make his way in the world. Like many creative people, he found a career in the entertainment business. Public playhouses and professional full-time acting companies reliant on the market for their income were born in Shakespeare's childhood. When he arrived in London as a man, sometime in the late 1580s, a new phenomenon was in the making: the actor who is so successful that he becomes a 'star'. The word did not exist in its modern sense, but the pattern is recognizable: audiences went to the theatre not so much to see a particular show as to witness the comedian Richard Tarlton or the dramatic actor Edward Alleyn.

Shakespeare was an actor before he was a writer. It appears not to have been long before he realized that he was never going to grow into a great comedian like Tarlton or a great tragedian like Alleyn. Instead, he found a role within his company as the man who patched up old plays, breathing new life, new dramatic twists, into tired repertory pieces. He paid close attention to the work of the university-educated dramatists who were writing history plays and tragedies for the public stage in a style more ambitious, sweeping and poetically grand than anything which had been seen before. But he may also have noted that what his friend and rival Ben Jonson would call 'Marlowe's mighty line' sometimes faltered in the mode of comedy. Going to university, as Christopher Marlowe did, was all well and good for honing the arts of rhetorical elaboration and classical allusion, but it could lead to a loss of the common touch. To stay close to a large segment of the potential audience for public theatre, it was necessary to write for clowns as well as kings and to intersperse the flights of poetry with the humour of the tavern, the privy and the brothel: Shakespeare was the first to establish himself early in his career as an equal master of tragedy, comedy and history. He realized that theatre could be the medium to make the national past available to a wider audience than the elite who could afford to read large history books: his signature early works include not only the classical tragedy *Titus Andronicus* but also the sequence of English historical plays on the Wars of the Roses.

He also invented a new role for himself, that of in-house company dramatist. Where his peers and predecessors had to sell their plays to the theatre managers on a poorly-paid piecework basis, Shakespeare took a percentage of the box-office income. The Lord Chamberlain's Men constituted themselves in 1594 as a joint stock company, with the profits being distributed among the core actors who had invested as sharers. Shakespeare acted himself – he appears in the cast lists of some of Ben Jonson's plays as well as the list of actors' names at the beginning of his own collected works – but his principal duty was to write two or three plays a year for the company. By holding shares, he was effectively earning himself a royalty on his work, something no author had ever done before in England. When the Lord Chamberlain's Men collected their fee for performance at court in the Christmas season of 1594, three of them went along to the Treasurer of the Chamber: not just Richard Burbage the tragedian and Will Kempe the clown, but also Shakespeare the scriptwriter. That was something new.

The next four years were the golden period in Shakespeare's career, though overshadowed by the death of his only son Hamnet, aged eleven, in 1596. In his early thirties and in full command of both his poetic and his theatrical medium, he perfected his art of comedy, while also developing his tragic and historical writing in new ways. In 1598, Francis Meres, a Cambridge University graduate with his finger on the pulse of the London literary world, praised Shakespeare for his excellence across the genres:

> As Plautus and Seneca are accounted the best for comedy and tragedy among the Latins, so Shakespeare among the English is the most excellent in both kinds for the stage; for comedy, witness his *Gentlemen of Verona*, his *Errors*, his *Love Labours Lost*, his *Love Labours Won*, his *Midsummer Night Dream* and his *Merchant of Venice*: for tragedy his *Richard the 2*, *Richard the 3*, *Henry the 4*, *King John*, *Titus Andronicus* and his *Romeo and Juliet*.

For Meres, as for the many writers who praised the 'honey-flowing vein' of *Venus and Adonis* and *Lucrece*, narrative poems written when the theatres were closed due to plague in 1593–94, Shakespeare was marked above all by his linguistic skill, by the gift of turning elegant poetic phrases.

PLAYHOUSES

Elizabethan playhouses were 'thrust' or 'one-room' theatres. To understand Shakespeare's original theatrical life, we have to forget about the indoor theatre of later times, with its proscenium arch and curtain that would be opened at the beginning and closed at the end of each act. In the proscenium arch theatre, stage and auditorium are effectively two separate rooms: the audience looks from one world into another as if through the imaginary 'fourth wall' framed by the proscenium. The picture-frame stage, together with the elaborate scenic effects and backdrops beyond it, created the illusion of a self-contained world – especially once nineteenth-century developments in the control of artificial lighting meant that the auditorium could be darkened and the spectators made to focus on the lighted stage. Shakespeare, by contrast, wrote for a bare platform stage with a standing audience gathered around it in a courtyard in full daylight. The audience were always conscious of themselves and their fellow-spectators, and they shared the same 'room' as the actors. A sense of immediate presence and the creation of rapport with the audience were all-important. The actor could not afford to imagine he was in a closed world, with silent witnesses dutifully observing him from the darkness.

Shakespeare's theatrical career began at the Rose Theatre in Southwark. The stage was wide and shallow, trapezoid in shape, like a lozenge. This design had a great deal of potential for the theatrical equivalent of cinematic split-screen effects, whereby one group of characters would enter at the door at one end of the tiring-house wall at the back of the stage and another group through the door at the other end, thus creating two rival tableaux. Many of the battle-heavy and faction-filled plays that premiered at the Rose have scenes of just this sort.

At the rear of the Rose stage, there were three capacious exits, each over ten feet wide. Unfortunately, the very limited excavation of a fragmentary portion of the original Globe site, in 1989, revealed nothing about the stage. The first Globe was built in 1599 with similar proportions to those of another theatre, the Fortune, albeit that the former was polygonal and looked circular, whereas the latter was rectangular. The building contract for the Fortune survives and allows us to infer that the stage of the Globe was probably substantially wider than it was deep (perhaps forty-three feet wide and twenty-seven feet deep). It may well have been tapered at the front, like that of the Rose.

The capacity of the Globe was said to have been enormous, perhaps in excess of three thousand. It has been conjectured that about eight hundred people may have stood in the yard, with two thousand or more in the three layers of covered galleries. The other 'public' playhouses were also of large capacity, whereas the indoor Blackfriars theatre that Shakespeare's company began using in 1608 – the former refectory of a monastery – had overall internal dimensions of a mere forty-six by sixty feet. It would have made for a much more intimate theatrical experience and had a much smaller capacity, probably of about six hundred people. Since they paid at least sixpence a head, the Blackfriars attracted a more select or 'private' audience. The atmosphere would have been closer to that of an indoor performance before the court in the Whitehall Palace or at Richmond. That Shakespeare always wrote for indoor production at court as well as outdoor performance in the public theatre should make us cautious about inferring, as some scholars have, that the opportunity provided by the intimacy of the Blackfriars led to a significant change towards a 'chamber' style in his last plays – which, besides, were performed at both the Globe and the Blackfriars. After the occupation of the Blackfriars a five-act structure seems to have become more important to Shakespeare. That was because of artificial lighting: there were musical interludes between the acts, while the candles were trimmed and replaced. Again, though, something similar must have been necessary for indoor court performances throughout his career.

Front of house there were the 'gatherers' who collected the money from audience members: a penny to stand in the open-air yard, another penny for a place in the covered galleries, sixpence for the prominent 'lord's rooms' to the side of the stage. In the indoor 'private' theatres, gallants from the audience who fancied making themselves part of the spectacle sat on stools on the edge of the stage itself. Scholars debate as to how widespread this practice was in the public theatres such as the Globe. Once the audience were in place and the money counted, the gatherers were available to be extras on stage. That is one reason why battles and crowd scenes often come later rather than early in Shakespeare's plays. There was no formal prohibition upon performance by women, and there certainly were women among the gatherers, so it is not beyond the bounds of possibility that female crowd members were played by females.

The play began at two o'clock in the afternoon and the theatre had to be cleared by five. After the main show, there would be a jig – which consisted not only of dancing, but also of knockabout comedy (it is the origin of the farcical 'afterpiece' in the eighteenth-century theatre). So the time available for a Shakespeare play was about two and a half hours, somewhere between the 'two hours' traffic' mentioned in the prologue to *Romeo and Juliet* and the 'three hours' spectacle' referred to in the preface to the 1647 Folio of Beaumont and Fletcher's plays. The prologue to a play by Thomas Middleton refers to a thousand lines as 'one hour's words', so the likelihood is that about two and a half thousand, or a maximum of three thousand lines made up the performed text. This is indeed the length of most of Shakespeare's comedies, whereas many of his tragedies and histories are much longer, raising the possibility that he wrote full scripts, possibly with eventual publication in mind, in the full knowledge that the stage version would be heavily cut. The short Quarto texts published in his lifetime – they used to be called 'Bad' Quartos – provide fascinating evidence as to the kind of cutting that probably took place. So, for instance, the First Quarto of *Hamlet* neatly merges two occasions when Hamlet is overheard, the 'Fishmonger' and the 'nunnery' scenes.

The social composition of the audience was mixed. The poet Sir John Davies wrote of 'A thousand townsmen, gentlemen and whores, / Porters and servingmen' who would 'together throng' at the public playhouses. Though moralists associated female play-going with adultery and the sex trade, many perfectly respectable citizens' wives were regular attendees. Some, no doubt, resembled the modern groupie: a story attested in two different sources has one citizen's wife making a post-show assignation with Richard Burbage and ending up in bed with Shakespeare – supposedly eliciting from the latter the quip that William the Conqueror was before Richard III. Defenders of theatre liked to say that by witnessing the comeuppance of villains on the stage, audience members would repent of their own wrongdoings, but the reality is that most people went to the theatre then, as they do now, for entertainment more than moral edification. Besides, it would be foolish to suppose that audiences behaved in a homogeneous way: a pamphlet of the 1630s tells of how two men went to see *Pericles* and one of them laughed while the other wept. Bishop John Hall complained that people went to church for the same reasons that they went to the theatre: 'for company, for custom, for recreation . . . to feed his eyes or his ears . . . or perhaps for sleep'.

Men-about-town and clever young lawyers went to be seen as much as to see. In the modern popular imagination, shaped not least by *Shakespeare in Love* and the opening sequence of Laurence Olivier's *Henry V* film, the penny-paying groundlings stand in the yard hurling abuse or encouragement and hazelnuts or orange peel at the actors, while the sophisticates in the covered galleries appreciate Shakespeare's soaring poetry. The reality was probably the other way round. A 'groundling' was a kind of fish, so the nickname suggests the penny audience standing below the level of the stage and gazing in silent open-mouthed wonder at the spectacle unfolding above them. The more difficult audience members, who kept up a running commentary of clever remarks on the performance and who occasionally got into quarrels with players, were the gallants. Like Hollywood movies in modern times, Elizabethan and Jacobean plays exercised a powerful influence on the fashion and behaviour of the young. John Marston mocks the lawyers who would open their lips, perhaps to court a girl, and out would 'flow / Naught but pure Juliet and Romeo'.

THE ENSEMBLE AT WORK

In the absence of typewriters and photocopying machines, reading aloud would have been the means by which the company got to know a new play. The tradition of the playwright reading his complete script to the assembled company endured for generations. A copy would then have been taken to the Master of the Revels for licensing. The theatre book-holder or prompter would then have copied the parts for distribution to the actors. A partbook consisted of the character's lines, with each speech preceded by the last three or four words of the speech before, the so-called 'cue'. These would have been taken away and studied or 'conned'. During this period of learning the parts, an actor might have had some one-to-one instruction, perhaps from the dramatist, perhaps from a senior actor who had played the same part before, and, in the case of an apprentice, from his master. A high percentage of Desdemona's lines occur in dialogue with Othello, of Lady Macbeth's with Macbeth, Cleopatra's with Antony and Volumnia's with Coriolanus. The roles would almost certainly have been taken by the apprentice of the lead actor, usually Burbage, who delivers the majority of the cues. Given that apprentices lodged with their masters, there would have been

9. Hypothetical reconstruction of the interior of an Elizabethan playhouse during a performance.

ample opportunity for personal instruction, which may be what made it possible for young men to play such demanding parts.

After the parts were learned, there may have been no more than a single rehearsal before the first performance. With six different plays to be put on every week, there was no time for more. Actors, then, would go into a show with a very limited sense of the whole. The notion of a collective rehearsal process that is itself a process of discovery for the actors is wholly modern and would have been incomprehensible to Shakespeare and his original ensemble. Given the number of parts an actor had to hold in his memory, the forgetting of lines was probably more frequent than in the modern theatre. The book-holder was on hand to prompt.

Backstage personnel included the property man, the tire-man who oversaw the costumes, call-boys, attendants and the musicians, who might play at various times from the main stage, the rooms above and within the tiring-house. Scriptwriters sometimes made a nuisance of themselves backstage. There was often tension between the acting companies and the freelance playwrights from whom they purchased scripts: it was a smart move on the part of Shakespeare and the Lord Chamberlain's Men to bring the writing process in-house.

Scenery was limited, though sometimes set-pieces were brought on (a bank of flowers, a bed, the mouth of hell). The trapdoor from below, the gallery stage above and the curtained discovery-space at the back allowed for an array of special effects: the rising of ghosts and apparitions, the descent of gods, dialogue between a character at a window and another at ground level, the revelation of a statue or a pair of lovers playing at chess. Ingenious use could be made of props, as with the ass's head in *A Midsummer Night's Dream*. In a theatre that does not clutter the stage with the material paraphernalia of everyday life, those objects that are deployed may take on powerful symbolic weight, as when Shylock bears his weighing scales in one hand and knife in the other, thus becoming a parody of the figure of Justice who traditionally bears a sword and a balance. Among the more significant items in the property cupboard of Shakespeare's company, there would have been a throne (the 'chair of state'), joint stools, books, bottles, coins, purses, letters (which are brought on stage, read or referred to on about eighty occasions in the complete works), maps, gloves, a set of stocks (in which Kent is put in *King Lear*), rings, rapiers, daggers, broadswords, staves, pistols, masks and vizards, heads and skulls, torches and tapers and lanterns which served to signal night scenes on the daylit stage, a buck's head, an ass's head, animal costumes. Live animals also put in appearances, most notably the dog Crab in *The Two Gentlemen of Verona* and possibly a young polar bear in *The Winter's Tale*.

The costumes were the most important visual dimension of the play. Playwrights were paid between £2 and £6 per script, whereas Alleyn was not averse to paying £20 for 'a black velvet cloak with sleeves embroidered all with silver and gold'. No matter the period of the play, actors always wore contemporary costume. The excitement for the audience came not from any impression of historical accuracy, but from the richness of the attire and perhaps the transgressive thrill of the knowledge that here were commoners like themselves strutting in the costumes of courtiers in effective defiance of the strict sumptuary laws whereby in real life people had to wear the clothes that befitted their social station.

To an even greater degree than props, costumes could carry symbolic importance. Racial characteristics could be suggested: a breastplate and helmet for a Roman soldier, a turban for a Turk, long robes for exotic characters such as Moors, a gabardine for a Jew. The figure of Time, as in *The Winter's Tale*, would be equipped with hourglass, scythe and wings; Rumour, who speaks the prologue of *2 Henry IV*, wore a costume adorned with a thousand tongues. The wardrobe in the tiring-house of the Globe would have contained much of the same stock as that of rival manager Philip Henslowe at the Rose: green gowns for outlaws and foresters, black for melancholy men such as Jaques and people in mourning such as the Countess in *All's Well that Ends Well* (at the beginning of *Hamlet*, the prince is still in mourning black when everyone else is in festive garb for the wedding of the new king), a gown and hood for a friar (or a feigned friar like the duke in *Measure for Measure*), blue coats and tawny to distinguish the followers of rival factions, a leather apron and ruler for a carpenter (as in the opening scene of *Julius Caesar* – and in *A Midsummer Night's Dream*, where this is the only sign that Peter Quince is a carpenter), a cockle hat with staff and a pair of sandals for a pilgrim or palmer (the disguise assumed by Helen in *All's Well*), bodices and kirtles with farthingales beneath for the boys who are to be dressed as girls. A gender switch such as that of Rosalind or Jessica seems to have taken between fifty and eighty lines of dialogue – Viola does not resume her 'maiden weeds', but remains in her boy's costume to the end of *Twelfth Night* because a change would have slowed down the action at just the moment it was speeding to a climax. Henslowe's inventory also included 'a robe for to go invisible': Oberon, Puck and Ariel must have had something similar.

As the costumes appealed to the eyes, so there was music for the ears. Comedies included many songs. Desdemona's willow song, perhaps a late addition to the text, is a rare and thus exceptionally poignant example from tragedy. Trumpets and tuckets sounded for ceremonial entrances, drums denoted an army on the march. Background music could create atmosphere, as at the beginning of *Twelfth Night*, during the lovers' dialogue near the end of *The Merchant of Venice*, when the statue seemingly comes to life in *The Winter's Tale*, and for the revival of Pericles and of Lear (in the Quarto text, but not the Folio). The haunting sound of the hautboy suggested a realm beyond the human, as when the god Hercules is imagined deserting Mark Antony. Dances symbolized the harmony of the end of a comedy – though in Shakespeare's world of mingled joy and sorrow, someone is usually left out of the circle.

The most important resource was, of course, the actors themselves. They needed many skills: in the words of one contemporary commentator, 'dancing, activity, music, song, elocution, ability of body, memory, skill of weapon, pregnancy of wit'. Their bodies were as significant as their voices. Hamlet tells the player to 'suit the action to the word, the word to the action': moments of strong emotion, known as 'passions', relied on a repertoire of dramatic gestures as well as a modulation of the voice. When Titus Andronicus has had his hand chopped off, he asks 'How can I grace my talk, / Wanting a hand to give it action?' A pen portrait of 'The Character of an Excellent Actor' by the dramatist John Webster is almost certainly based on his impression of Shakespeare's leading man, Richard Burbage: 'By a full and significant action of body, he charms our attention: sit in a full theatre, and you will think you see so many lines drawn from the circumference of so many ears, whiles the actor is the centre . . . .'

Though Burbage was admired above all others, praise was also heaped upon the apprentice players whose alto voices fitted them for the parts of women. A spectator at Oxford in 1610 records how the audience were reduced to tears by the pathos of Desdemona's death. The puritans who fumed about the biblical prohibition upon crossdressing and the encouragement to sodomy constituted by the sight of an adult male kissing a teenage boy on stage were a small minority. Little is known, however, about the characteristics of the leading apprentices in Shakespeare's company. It may perhaps be inferred that one was a lot taller than the other, since Shakespeare often wrote for a pair of female friends, one tall and fair, the other short and dark (Helena and Hermia, Rosalind and Celia, Beatrice and Hero).

We know little about Shakespeare's own acting roles – an early allusion indicates that he often took royal parts, and a venerable tradition gives him old Adam in *As You Like It* and the ghost of old King Hamlet. Save for Burbage's lead roles and the generic part of the clown, all such castings are mere speculation. We do not even know for sure whether the original Falstaff was Will Kempe or another actor who specialized in comic roles, Thomas Pope.

Kempe left the company in early 1599. Tradition has it that he fell out with Shakespeare over the matter of excessive improvisation. He was replaced by Robert Armin, who was less of a clown and more of a cerebral wit: this explains the difference between such parts as Lancelet Gobbo and Dogberry, which were written for Kempe, and the more verbally sophisticated Feste and Lear's Fool, which were written for Armin.

One thing that is clear from surviving 'plots' or story-boards of plays from the period is that a degree of doubling was necessary. *2 Henry VI* has over sixty speaking parts, but more than half of the characters only appear in a single scene and most scenes have only six to eight speakers. At a stretch, the play could be performed by thirteen actors. When Thomas Platter saw *Julius Caesar* at the Globe in 1599, he noted that there were about fifteen. Why doesn't Paris go to the Capulet ball in *Romeo and Juliet*? Perhaps because he was doubled with Mercutio, who does. In *The Winter's Tale*, Mamillius might have come back as Perdita and Antigonus been doubled by Camillo, making the partnership with Paulina at the end a very neat touch. Titania and Oberon are often played by the same pair as Hippolyta and Theseus, suggesting a symbolic matching of the rulers of the worlds of night and day, but it is questionable whether there would have been time for the necessary costume changes. As so often, one is left in a realm of tantalizing speculation.

THE KING'S MAN

On Queen Elizabeth's death in 1603, the new king, James I, who had held the Scottish throne as James VI since he had been an infant, immediately took the Lord Chamberlain's Men under his direct patronage. Henceforth they would be the King's Men, and for the rest of Shakespeare's career they were favoured with far more court performances than any of their rivals. There even seem to have been rumours early in the reign that Shakespeare and Burbage were being considered for knighthoods, an unprecedented honour for mere actors – and one that in the event was not accorded to a member of the profession for nearly three hundred years, when the title was bestowed upon Henry Irving, the leading Shakespearean actor of Queen Victoria's reign.

Shakespeare's productivity rate slowed in the Jacobean years, not because of age or some personal trauma, but because there were frequent outbreaks of plague, causing the theatres to be closed for long periods. The King's Men were forced to spend many months on the road. Between November 1603 and 1608, they were to be found at various towns in the south and Midlands, though Shakespeare probably did not tour with them by this time. He had bought a large house back home in Stratford and was accumulating other property. He may indeed have stopped acting soon after the new king took the throne. With the London theatres closed so much of the time and a large repertoire on the stocks, Shakespeare seems to have focused his energies on writing a few long and complex tragedies that could have been played on demand at court: *Othello*, *King Lear*, *Antony and Cleopatra*, *Coriolanus* and *Cymbeline* are among his longest and poetically grandest plays. *Macbeth* only survives in a shorter text, which shows signs of adaptation after Shakespeare's death. The bitterly satirical *Timon of Athens*, apparently a collaboration with Thomas Middleton that may have failed on the stage, also belongs to this period. In comedy, too, he wrote longer and morally darker works than in the Elizabethan period, pushing at the very bounds of the form in *Measure for Measure* and *All's Well that Ends Well*.

From 1608 onwards, when the King's Men began occupying the indoor Blackfriars playhouse (as a winter house, meaning that they only used the outdoor Globe in summer?), Shakespeare turned to a more romantic style. His company had a great success with a revived and altered version of an old pastoral play called *Mucedorus*. It even featured a bear. The younger dramatist John Fletcher, meanwhile, sometimes working in collaboration with Francis Beaumont, was pioneering a new style of tragicomedy, a mix of romance and royalism laced with intrigue and pastoral excursions. Shakespeare experimented with this idiom in *Cymbeline* and it was presumably with his blessing that Fletcher eventually took over as the King's Men's company dramatist. The two writers apparently collaborated on three plays in the years 1612–14: a lost romance called *Cardenio* (based on the love-madness of a character in Cervantes' *Don Quixote*), *Henry VIII* (originally staged with the title 'All is True'), and *The Two Noble Kinsmen*, a dramatization of Chaucer's 'Knight's Tale'. These were written after Shakespeare's two final solo-authored plays, *The Winter's Tale*, a self-consciously old-fashioned work dramatizing the pastoral romance of his old enemy Robert Greene, and *The Tempest*, which at one and the same time drew together multiple theatrical traditions, diverse reading and contemporary interest in the fate of a ship that had been wrecked on the way to the New World.

The collaborations with Fletcher suggest that Shakespeare's career ended with a slow fade rather than the sudden retirement supposed by the nineteenth-century Romantic critics who read Prospero's epilogue to *The Tempest* as Shakespeare's personal farewell to his art. In the last few years of his life Shakespeare certainly spent more of his time in Stratford-upon-Avon, where he became further involved in property dealing and litigation. But his London life also continued. In 1613 he made his first major London property purchase: a freehold house in the Blackfriars district, close to his company's indoor theatre. *The Two Noble Kinsmen* may have been written as late as 1614, and Shakespeare was in London on business a little over a year before he died of an unknown cause at home in Stratford-upon-Avon in 1616, probably on his fifty-second birthday.

About half the sum of his works were published in his lifetime, in texts of variable quality. A few years after his death, his fellow-actors began putting together an authorized edition of his complete *Comedies, Histories and Tragedies*. It appeared in 1623, in large 'Folio' format. This collection of thirty-six plays gave Shakespeare his immortality. In the words of his fellow-dramatist Ben Jonson, who contributed two poems of praise at the start of the Folio, the body of his work made him 'a monument without a tomb':

And art alive still while thy book doth live
And we have wits to read and praise to give ...
He was not of an age, but for all time!

SHAKESPEARE'S WORKS: A CHRONOLOGY

1589–91	*? Arden of Faversham* (possible part authorship)
1589–92	*The Taming of the Shrew*
1589–92	*? Edward the Third* (possible part authorship)
1591	*The Second Part of Henry the Sixth*, originally called *The First Part of the Contention betwixt the Two Famous Houses of York and Lancaster* (element of co-authorship possible)
1591	*The Third Part of Henry the Sixth*, originally called *The True Tragedy of Richard Duke of York* (element of co-authorship probable)
1591–92	*The Two Gentlemen of Verona*
1591–92 perhaps revised 1594	*The Lamentable Tragedy of Titus Andronicus* (probably co-written with, or revising an earlier version by, George Peele)
1592	*The First Part of Henry the Sixth*, probably with Thomas Nashe and others
1592/94	*King Richard the Third*
1593	*Venus and Adonis* (poem)
1593–94	*The Rape of Lucrece* (poem)
1593–1608	*Sonnets* (154 poems, published 1609 with *A Lover's Complaint*, a poem of disputed authorship)
1592–94/ 1600–03	*Sir Thomas More* (a single scene for a play originally by Anthony Munday, with other revisions by Henry Chettle, Thomas Dekker and Thomas Heywood)
1594	*The Comedy of Errors*
1595	*Love's Labour's Lost*

1595–97	*Love's Labour's Won* (a lost play, unless the original title for another comedy)
1595–96	*A Midsummer Night's Dream*
1595–96	*The Tragedy of Romeo and Juliet*
1595–96	*King Richard the Second*
1595–97	*The Life and Death of King John* (possibly earlier)
1596–97	*The Merchant of Venice*
1596–97	*The First Part of Henry the Fourth*
1597–98	*The Second Part of Henry the Fourth*
1598	*Much Ado about Nothing*
1598–99	*The Passionate Pilgrim* (20 poems, some not by Shakespeare)
1599	*The Life of Henry the Fifth*
1599	'To the Queen' (epilogue for a court performance)
1599	*As You Like It*
1599	*The Tragedy of Julius Caesar*
1600–01	*The Tragedy of Hamlet, Prince of Denmark* (perhaps revising an earlier version)
1600–01	*The Merry Wives of Windsor* (perhaps revising version of 1597–99)
1601	'Let the Bird of Loudest Lay' (poem, known since 1807 as 'The Phoenix and Turtle' (turtle-dove))
1601	*Twelfth Night, or What You Will*
1601–02	*The Tragedy of Troilus and Cressida*
1604	*The Tragedy of Othello, the Moor of Venice*
1604	*Measure for Measure*
1605	*All's Well that Ends Well*
1605	*The Life of Timon of Athens*, with Thomas Middleton
1605–06	*The Tragedy of King Lear*
1605–08	? contribution to *The Four Plays in One* (lost, except for *A Yorkshire Tragedy*, mostly by Thomas Middleton)
1606	*The Tragedy of Macbeth* (surviving text has additional scenes by Thomas Middleton)
1606–07	*The Tragedy of Antony and Cleopatra*
1608	*The Tragedy of Coriolanus*

1608	*Pericles, Prince of Tyre*, with George Wilkins
1610	*The Tragedy of Cymbeline*
1611	*The Winter's Tale*
1611	*The Tempest*
1612–13	*Cardenio*, with John Fletcher (survives only in later adaptation called *Double Falsehood* by Lewis Theobald)
1613	*Henry VIII (All is True)*, with John Fletcher
1613–14	*The Two Noble Kinsmen*, with John Fletcher

FURTHER READING
AND VIEWING

CRITICAL APPROACHES

Bloom, Harold, ed., *Modern Critical Interpretations: William Shakespeare's Much Ado About Nothing* (1988). Excellent collection of critical essays offering variety of interpretations.

Callaghan, Dympna, ed., *A Feminist Companion to Shakespeare* (2000). Includes a short essay on *Much Ado* – 'Gender, Class, and the Ideology of Comic Form: *Much Ado About Nothing* and *Twelfth Night*' – by Mihoko Suzuki which focuses on class/gender relations.

Clamp, Mike, *Cambridge Student Guide: Much Ado About Nothing* (2002). Useful commentary with basic critical and contextual information.

Everett, Barbara, '*Much Ado About Nothing*: The Unsociable Comedy', in *English Comedy*, ed. Michael Cordner, Peter Holland and John Kerrigan (1994), pp. 68–84. Intricately grounded reading.

Howard, Jean E., 'Renaissance Antitheatricality and the Politics of Gender and Rank in *Much Ado About Nothing*', in *Shakespeare Reproduced: The Text in History and Ideology*, ed. Jean E. Howard and Marion F. O'Connor (1987), pp. 163–87. Strong political reading.

Mangan, Michael, *A Preface to Shakespeare's Comedies 1594–1603* (1996). Part 1 gives a broad overview of the role of comedy; Part 2 offers a basic critical discussion of individual plays – *Much Ado* is on pp. 179–201.

Wynne-Davies, Marion, ed., *New Casebooks: Much Ado About Nothing and The Taming of the Shrew* (2001). Selection of five modern critical essays focusing on gender politics and early modern society; number four by Penny Gay discusses post-Second World War productions in relation to the changing social climate, reproduced from her *As She Likes It: Shakespeare's Unruly Women* (1994).

THE PLAY IN PERFORMANCE

Branagh, Kenneth, *Much Ado About Nothing by William Shakespeare* (1993). Screenplay of Branagh's film with notes and photographs.

Cox, John F., ed., *Shakespeare in Production: Much Ado About Nothing* (1997). Excellent introductory account of the play's stage history.

Mason, Pamela, *Text and Performance: Much Ado About Nothing,* (1992). Part 1 offers a useful overview of the play; part 2 discusses important productions from 1949 to 1990.

Raccah, Dominique, and Maria Macaisa, eds, *Shakespeare in Performance: Much Ado About Nothing* (2007). Useful student guide with accompanying CD.

Reeves, Saskia, *Actors on Shakespeare: Much Ado About Nothing* (2003). Entertaining, thoughtful account of the author's experience of playing Beatrice in Cheek by Jowl's 1998 production.

AVAILABLE ON DVD

Much Ado About Nothing directed by Joseph Papp (1980, DVD 2002). Film of 1973 New York Shakespeare Festival production: updates the play to 1910 America with Sam Waterston as Benedick and Kathleen Widdoes as Beatrice; Dogberry and the Watch are played as Keystone Kops. Lively and entertaining, but divided the critics.

Much Ado about Nothing directed by Stuart Burge (1984, DVD 2006). Lacklustre version for the BBC television Complete Shakespeare series.

Much Ado About Nothing directed by Kenneth Branagh (1993, DVD 2003). Lush romantic version set in gorgeous Tuscan landscape. Very popular box-office success.

REFERENCES

1 *Much Ado* was not one of Shakespeare's plays listed in Francis Meres' commonplace book *Palladis Tamia* (1598), but Will Kempe left the Chamberlain's Men in 1599, which suggests that the play was written between these dates, a theory borne out by stylistic and linguistic evidence.
2 Robert Latham and William Matthews, eds, *The Diary of Samuel Pepys*, Volume 3 (1970), p. 32. This diary entry may have referred to the premiere on 15 February 1662 or a later performance on 17 December in the same year.
3 Arthur Murphy, *The Life of David Garrick, Esq.*, Volume I (1801), p. 389.
4 Charles E. L. Wingate, 'Beatrice', in his *Shakespeare's Heroines on the Stage* (1895), pp. 31–58.
5 Georg Christoph Lichtenberg, *Lichtenberg's Visits to England*, ed. and trans. Margaret L. Marc and W. H. Quarrell (1938), quoted in George Winchester Stone, Jr. and George M. Kahrl, 'Garrick's Greatest Comic Roles', in *David Garrick: A Critical Biography* (1979), pp. 473–514.
6 Jeffrey Kahan, *Much Ado About Nothing: Shakespeare in Performance* (2007), p. 8.
7 Clement Scott, 'Much Ado about Nothing', in *From 'The Bells' to 'King Arthur'* (1897), pp. 247–58.
8 Vincent Sternroyd and Harcourt Williams, 'Irving as Benedick', in *We Saw Him Act: A Symposium on the Art of Sir Henry Irving*, ed. H. A. Saintsbury and Cecil Palmer (1939, repr. 1969), pp. 229–38.
9 Vincent Sternroyd in Sternroyd and Williams, 'Irving as Benedick', pp. 229–38.
10 Scott, 'Much Ado about Nothing' pp. 247–58.
11 Ellen Terry, *The Story of My Life* (1908). Can be downloaded at www.gutenberg.org/etext/12326.
12 Terry, *The Story of My Life*, VIII, 'Work at the Lyceum'.
13 F. H. Mares in the introduction to his Cambridge edition of *Much Ado about Nothing* (1988), pp. 1–52.
14 J. C. Trewin, *Shakespeare on the English Stage 1900–1964* (1964).
15 G. B. Shaw, in a letter to Ellen Terry, 3 June 1903, in their *Ellen Terry and Bernard Shaw: A Correspondence*, ed. Christopher St. John (1932), pp. 293–4.
16 *The Times*, London, 23 April 1904.
17 G. B. Shaw, *Saturday Review*, 11 February 1905.
18 *The Times*, London, 22 July 1955.
19 John Gielgud, '1946–1954', in *Gielgud: An Actor and His Time* (1980), pp. 157–87.
20 Brooks Atkinson, *New York Times*, 8 August 1957.
21 Henry Hewes, *Saturday Review*, 24 August 1957.
22 V. S. Pritchett, *New Statesman*, 6 September 1958.
23 *The Times*, London, 27 August 1958.

24 Alan Brien, *Spectator*, 5 September 1958, pp. 305–6.
25 Brooks Atkinson, *New York Times*, 26 June 1958.
26 Penelope Gilliatt, 'Prodigals: Shakespeare in Italy', in her *Unholy Fools, Wits, Comics, Disturbers of the Peace: Film & Theatre* (1973), pp. 330–3.
27 *The Times*, London, 17 February 1965.
28 B. A. Young, *Financial Times*, 17 February 1965.
29 Mel Gussow, *New York Times*, 18 August 1972.
30 Stanley Kauffman, *New Republic*, 9 September 1972, pp. 20, 33–4.
31 H. R. Coursen, 'Anachronism and Papp's *Much Ado*', in *Shakespeare on Television: An Anthology of Essays and Reviews*, ed. J. C. Bulman and H. R. Coursen (1988), pp. 151–5.
32 Leslie Bennetts, *New York Times*, Section 2, 10 July 1988, pp. 1, 5.
33 Page R. Laws, *Theatre Journal*, 54, no. 2 (2002), pp. 305–7.
34 Markland Taylor, *Variety*, 388, no. 7 (30 September–6 October 2002), p. 36.
35 Martha Tuck Rozett, *Shakespeare Bulletin*, 21, no. 3 (Fall 2003), pp. 131–3.
36 Kenneth Branagh, *Introduction to Much Ado About Nothing, by William Shakespeare, with Screenplay, Introduction, and Notes on the Making of the Movie* (1993), pp. vi–xvi.
37 W. A. Darlington, *Daily Telegraph*, 5 April 1961.
38 Michael Billington, *Guardian*, 29 May 1971.
39 Michael Billington, *Guardian*, 9 April 1976.
40 J. F. Cox, *Shakespeare in Production: Much Ado About Nothing* (1997), p. 71.
41 Ralph Berry, *On Directing Shakespeare: Interviews with Contemporary Directors* (1977), p. 78.
42 Michael Coveney, *Financial Times*, 28 April 1982.
43 Michael Billington, *Guardian*, 21 April 1982.
44 Michael Billington *Guardian*, 12 April 1990.
45 Billington *Guardian*, 12 April 1990.
46 Benedict Nightingale, *The Times*, London, 11 April 1990.
47 Benedict Nightingale, *The Times*, London, 29 November 1996.
48 Charles Spencer, *Daily Telegraph*, 29 November 1996.
49 Nicholas de Jongh, *Evening Standard*, 27 November 1996.
50 De Jongh, *Evening Standard*, 27 November 1996.
51 Robert Smallwood, *Shakespeare Quarterly*, 40 (1989), p. 84.
52 Patrick Marmion, *Mail on Sunday*, 4 August 2002.
53 Kate Bassett, *Independent on Sunday*, 19 May 2002.
54 Paul Taylor, *Independent*, 25 May 2006.
55 Michael Billington *Guardian*, 19 May 2006.
56 Taylor, *Independent*, 25 May 2006.
57 *The Times*, London, 5 April 1961.
58 Cox, *Much Ado About Nothing*, p. 69.
59 Peter Lewis, *Daily Mail*, 9 April 1976.
60 Don Chapman, *Oxford Mail*, 15 October 1968.
61 Chapman, *Oxford Mail*, 15 October 1968.
62 Maureen Paton, *Daily Express*, 15 April 1988
63 Don Chapman, *Oxford Mail*, 14 April 1988.
64 Irving Wardle, *The Times*, London, 14 April 1988.
65 Maggie Steed in *Players of Shakespeare 3*, ed. Russell Jackson and Robert Smallwood (1993), pp. 42–52.
66 Marmion, *Mail on Sunday*, 4 August 2002.

67 Paul Taylor, *Independent*, 15 May 2002.

68 Ian Johns, *The Times*, London, 5 August 2002.

69 Patrick Marmion, *Mail on Sunday*, 4 August 2002.

70 B. A. Young, *Financial Times*, 15 October 1968.

71 Billington, *Guardian*, 21 April 1982.

72 Sinead Cusack in Carol Rutter's *Clamorous Voices* (1988), p. xvi.

73 Billington, *Guardian*, 21 April 1982.

74 Alastair Macaulay, *Financial Times*, 29 November 1996.

75 Charles Spencer, *Daily Telegraph*, 3 August 1996.

76 Alastair Macaulay, *Financial Times*, 29 November 1996.

77 Susan Fleetwood, interviewed with her Benedick, Roger Allam, *Leicester Mercury*, 6 April 1990.

78 Billington, *Guardian*, 19 May 2006.

79 Nicholas de Jongh, *Evening Standard*, 19 May 2006.

80 Alastair Macaulay, *Financial Times*, 23 May 2006.

81 Chapman, *Oxford Mail*, 15 October 1968.

82 Billington, *Guardian*, 12 April 1990.

83 Michael Billington, *Guardian*, 10 May 2002.

84 Billington, *Guardian*, 9 April 1976.

85 Wardle, *The Times*, 14 April 1988.

86 Spencer, *Daily Telegraph*, 3 August 2002.

87 Spencer, *Daily Telegraph*, 3 August 2002.

88 Charles Spencer, *Daily Telegraph*, 22 May 2006.

89 W.A. Darlington, *Daily Telegraph*, 5 April 1961.

90 Macaulay, *Financial Times*, 29 November 1996.

91 De Jongh, *Evening Standard*, 27 November 1996.

92 Billington, *Guardian*, 12 April 1990.

93 Billington, *Guardian*, 21 April 1982.

94 Peter Lewis, *Daily Mail*, 9 April 1976.

95 Christopher Hart, *Sunday Times*, London, 21 May 2006.

ACKNOWLEDGEMENTS AND PICTURE CREDITS

Preparation of 'Much Ado in Performance' was assisted by a generous grant from the CAPITAL Centre (Creativity and Performance in Teaching and Learning) of the University of Warwick for research in the RSC archive at the Shakespeare Birthplace Trust. The Arts and Humanities Research Council (AHRC) funded a term's research leave that enabled Jonathan Bate to work on 'The Director's Cut'.

Picture research by Michelle Morton. Grateful acknowledgement is made to the Shakespeare Birthplace Trust for assistance with picture research (special thanks to Helen Hargest) and reproduction fees.

Images of RSC productions are supplied by the Shakespeare Centre Library and Archive, Stratford-upon-Avon. This Library, maintained by the Shakespeare Birthplace Trust, holds the most important collection of Shakespeare material in the UK, including the Royal Shakespeare Company's official archive. It is open to the public free of charge.

For more information see www.shakespeare.org.uk.

1. Directed by John Gielgud (1949) Angus McBean © Royal Shakespeare Company
2. Directed by Douglas Seale (1958) Angus McBean © Royal Shakespeare Company
3. Directed by Trevor Nunn (1968) Tom Holte © Shakespeare Birthplace Trust
4. Directed by Terry Hands (1982) Joe Cocks Studio Collection © Shakespeare Birthplace Trust

5. Directed by Di Trevis (1988) Joe Cocks Studio Collection © Shakespeare Birthplace Trust
6. Directed by Nicholas Hytner (2007) © Donald Cooper/photostage.co.uk
7. Directed by Marianne Elliott (2006) Simon Annand © Royal Shakespeare Company
8. Directed by Gregory Doran (2002) Jonathan Dockar-Drysdale © Royal Shakespeare Company
9. Reconstructed Elizabethan playhouse © Charcoalblue